# Paul Kiparsky

# Explanation in Phonology

1982
FORIS PUBLICATIONS
Dordrecht - Holland/Cinnaminson - U.S.A.

*Published by:*
Foris Publications Holland
P.O. Box 509
3300 AM Dordrecht, The Netherlands

*Sole distributor for the U.S.A. and Canada:*
Foris Publications U.S.A.
P.O. Box C-50
Cinnaminson N.J. 08077
U.S.A.

The editors are grateful to Mieke Trommelen for her assistance in the production of this monograph.

ISBN 90 70176 37 8 (Bound)
ISBN 90 70176 24 6 (Paper)

Printed in the Netherlands by Intercontinental Graphics, H.I. Ambacht.

# Contents

# Preface

The essays reprinted in this volume are concerned with exploring the connections between synchronic phonology and change. The strategy is to identify structure-dependent properties of change and to use them in turn to test hypotheses about structure. For example, if the right way to look at analogical change is not as the projection of surface regularities but as the elimination of arbitrary complexity from the system, in a sense of complexity independently defined in the theory of grammar, then it follows that particular instances of change can show something about the grammars of the languages in question and about the precise way the theory of grammar should be formulated.

This straightforward research program has turned out to be as interesting as anticipated but much trickier to work out properly. It is hardly necessary to caution the reader that there are some false steps taken at various points in these efforts, but it may be useful to indicate briefly what I think they are. In retrospect, the main weakness here is perhaps the tendency to elevate generalizations about change directly into so many autonomous principles of grammar, such as the "paradigm conditions" or the Alternation Condition. It now seems that versions of the generalizations in question are derivable from the interaction of more basic factors, both grammatical and extragrammatical. This is particularly so if we adopt the more highly structured models of the lexicon that have been proposed recently. In the framework of lexical phonology, word formation and word phonology are located in the lexicon in a way which incorporates the essential insights of level-ordered morphology and cyclic phonology. What I tried to accomplish by enriching the evaluation measure and imposing restrictions on the "abstractness" of underlying representations largely follows within lexical phonology from the organization of the grammar itself. Other facts fall into place when we bring the use and acquisition of language into the picture, naturally dropping for this purpose the simplifying idealizations that speech communities are homogeneous and language is learned instantaneously. For example, some innovations may be projections of "wrong" analyses which are optimal only for an incomplete set of data under consideration at some intermediate stages of language acquisition. Taking this into account relieves the theory of grammar of explanatory burdens it is not really designed to carry and allows it to be greatly simplified. While that is of course a happy outcome, it does mean that linguistic change is not as direct a "window" on linguistic structure as one might have hoped. But insofar as we can specify the roles played by the other variables in change, it still gives us an accurate source of evidence whose importance grows as our conception of grammar becomes more richly articulated.

# ACKNOWLEDGEMENTS

Foris Publishers and the editors of the *Publications in Language Sciences* series wish to thank the following publishers and persons for their permission to reprint copyright material:

Holt, Rinehart, and Winston, New York, N.Y., and Professors E. Bach and R.T. Harms for their permission to reprint "Linguistic Universals and Linguistic Change", from E. Bach and R.T. Harms (eds.), *Universals in Linguistic Theory*, 1968.

Penguin Books Ltd., Harmondsworth, Middlesex, England, and Professor J. Lyons for their permission to reprint "Historical Linguistics", from J. Lyons (ed.), *New Horizons in Linguistics*, 1970.

Greylock Publishers, Stamford, Connecticut, for their permission to reprint "Historical Linguistics", from W.O. Dingwall (ed.), *A Survey of Linguistic Science*, 1978.

Prentice-Hall Inc., Englewood Cliffs, N.J., for their permission to reprint "Explanation in Phonology", from S. Peters (ed.), *Goals in Linguistic Theory*, 1972.

LABO Co. for Language and Educational Research, TEC Co., Ltd., Tokyo, for their permission to reprint "How Abstract is Phonology?", from O. Fujimura (ed.), *Three Dimensions of Linguistic Theory*, 1973.

Mouton Publishers, The Hague, for their permission to reprint "Productivity in Phonology", from M.J. Kenstowicz and Ch.W. Kisseberth (eds.), *Issues in Phonological Theory*, 1973.

Indiana University Press, Bloomington, Indiana, for their permission to reprint "From Paleogrammarians to Neogrammarians", from D. Hymes (ed.), *Studies in the History of Linguistics, Traditions and Paradigms*, 1974.

The Chicago Linguistic Society, Chicago, Illinois, for their permission to reprint "On the Evaluation Measure", from A. Bruck, R.A. Fox, and Michael W. LaGaly (eds.), *Papers from the Parasession on Natural Phonology*, 1974.

North-Holland Publishing Co., Amsterdam, for their permission to reprint "Remarks on Analogical Change", from J.M. Anderson and Ch. Jones (eds.), *Historical Linguistics II*, 1974.

The Editors of the *Studies in the Linguistic Sciences*, Department of Linguistics, University of Illinois, Urbana, Illinois, for their permission to reprint "Analogical Change as a Problem for Linguistic Theory", from *Studies in the Linguistic Sciences* Vol. 8:2, "Linguistics in the Seventies: Directions and Prospects", 1978.

# Chapter 1

# Sound Change*

## 1. The Neogrammarian Theory

The clearest and most influential formulation of the Neogrammarian theory of phonological change is found in the third chapter of Paul's *Prinzipien der Sprachgeschichte*. According to Paul, phonological information is stored by the speaker in two forms: as *auditory representations* (*Lautbilder*) and as *articulatory representations* (*Bewegungsgefühle*). One form of phonological change (*Lautwandel*) takes place in that the execution of articulatory movements changes and that these changes in turn lead to changes in the articulatory representations themselves. There are two ways in which the execution of articulatory movements can change and accordingly two major manifestations of *Lautwandel: articulatory drift* (*Verschiebung des Bewegungsgefühles*) and *replacement* (*Vertauschung der Elemente*).

In articulatory drift, the articulation of the minimal phonetic elements (it is not clear what these elements are) undergoes gradual shift. The shift is subject to the constraint that the resulting auditory deviation must not transcend the threshold of conscious perception (*Kontrolle des Lautbildes*). Phonological change takes place in that the articulatory representations are continually revised to match these shifts in their execution. Aware that merely random fluctuations of articulation could have no effect, Paul proposes that a tendency towards greater facility of articulation lends a directionality to the drift. But what facility of articulation is and how it is to be determined is left unspecified except for the statement that assimilation increases it, and that it depends in part on the phonological systems of the language. It has been long realized that this gap in Paul's theory is impossible to fill, there being no way of defining facility of articulation so that it would account for what sound changes actually happen. Hence the idea of articulatory drift is in effect quite empty.

In replacement, phonetic elements are replaced by others in individual

---

\*    Part of Chapter 1 of Kiparsky (1965).

productions of words because of slips of the tongue. These slips of the tongue become part of the language through being adopted as correct forms by oncoming generations of language learners. As examples of replacement Paul mentions metathesis, assimilation and dissimilation, and presumably epenthesis and apocopation should be added to complete his list.

But there is another way, according to Paul, in which phonological changes amounting to the same effect, largely, as articulatory drift and replacement may take place. This is that children deviate from their linguistic models and from the beginning form articulatory representations which differ from those of the speakers who provide their linguistic experience. Changes of this type must be sufficiently insignificant to escape correction; they can thus either result in the kinds of metatheses, assimilations, etc. brought about by replacement or else in differences of articulatory representation with minimal acoustic consequences, such as that of dorsal and alveolar *t* [sic].

In this respect, there is a curious equivocation in Paul as to which of the postulated mechanisms is to be considered the basic form of phonological change. On the one hand, he very clearly points out that articulatory drift in mature speakers cannot lead to changes of any consequence:

> Innerhalb der nämlichen Generation werden auf diese Weise[sc. by articulatory drift] immer nur sehr geringfügige Verschiebungen zu Stande kommen. Merklichere Verschiebungen erfolgen erst, wenn eine ältere Generation durch eine neu heranwachsende verdrängt ist. (62-63)

He emphasizes that it is by imperfect learning that phonological change in practice most commonly takes place:

> Man wird also sagen können, dass die *Hauptveranlassung zum Lautwandel in der Uebertragung der Laute auf neue Individuen liegt.* [His emphasis]. Für diesen Vorgang ist also der Ausdruck Wandel, wenn man sich an das wirklich tatsächliche hält, gar nich zutreffend, es ist vielmehr eine abweichende Neuerzeugung. (63)

On the other hand, the famous principle of regularity is claimed only for articulatory drift in mature speakers (§47-8), i.e. for a form of phonological change which in the above quotations is dismissed as insignificant. However, when discussing regularity Paul contradicts his earlier statements by implying that articulatory drift in mature speakers is on the contrary the major form of phonological change:

> Es bleiben nun allerdings einige Arten von lautlichen Veränderungen übrig, für die sich konsequente Durchführung theoretisch nicht als notwendig erweisen lässt. Diese bilden aber eine verhältnismässig geringen Teil der gesamtem Laut-

veränderungen, und sie lassen sich genau abgrenzen. Einerseits also gehören hierher die Fälle, in denen ein Laut vermittelst einer abweichenden Artikulation nachgeahmt wird, anderseits die §45 besprochenen Metathesen, Assimilationen und Dissimilationen. (73)

As more important than the inadequacies and inconsistencies of Paul's theory I would regard his fundamental insight that the phonology of a language can change in two ways: by *Lautwandel* and by *abweichende Neuerzeugung*. I will translate them as *sound change* and *imperfect learning*, respectively, subsuming both under the general term *phonological change*. Sound change is brought about by the joint operation of *innovation* and subsequent *restructuring*. Innovation in phonology is change in the way phonological representations are executed by speakers of a language; restructuring is the resulting revision in the phonological representations. As the latter were considered to be phonetic by Paul, and restructuring immediately followed on innovation, the distinction between innovation and restructuring was to him purely theoretical and devoid of any practical consequences. But with richer conceptions of phonological structure it takes on a cardinal importance for diachronic phonology.[1] Imperfect learning is due to the fact that the child does not learn a grammar directly but must recreate it for himself on the basis of a necessarily limited and fragmentary experience with speech. It is in no way surprising that the grammar should change in the process of transmission across generations of speakers.

In the following discussion of phonological change I accept these basic concepts, though interpreting them (particularly the concept of imperfect learning) very differently from Paul. This chapter deals with restructuring and innovation, the presentation taking the form of a confrontation of the taxonomic and generative phonological views of these processes.

## 2. Restructuring

Take the case of Old High German umlaut, a canonical example of diachronic phonemics.[2] In Old High German, vowels became nongrave before *i*; short vowels were in addition made noncompact. Subsequently unstressed vowels were reduced to *e* (probably phonetically *ə*). Cf., with change of gravity,

(1)  wurmi   >  würmi   >  würme  (nom. pl. of *wurm* 'worm')
     tāti    >  tǟti    >  tǟte   (nom. pl. of *tāt*  'deed')
     nōti    >  nȫti    >  nȫte   (nom. pl. of *nōt*  'distress')

and with change of both gravity and compactness,

(2)  slagi  >  slegi  >  slege   (nom. pl. of *slag*  'stroke')
     gasti  >  gesti  >  geste   (nom. pl. of *gast*  'guest')

What is the effect of these two sound changes on the grammar ?

After umlaut, taxonomic phonemics requires a restructuring of phonetic representations in the case of just one of the vowels affected by the
change. Changes like (1) involve merely the introduction of new allophones
before *i*, but the change of *a* to *e* as in (2) must be regarded as a phonemic
change because *a* and *e* contrast in other environments. Thus a taxonomic
grammar must at this stage phonemically represent *nōti* as /nōti/ but
*slegi* as /slegi/ and must, if it is to account for the regularities of the
language, contain two separate umlaut rules, a *morphophonemic* umlaut
rule turning *a* into *e* (e.g /slagi/ > /slegi/) to provide the phonemic level
of representation, and a *phonemic* umlaut rule affecting the remaining
vowels (e.g. /nōti/ > [nŏti]) to provide the phonetic level of representation. Vowel reduction then creates minimal pairs between each umlaut
vowel and its underlying counterpart, cf. nom. pl. *würme* with dat. sg.
*wurme*. With this second innovation all umlaut vowels become phonemic
and umlaut is henceforth entirely a 'nonautomatic' morphophonemic
alternation.

The theory of generative grammar suggests a radically different picture.
Since a grammar is a system of rules, it becomes natural to regard innovations as added rules (Halle 1962; Klima 1964a). Thus, umlaut is the
addition of the following phonological rule to the grammar of Old High
German:

$$
(3) \quad \begin{bmatrix} -\text{consonantal} \\ <-\text{long}> \end{bmatrix} \rightarrow \begin{bmatrix} -\text{grave} \\ <-\text{compact}> \end{bmatrix} \Big/ \quad \underline{\qquad} C_n \, i
$$

(Material in angled brackets must be either all present or all absent in
applying rules; $C_n$ denotes 'n or more consonants'.)

Once we abandon proceduralism and with it the level of taxonomic
phonemics there no longer remains the slightest reason to suppose that
the phonemic representations of Old High German were revised as a result
of (3), and that the grammar came to contain two separate umlaut rules.
The grammar of this stage, in fact, has the same phonemic representations
as the pre-umlaut stage (e.g. /slagi, nōti/) and contains the phonological
rule (3) which derives the correct phonetic forms (e.g. *slegi, nŏti*). Nor
does the subsequent development of minimal pairs like *würme : wurme* by
the addition of the vowel reduction rule

$$
(4) \quad \begin{bmatrix} +\text{vocalic} \\ -\text{consonantal} \\ -\text{stressed} \end{bmatrix} \rightarrow \quad [ə]
$$

necessarily mean that the umlaut vowels have become phonemic and that the occurrence of umlaut is no longer predictable. There is the relevant fact that any grammar will at that stage still have to contain both rules (3) and (4) for reasons that are quite independent of such forms as (1) and (2). (3) is required in the grammar because umlaut is still phonologically conditioned by *i* in those suffixes that were protected from (4) by a secondary stress. Cf., with umlaut before *i*, *tȫrìsch* 'foolish' (*tȫre* 'fool'), *bÉstīn* 'made of bast' (*bast* 'bast'), *géstìnne* 'female guest' (*gast* 'guest'), *tüechìn* 'cloth (dim.)' (*tuoch* 'cloth'); but, without umlaut, *mánùnge* 'exhortation' (*manen* 'exhort'), *ármùot* 'poverty (*arm* 'poor'). And (4) is a phonological rule because stress alternations such as those between prefix and stem are accompanied by automatic shifts in vowel quality, e.g. *ántlàz* 'absolution', *entlázen* 'absolve'; *ímbīz* 'partaking', *embīzen* 'partake'; *úrteìl* 'judgment', *ertéilen* 'judge'. Given the necessity of including (3) and (4) in the grammar, it is now only necessary to make two further assumptions in order to account for forms like (1) and (2): that the plural ending in these forms is phonemically *i*, and that the rules apply in the order (3, 4). This would in fact seem to be the correct solution for Middle High German, though no longer for Modern German.

In this way the more highly structured form of language postulated by the theory of generative grammar, together with the goal of giving in a grammar an explicit account of the regularities of a language, often leads to a synchronically motivated retention of earlier underlying representations and incorporation of innovations as phonological rules, often in a synchronic order that matches their relative chronology, in situations where a taxonomic account would require immediate restructuring. By the same token, it follows from generative grammatical theory that restructurings, when they do take place, can be of a far more radical nature than taxonomic phonemics would have one suspect. Clearly, too, it depends on the structure of the language whether an innovation leads to restructuring. Other things being equal, an innovation is more likely to remain as a synchronic rule in a language with a complicated phonology than in one with very few rules. Thus complicated phonologies tend to remain complicated and simple phonologies tend to remain simple: hence the relative stability of typological properties such as agglutination, inflection and isolation.

The sequence of sound changes known as Grimm's Law furnishes a good illustration of restructuring.[3] For a stage of Pre-Germanic preceding the operation of Grimm's Law we can assume the existence of the verb stems *skab* 'shape', *nas* 'save', with infinitive and part participle forms

(5)  skabian    skabtas    nasian    nasitas

phonetically realized as

(6)   skabjan      skaptas      nasjan      nasitas.

The devoicing of *b* in *skaptas* is due to a rule of regressive assimilation of Indo-European origin:

$$(7) \quad [+ \text{obstruent}] \rightarrow [a \text{ voiced}] / \underline{\phantom{xxx}} \begin{bmatrix} + \text{obstruent} \\ a \text{ voiced} \end{bmatrix}$$

The vowel *i* automatically becomes a glide before vowels by a rule that I will tacitly assume to apply in the following.

The first step of Grimm's Law is that voiceless stops are aspirated (made tense) everywhere except after obstruents:

$$(8) \quad \begin{bmatrix} - \text{continuant} \\ + \text{obstruent} \\ - \text{voiced} \end{bmatrix} \rightarrow [+ \text{tense}] / \left\{ \begin{matrix} [- \text{obstruent}] \\ \# \end{matrix} \right\} \underline{\phantom{xxx}}$$

Rule (8) changes *skaptas* to *skap$^h$tas* and *nasitas* to *nasit$^h$as*, thus introducing an alternation *tas* : *t$^h$as* in the past participle morpheme. It does not lead to restructuring; the result of adding (8) is a grammar with the underlying representations (5) and the rules (7) and (8), in that order, yielding the phonetic forms

(9)   skabjan      skap$^h$tas      nasjan      nasit$^h$as.

By the next step of Grimm's Law, aspirated stops turn into continuants:

$$(10) \quad \begin{bmatrix} + \text{tense} \\ + \text{obstruent} \end{bmatrix} \rightarrow [+ \text{continuant}]$$

This rule applies both to the voiceless aspirates which arose by (8), e.g. *skap$^h$tas* > *skaftas* and *nasit$^h$as* > *nasiθas*, and to the voiced aspirates inherited from Indo-European, e.g. *b$^h$eran* > *βeran* (cf. Sanskrit *bharati*, Engl. *bear*). The alternation of aspiration now appears as a stop-continuant alternation. One possible grammar for this stage of course has the same dictionary representations as before, with the rules (7, 8, 10). But at this point there is a quite different grammar which accounts for the same language in a simpler way. The old voiced aspirates *b$^h$* etc. are replaced in the dictionary representations by the corresponding continuants *β* etc. The restructured grammar has the rule (7), by which *skabtas* > *skaptas*, followed by a new rule (11) that combines the effect of (8) and (10), turning *skaptas* > *skaftas* and *nasitas* > *nasiθas*.

(11)
$$\begin{bmatrix} + \text{obstruent} \\ -\text{voiced} \end{bmatrix} \rightarrow [+ \text{continuant}]/ \begin{Bmatrix} [- \text{obstruent}] \\ \# \end{Bmatrix} \underline{\quad\quad}$$

With this restructuring the feature of tenseness has ceased to play a role in the obstruent system, and has been replaced by the feature of continuance. Thus the very simple rule (10) has triggered considerable revision in both the rules and underlying representations of the language.

The final part of Grimm's Law makes the voiced stops unvoiced (*skabjan* > *skapjan*):

(12)
$$\begin{bmatrix} + \text{obstruent} \\ -\text{continuant} \end{bmatrix} \rightarrow [-\text{voiced}]$$

This gives the phonetic forms

(13) skapjan    skaftas    nasjan    nasiθas

Again a possible grammar for this stage would retain the same phonemic system with the phonological rules (7, 11, 12). But there is a simpler grammar in which the old voiced stops *b* etc. are replaced by the corresponding voiceless stops *p* etc. in the dictionary entries; and the old voiceless stops *p* etc. are replaced by the corresponding continuants *f* etc., so that the underlying forms become

(14) skapian    skapθas    nasian    nasiθas

The phonetic forms (13) are derived from (14) by rule (15), a kind of anti-Grimm's Law:

(15) $[ + \text{obstruent}]$
$$\begin{bmatrix} + \text{obstruent} \\ - \text{strident} \end{bmatrix} \rightarrow [+ \text{continuant}] \quad [- \text{continuant}]$$

(Rule (7) remains in the language for other reasons.)

It is facts of this kind that constitute the ultimate linguistic justification for the distinction between innovation and restructuring. To attain the level of descriptive adequacy, a theory of linguistic change must express the limitations that obtain on the possible differences of successive grammars of a language, which are very severe indeed. It would be totally impossible to do this under the assumption that successive optimal grammars of a language somehow directly change into each other, e.g. by metarules that map grammars directly into their successors. The significant regularities do not lie in any direct relation between successive grammars but rather in the form of the innovations that bring the changes about. Cf.

Saussure's remark that 'there is no inner bond between the initial fact and the effect that it may subsequently produce on the whole system' (1959: 87).

This is also what invalidates P. Garde's assertion: "ou bien les 'règles synchroniques' sont une nouvelle formulation des lois diachroniques, ou bien elles sont fausses" (1965). The synchronic rules of a grammar not only need not be reformulations of past innovations but need not even bear the slightest resemblance to them, as the above examples show. A corollary and equally obvious moral to be drawn from restructuring is that there is no point in trying to do internal reconstruction by mindlessly translating the rules of a grammar into historical statements (or conversely trying to write generative grammars by providing the arrowheads of historical grammars with shafts). Explicit linguistic descriptions are a prerequisite but not a substitute for linguistic reconstruction.

## 3. Innovation

There is one central difference which above all marks off Halle's conception of linguistic innovation from virtually all of Neogrammarian and American structuralist thinking on the subject. This difference is that in Halle's view linguistic innovations, since they are added grammatical rules, originate in *langue*, in direct contradiction to the view which is quite explicit in Saussure and implicit in Neogrammarian and American structuralist theory that linguistic innovations originate in *parole*. In the linguistic theory of Saussure, the idea that change in language originates in *parole* is internally well-motivated by two specific aspects of the way in which he conceived of the difference between *langue* and *parole*. The first of these is Saussure's view of *langue* as a social phenomenon in contrast to *parole* as an individual phenomenon. Since innovations begin with individual speakers and are only later adopted by the whole speech community, it then follows that innovations are part of *parole* before they become part of *langue*:

> Once in possession of this double principle of classification, we can add that everything diachronic in language is diachronic only by virtue of speaking. It is in speaking that the germ of all change is found. Each change is launched by a certain number of individuals before it is accepted for general use. (98)

The second, which pertains specifically to sound change, is Saussure's exclusion of phonetics from the domain of *langue*:

> An argument against separating phonation from language might be phonetic changes, the alterations of the sounds which occur in speaking and which exert

such a profound influence on the future of language itself. Do we really have the right to pretend that language exists independently of phonetic change? Yes, for they affect only the material substance of words. If they attack language as a system of signs, it is only indirectly, through subsequent changes of interpretations; there is nothing phonetic in the phenomenon. (18)

Thus Saussure regards sound change as an ultimately extra-linguistic phenomenon. It can hence consist only of the kinds of phenomena that may conceivably be brought about by extraneous deviations of the speech mechanism, i.e. precisely slips of the tongue and imperceptible articulatory drifts. Thus Saussure has from a rather different theoretical basis arrived at essentially the Neogrammarian constraints on sound change.

But the view which ascribed innovation to *parole* is only as sound as the presuppositions on which it is based. Both the idea of *langue* and *parole* as social and individual phenomena respectively and the exclusion of phonetics from the domain of *langue* are facets of Saussurian theory that have been at least in practice correctly rejected in much of modern structuralism. The conclusion from this, namely that it is unmotivated to regard linguistic innovations as aspects of *parole*, was duly drawn by Jakobson (1929) who emphasized the systematic aspect of linguistic change and observed that the ultimate historical source — as distinct from theoretical basis — of Saussurian diachrony is to be found in the Neogrammarian doctrines of the 19th century.

The same historical dependence on the Neogrammarians is even more striking in the case of American structuralism (cf. Postal 1968: Part II). Bloomfield in the main accepted Paul's position (explicitly rejecting, however, his reliance on facility of articulation, and making no mention of imperfect learning). But his way of justifying it is quite different from that of Paul and Saussure. The first argument which Bloomfield offers in favor of the Neogrammarian theory is that it led to discoveries like Grassmann's Law (1933: 355) and Verner's Law (359). Alchemy, too, led to many important discoveries; and besides, Bloomfield's argument is historically false as neither Grassmann nor Verner are known to have held the Neogrammarian position either implicitly or explicitly.

The second, much more interesting argument is the principle of separation of levels:

Theoretically, we can understand the regular change of phonemes, if we suppose that language consists of two layers of habit. One layer is phonemic: the speakers have certain habits of voicing, tongue-movement, and so on. These habits make up the phonetic system of the language. The other layer consists of formal-semantic habits: the speakers habitually utter certain combinations of phonemes in response to certain types of stimuli, and respond appropriately when they hear these same combinations. These habits make up the grammar and lexicon of the language. (364-5)

If this statement is to make any sense as a defense of the Neogrammarian position, it must be interpreted to mean not merely that there are two layers, but also that the phonemic layer is independent of the grammatical-lexical layer in the sense that the phonological structure of utterances in languages is not determined in part by their grammatical-lexical structure. But that is an untenable view, as Bloomfield in effect acknowledged on the very next page, where he observed that some speakers of American English use 'a shorter variant of the phoneme [a] . . . before the clusters [rd, rt] followed by a primary suffix [-r, -n], as in *barter, Carter, garden, marten (Martin).* Before a secondary suffix [-r, -n], however, the longer variant is used, as in *starter, carter* ('one who carts'), *harden;* here the existence of the simple words (*start, cart, hard*), whose [a] is not subject to shortening, has led to the favoring of the normal, longer variant. The word *larder* (not part of the colloquial vocabulary) could be read with the shorter variant, but the agent-noun *larder* ('one who lards') could be formed only with the longer type of the [a]-phoneme.' Bloomfield explicitly pointed out that long and short [a] are 'sub-phonemic variants', being predictable from the nature of the suffix and hence in spite of such minimal pairs, not distinctive.[4] But diachronically, Bloomfield did not come to the obvious corresponding conclusion that the shortening failed to take place before the secondary suffixes but rather assumed that it took place even there, with the long allophone later being introduced analogically on the basis of the corresponding simplexes.

Thus Bloomfield still took the principle of separation of levels much more seriously in diachronic phonology than in synchronic phonology, ignoring it in this and many other instances in his actual descriptions while simultaneously insisting on it in an exactly parallel historical situation. The contribution of his disciples was to take seriously the principle in synchrony as well.[5] Thus the Neogrammarian theory of sound change is indubitably one source of taxonomic phonemics in America.

At any rate, in spite of various uncertainties of interpretation, we can say that the Neogrammarian, Saussurian, and Bloomfieldian theories of sound change place equivalent or very similar limitations on what kinds of sound change may happen. The theoretical justification for this shared position — let me call it the taxonomic position — is in each case based on assumptions which for independent reasons are untenable: in Paul, the absence of any level of higher-level, nonphonetic representation; in Saussure, a particular view of *langue* and *parole*; in Bloomfield, a form of separation of levels. Thus, there is no reason to believe that these limitations on phonological change are correct.

## Notes

1.    Saussure (1959: 83-7), Jakobson (1929, 1931), Halle (1962).
2.    Saussure (1959: 83-5), Twaddell (1938), Penzl (1949). Needless to say, my discussion of umlaut here is extremely schematic and I omit, for example, consideration of secondary umlaut. This will not affect the point being made.
3.    I cite this example here merely to illustrate the mechanics of restructuring, ignoring at this point the serious questions of relative chronology that must be raised with regard to the different steps of Grimm's Law. To some of these I return in Chapter 3 of Kiparsky (1965). The facts are clearly presented in Streitberg (1963); for illuminating comments, see Halle (1961, 1962).
4.    The exact difference is that secondary suffixes are preceded by word boundaries, i.e., act as enclitics. This fact has many striking reflexes in English phonology: for example, /ng/ retains its word-final form [ŋ] before agentive -r (hence *singer* [siŋər] but *finger* [fiŋgər]. See Chomsky and Halle (1968).
5.    This whole passage of Bloomfield's is rejected by C. Hockett (1965: fn. 20). His theory of sound change is essentially an impoverished version of Paul's and Bloomfield's, with articulatory drift as the only form of sound change. Hockett perhaps intended to meet the obvious objection that metathesis, assimilation, dissimilation etc. cannot conceivably be due to articulatory drift by his bizarre though unsupported remark that these are 'allied more closely to analogy than to borrowing or to sound change' (1958: 390). To clarify this, it should be remarked that Hockett distinguished three mutually exclusive forms of linguistic change: sound change, analogy, and borrowing, rather as if one were to partition the class of animals into mammals, insects and pets. One of the consequences of Hockett's view would be that sound changes cannot be borrowed; another would be that syntactic and semantic change either do not exist or are always due to analogy or borrowing. It is not clear to me whether Hockett actually would accept these absurd consequences. For a commentary on Hockett's theory of sound change, see Postal (1968: Part II).

# Chapter 2

# Linguistic Universals and Linguistic Change*

## *1. The Psychological Reality Problem*

Suppose that someone succeeds in writing a grammar which correctly enumerates the sentences of a language and assigns them the right structural descriptions. Such a grammar would ipso facto correctly represent the substance of a fluent speaker's knowledge of this language. But it would not necessarily represent the form of this knowledge in the sense of actually corresponding to the system of rules which is internalized by the speaker and constitutes part of what enables him to produce and understand arbitrary utterances in the language. Similarly, the knowledge of someone who has learned arithmetic, that is, the infinite set of correct arithmetical computations, could be defined by many different systems of rules, including both psychologically incorrect ones, such as certain axioms of set theory, computer programs, and so on, and the psychologically correct one, namely whatever knowledge is actually used in arithmetical performance, such as the rules of school arithmetic and the multiplication table. How do we know that generative grammar is not psychologically as wrong a model of linguistic competence as set theory is of arithmetical competence?

The linguistic universals which linguistic theory specifies include fixed notations in which grammars are written and an evaluation measure, which together establish a hypothesis about which of the innumerable grammars that might characterize the sentences of a language possesses psychological reality in the sense of representing the form rather than just the substance of a fluent speaker's competence. From among the pile of generalizations that might be made about the sentences of a language they select certain ones as being linguistically significant and corresponding to the generalizations that a child hearing such utterances would actually arrive at in

* This paper was read at the Symposium Universals in Linguistic Theory at the University of Texas at Austin, 13-15 April, 1967. I would like to thank J.R. Ross and W.G. Moulton for suggesting to me many improvements. But they do not necessarily agree with me, and the responsibility is mine alone. This work was supported in part by the National Institutes of Health (Grant MH 13390-02).

constructing his grammar. The question, then, is how the various aspects of this hypothesis are justified.

For many features of universal grammar there is justification enough in the fact that without them it would simply not be possible to write grammars that account for the sentences of a language. Particularly in syntax, as Chomsky has pointed out, the typical problem is not choosing the right one among various theories that work but finding even one that will work at all. But with conventions which are essentially abbreviatory in nature, such as braces and parentheses, among others, real problems of empirical justification can arise. A grammar can always be replaced by another, descriptively equivalent one, in which any one of these abbreviatory notations is not made use of. There could not be a language whose sentences could be enumerated one way but not the other. Then what is the empirical force, if any, of such notational conventions?

For example, most linguists would agree that two rules of the form

$$X \rightarrow Y$$
$$Z \rightarrow Y$$

if not separated in the ordering by any other rule, should be combined by factoring out their common right hand side as follows:

$$\left\{ \begin{matrix} X \\ Z \end{matrix} \right\} \rightarrow Y$$

We would say that the braces represent a linguistically significant generalization about these two rules. But how do we know that they do? How would we justify this convention to some linguist $A$ who maintained that it was wrong and that the two rules should be kept separate? Or, to take a more likely contingency, how would we justify it to another linguist $B$ who maintained that neither theory makes any verifiable truth claim as against the other, that since they are mutually convertible notational variants of each other, they represent equivalent hypotheses about the speaker's internalized grammar?

There are no conscious a priori ideas of generality that we can appeal to here in the way that we can appeal to intuitions that reflect features of structural descriptions, such as ambiguity and synonymy. The processes of normal language learning being unconscious, we have absolutely no ideas about the form of grammars, though we have clear ideas about the forms of sentences which grammars account for. It is true that the practicing linguist soon acquires ideas about the form of grammars and such concepts as generality. But these ideas are somehow the result of his work on languages, and we would like to know what the ideas are based on.

Nor is the fact that a generalization can be stated enough to show that it is real. All sorts of absurd notational conventions can easily be dreamed up which would express the kinds of spurious generalizations that we would want to exclude from grammars. It is necessary to justify conventions by showing that the generalizations they allow one to express do not hold accidentally. One might try to do this by arguing that a convention which can be used frequently in grammars cannot represent an accidental fact about language. But many presumably spurious conventions would come in handy very often in linguistic descriptions. For example, what about a linguist $C$ who says that the brace notation should be extended to collapse rules of the form

$$X \rightarrow Y$$
$$Z \rightarrow X$$

into the form

$$Z \rightarrow \left\{ X \right\}^{\rightarrow Y}$$

He will be able to show us just as many cases where such braces could be used in grammars to group rules together. Or, to cite an actual linguist, Pāṇini often makes use of an abbreviatory convention which corresponds to the following kind of use of braces, ruled out in generative grammar:[1]

$$A \rightarrow B \atop D \rightarrow \left\{ {E \atop F} \right\} / - C \atop / - G$$

What seems wrong about this is that it allows collapsing rules which represent heterogeneous processes. Of the rules combined here, two have absolutely nothing in common with each other: the top rule

$$A \rightarrow B / - C$$

and the bottom rule

$$(D \rightarrow F / - G)$$

But we would like the rules in a grammar to form blocks whose parts are related in some sense that goes beyond just partial identity. Ideally, the rules should be grouped into natural blocks whose parts represent different aspects of the same basic process.

Can psycholinguistics provide experimental evidence on the form of grammars? Recent psycholinguistic experiments designed to test the psychological reality of generative grammar have been concerned mainly with two questions. One group of experiments has sought behavioral correlates to the structural descriptions postulated by generative grammar. Bever, Fodor, and Garrett have, for example, carried out a series of experiments in which they found that the location at which a burst of sound is perceived in a synchronously presented sentence differs from its objective location in a way that can be predicted from the surface constituent structure of the sentence. The goal of another group of experiments was to find evidence bearing on the claim that a system of rules such as that postulated by generative grammar is involved in producing and understanding utterances. In contrast with the successful experiments concerned with the psychological reality of structural descriptions, those concerned with the psychological reality of grammars have on the whole been a failure (Fodor and Garrett 1966). It is true that there was an initial spate of successes in which a clear relationship seemed to emerge between the grammatical complexity of a sentence, as measured by the number of rules of the grammar that contribute to its formation, and its perceptual complexity, as measured by various experimentally obtained performance parameters. But in recent experiments with more complex linguistic material this relationship has all but disappeared. It stands to reason that the utilization of the speaker's internalized grammatical rules is a highly complex process involving elaborate ways of tracking down the relevant rules and processing sentences in such a way that parameters which tap performance directly are not going to be related at all directly to such crude grammatical properties of sentences as the number of rules involved in their derivation. The fact that grammars are not performance models presumably means that the answer to the question of whether they are correct competence models is not likely to be forthcoming by any currently known experimental techniques until the contributions of competence can be separated out from the facts about performance.

What we really need is a window on the form of linguistic competence that is not obscured by factors like performance, about which next to nothing is known. In linguistic change we have precisely such a window.

## 2. The Form of Linguistic Change

We can think of linguistic change in roughly the following terms. Grammars are subject to changes of two kinds: the addition of new rules to them and simplification of them. In phonology, the addition of rules corresponds roughly to the concept of 'sound change' (Halle 1962, Postal 1968). For example, the sound change whereby final obstruents in words became voiceless in German and many other Germanic languages is the addition of the rule

1.          [+ obstruent] → [− voiced] / —— #

Through alternations such as [bunt]:[bunde] (versus [bunt]:[bunte]), in which this rule is reflected, it is learned anew as part of the language by each generation of speakers, and even in modern German the underlying representations of most words retain the medially pronounced voiced segment. Yet the addition of Rule 1 does not leave the lexicon entirely unaffected. Words like *ab, ob*, and *weg*, which never came to stand before an inflectional ending that would cause the reappearance of an underlying voiced obstruent, are never heard after the sound change with anything but a voiceless final obstruent; in these isolated forms, succeeding generations of speakers therefore have no reason to set up underlying forms with voiced obstruents. The change thus brings about a restructuring in a tiny corner of the vocabulary.

I hope that this use of the term *generation* will not convey the absurd picture of a society horizontally segmented into a number of discrete age groups, each with its own grammar. The point is simply that a language is not some gradually and imperceptibly changing object which smoothly floats through time and space, as historical linguistics based on philological material all too easily suggests. Rather, the transmission of language is discontinuous, and a language is recreated by each child on the basis of the speech data it hears. Nor should the term *restructuring* be understood as denoting a change of some speaker's grammar into another grammar, for it refers just to a discontinuous linguistic change arising from the difference between the grammar constructed by a child and the grammar of those whose speech constituted his linguistic experience. In discussing linguistic change in these elementary terms we are, of course, missing a number of important factors which cannot in the long run be ignored. For example, as Jakobson has pointed out, metalinguistic information concerning such things as the social value of different speech forms is an important part of what a speaker knows, and Labov's recent studies (1963, 1965) show its diachronic relevance very clearly. A conception of grammar in which these broader aspects of competence are explicitly accounted for will hopefully provide a general basis for the study of their role in linguistic change.

A sound change that I will frequently refer to is umlaut in Germanic. By this rule, vowels were fronted before *i* (for example, Old High German *wurmi > würmi* 'worms', *täti > tǣti* 'deeds', *nōti > nȫti* 'needs'). Short *a* was not only fronted but also raised to *e* (for example, *slagi > slegi* 'strokes', *gasti > gesti* 'guests'). The original umlaut rule, then, was the following:[2]

2.       $$\left[\begin{array}{c} V \\ <\text{--long}> \end{array}\right] \to \left[\begin{array}{c} -\text{back} \\ <-\text{low}> \end{array}\right] \ / \!\!-\!\!-\! C_0 i$$

In modern German we encounter this rule in a somewhat different form. In the majority of dialects what we find as the productive umlaut of *a* is not *e*, as originally, but *æ*. For example, in the Low German dialect of Prignitz (Mackel 1905-1907) we have *gast:gæst, kraft:kræftig* with a low front vowel in the umlauted forms, rather than the expected *gast: gest, kraft:kreftig*. But the only *e*'s that have thus gone to *æ* are those that were productively umlauted from *a*. Phonemic *e*'s have remained unchanged. These include not only original Germanic *e* in words like *nest* but also *e* from historically umlauted *a* in words like *bet* 'bed', *net* 'net' where *e* has become phonemic since there was no reason to derive it synchronically from an underlying *a*. Analogous facts hold true in Old English as well. In terms of the grammar, this widespread change is a simplification of the umlaut rule from its original form of 2 to the form in 3:

3.       $V \to [-\text{back}] \ / \ldots$

(I leave open here the question of what exactly the environment of umlauting in modern German is, which is irrelevant for present purposes.)

The change from 2 to 3 is an instance of the second basic type of linguistic change, simplification.[3] I shall merely illustrate this type for the moment but hope to justify it in more detail later. Simplification is a generalized and reinterpreted version of the traditional concept of analogy (Matthews 1970, Kiparsky 1965, 1967). This is particularly evident in its simplest form, namely morphological regularization as in changes of the type *brought* > *bringed*, which amount to loss of the special mark associated with lexical entries like *bring* that singles them out as morphological exceptions and specifies the nature of their exceptional behavior. Much more interesting in many respects are cases in which the simplification affects the rules of the grammar rather than the lexicon. Quite commonly, such simplification leads to the loss of parts of rules from the grammar, as in the change of the umlaut rule just cited, where what is lost is the part of the rule which raises *a*. The process may even lead to the loss of entire rules. For example, Rule 1, which devoices word-final obstruents and once was common to all dialects of German, has been lost in some dialects of Northern Switzerland as well as in some varieties of Yiddish. In place of *bunt: bundes* they have *bund: bundes*, with the morphophonemic distinction of voicing now again appearing phonetically in word-final position. We know that these languages once possessed Rule 1, as it has permanently affected the handful of isolated words like *(a)vek* 'away', *ap* (Yidd. *op*) 'away', which had a voiced final obstruent but lost it even morphophonemically after the phonetic devoicing took place because retention was not motivated by any inflected forms. Hence there was also no basis for reintroducing the voicing in these words once Rule 1 had dropped out of the language by simplification.

It is also evident that the *order* of rules in a grammar is subject to historical change. Later, I will try to show that this is a special case of simplification; right now a few examples will do. By a historically fairly old rule of Finnish, underlying long mid vowels are diphthongized, for example, *vee* > *vie*. Subsequently, the loss of certain medial voiced continuants introduces new long mid vowels, for example, *teɣe* > *tee*. In standard Finnish, these new long mid vowels stay, and the rule introducing them must therefore follow the diphthongization. That is, the order is

*a*. diphthongization
*b*. loss of medial voiced continuants

Yet in many dialects of Finnish the new long mid vowels have subsequently come to join in the diphthongization, for example *teɣe* > *tee* > *tie*. What this means is that the order of the rules has changed to

*a*. loss of medial voiced continuants
*b*. diphthongization

Notice also what it does *not* mean. It does not mean what anyone coming from traditional historical linguistics automatically tends to think it means, namely, that in standard Finnish, where *tee* from *teɣe* does not diphthong-ize, the diphthongization rule is not 'productive'. On the contrary, it is perfectly productive since it must apply to underlying forms like *vee*, in which the underlying long mid vowel must be assumed because of morphophonemic rules such as those for past formation, for example, *vee + i* > *vei* like *saa + i* > *sai*, as McCawley (ms.) has shown. The difference between the two kinds of dialects has nothing to do with the productivity of the diphthongization rule but simply with its order with respect to the loss of medial voiced continuants.

An example of reordering which once again involves the umlaut is the following. In the dialects of Northeastern Switzerland the back mid-vowel *o* becomes lowered to *ɔ* if it immediately precedes a dental or palatal (nongrave, or what Halle now calls a coronal) true consonant or *r*. Compare, in the Kanton of Schaffhausen (Wanner 1941):

Retention of *o*:
before *l*: foll, holts, gold
before labials: grob, ops, hobəl, xnopf, dobə, ofə, xopf
before velars: xoxxə, xnoxxə, rokx, kflogə, bogə.

Lowering to ɔ:
  before *r*: hɔrn, tɔrn, šɔrə
  before dentals and palatals: rɔss, xrɔttə, lɔsə, ksɔttə, bɔdɔ, pəšt.

The distribution of allophones is given by the rule

4.
$$
\begin{bmatrix} V \\ -\text{high} \\ +\text{back} \end{bmatrix} \rightarrow [\,+\text{low}\,]\,/\!-\!\begin{bmatrix} +\text{consonantal} \\ -\text{grave} \\ -\text{lateral} \end{bmatrix}
$$

It is necessary to restrict 4 to the back vowels. The umlauted variant
*ö* of the vowel *o* is not lowered. The plurals of *bogə* and *bɔdə* are *bögə* and
*bödə*, both with a mid *ö*. Hence the relative order of 4 and umlaut must
be

  *a*. Rule 3 (umlaut)
  *b*. Rule 4 (lowering)

This is the situation in some dialects on the northern fringe of Switzerland. Elsewhere a different state of affairs obtains.
  I will take a dialect which in all other relevant respects is identical to
that of the Schaffhausen area, namely that of Kesswil, in neighboring
Oberthurgau (Enderlin 1913). Rule 4 operates in unmodified form here
too. All the vocabulary items cited above for the Schaffhausen dialects
are found, with the same distribution of *o* and *ɔ*, in Kesswil. But the
difference is that Kesswil, along with most of Northeastern Switzerland,
has *ö* as the umlauted form of *o*, but *ɔ̈* as the umlauted form of *ɔ*. In these
dialects the plural of *bogə* is *bögə*, but the plural of *bɔdə* is *bɔ̈də*.
  The solution which first might come to mind is that the lowering rule in
4 was simplified to apply to rounded vowels regardless of whether they are
front or back. But this fails since phonemic *ö* does not lower to *ɔ̈* in the
environment of 4. The crucial cases are such forms as *plötsli* and *fröšš*
'frog' (originally a plural form). The behavior of these isolated forms
whose vowels are not lowered shows conclusively that we are in reality not
dealing with a lowering of *ö* to *ɔ̈* at all, but rather with the umlauting of
*ɔ* as well as of *o*. That is, the order of the rules has now become

  *a*. Rule 4 (lowering)
  *b*. Rule 3 (umlaut)

Applying to the same underlying forms as before, these rules now produce
the segment *ɔ̈*, which did not arise under the old ordering.

## 3. A Criterion for Psychological Reality

Returning after this brief survey of some main types of phonological change to the initial question about the justification for assuming the psychological reality of generative grammar, suppose that we now raise this question about some aspect of generative grammar, such as the requirement that grammars contain a certain level of representation, or that they be written with the use of certain notational conventions. The conception of linguistic change sketched out above, in which linguistic structure crucially figures at several points, suggests as one test for determining the answer that we ask the question: Do the levels, the kinds of rules, and so on, which are required by this theory ever play a role in linguistic change? Taking as our example again the simple case of the brace notation, we can ask: Do blocks of rules collapsed by braces form units of a kind which can undergo systematic change? If they do, this will be a powerful argument for this notation, and if not, we will have prima facie evidence that it is a spurious notation. On such questions, evidence of the following kind can be found.

In English, underlying long vowels, which are otherwise realized as diphthongs, are shortened in two main phonological environments: before two or more consonants (for example, *keep:kept*) and in the third syllable from the end of the word (for example, *vain:vanity, severe:severity*). The rules which bring these shortenings about are the following:

5'. $\quad$ V → [ − long] / —— CC
5". $\quad$ V → [ − long] / —— C ... V ... V

The theory of generative grammar requires that 5' and 5" be collapsed into a single rule as follows:

5. $\quad$ V → [ − long] / —— C $\begin{Bmatrix} C \\ ...V...V \end{Bmatrix}$

It asserts that of the two descriptively equivalent grammars, one of which contains the two rules (5' and 5") as separate processes, and the other as a single process combined into 5 by factoring out their common part and enclosing the remainder in braces, it is the latter which is the psychologically correct one.

Rule 5 arose in Early Middle English as a generalization of a much more restricted process of shortening. In Old English, vowels were shortened before *three* or *more* consonants (for example, *gōdspell* > *godspell, brǣmblas* > *bræmblas*) and in the third syllable from the end provided they were followed by *two* consonants (for example, *blēdsian* > *bledsian*).[4] The corresponding rules were:

6'.      $V \rightarrow [-\text{long}] / \underline{\quad} CCC$
6".      $V \rightarrow [-\text{long}] / \underline{\quad} CC \ldots V \ldots V$

Again, these rules must be collapsed as before:

6.      $V \rightarrow [-\text{long}] / \underline{\quad} CC \begin{Bmatrix} C \\ \ldots V \ldots V \end{Bmatrix}$

On comparing the Old English rule in 6 and the Early Middle English (and indeed Modern English) rule in 5 we see that the only difference between them is that the later rule (5) has lost one of the required consonants in its environment. It represents a simpler, more general form of the Old English vowel-shortening process. It will apply in all cases where 6 applied but also in cases where 6 would not have applied. Evidently the change from 6 to 5 is an instance of simplification, which we have seen to be one of the basic mechanisms of linguistic change. But in a linguistic theory in which the brace notation plays no role, the relation between the Old English and the Early Middle English shortening processes is a different one. If the brace notation were not part of linguistic theory we would have two separate changes – namely, 6' > 5' and 6" > 5" – on our hands and we would be faced with the very peculiar fact that two separate, unrelated rules have undergone an identical modification at the same point in the history of English. The linguistic theory on which traditional historical grammar was based is an instance of such a theory, and traditional historical grammar has in fact failed to see the regularity here and has treated the change as two separate processes.

   In the same way, we can go on to ask whether rules of the form

$$\begin{Bmatrix} X \\ Y \end{Bmatrix} \rightarrow Z$$

can be added to grammars. On the assumption that sound changes are natural processes, and that the brace notation groups rules into natural blocks, we should predict that rules collapsed by braces should be capable of being added to grammars. There are of course numerous instances of this type of change. In fact, the addition of Rule 6 to the grammar of Old English is probably just such an instance. Similarly we should predict that rules collapsed by braces should participate in reordering as blocks.

   The proposed test also has the virtue of rendering such notations eminently vulnerable to potential counterevidence from historical change. The counterclaim which would be made by the theory which excludes braces is that rules like 5' and 5", or 6' and 6", when found together in a grammar with no necessarily intervening rules forcing them apart, should be able to undergo simplification individually, in such a way that the resulting pair of rules could not subsequently be collapsed by braces. Such a change, which in this theory would be a legitimate simplification, would be neither a possible sound change nor a simplification in a theory which allows collapsing by braces, and it would therefore be excluded in the latter. If such changes could be found, they would be clear counter-evidence against the brace notation and would suggest that the generalizations effected by means of braces are spurious ones. The position which excludes braces would also entail that a rule could be inserted between two rules collapsed by braces in such a way that they subsequently could no longer be so collapsed. And finally, it would also entail that the parts of rules collapsed in this way should be individually capable of reordering with other rules of the grammar. The fact that no such changes appear to exist is strong negative evidence which adds to the historical support for the essential correctness of this abbreviatory convention of generative grammar.

The aforementioned linguist *C*, who wanted to introduce abbreviations like

$$Z \rightarrow \left\{ \begin{matrix} X \end{matrix} \right\} \rightarrow Y$$

and Pāṇini, who supported other conventions which generative grammar does not countenance, now both get a real opportunity to prove their points by showing that the blocks of rules resulting from such conventions act as units in simplification (for example, by showing cases in which the joint environment X is simplified) or by showing that they are added as units to grammars, or reordered as units with respect to other rules. There is no evidence in sight that I know of to encourage them in this search.

One answer, then, to the question concerning the empirical basis for the notational conventions of linguistic theory is that these conventions are an essential part of any attempt to characterize what is a possible linguistic change and what is not a possible linguistic change. It involves in a sense only systematically drawing the conclusions from Halle's idea (1962) that the class of possible sound changes (qua added rules) is the same as the class of possible phonological rules and bringing in the additional evidence of simplification, whose role in linguistic change Halle did not consider.

In many crucial respects this criterion for rule naturalness lends support to the assumptions which are currently made in the theory of generative grammar. But accepting the equivalence of possible sound change and possible rule commits one to placing many restrictions on the notations of grammatical descriptions which are not at present acknowledged, and on the other hand, it suggests the need for many new conventions and new extensions of notations which should be incorporated into linguistic theory. For example, by saying that braces are needed we have only told half the story. We would like to limit the use of braces in such a way as to combine only processes which are indeed in some sense related and can jointly produce a sound change. Suppose, for example, that we found a language with three phonological processes that all applied before vowels and that did not have to be separated by other rules:

> *a.* voiced stops become continuants
> *b. s* becomes *h*
> *c.* vowels drop

For all three processes to take place before vowels is quite natural, and examples for each of them could be cited from dozens of languages. Yet there would be something wrong about combining all three by virtue of their shared environment. It is evident that *a* and *b* are more closely related than either of them is to *c*, and that an adequate theory should require the combining of *a* and *b* but not *c*. The basis for this feeling is, I think, nothing but the fact that *a* and *b* characteristically occur together in linguistic change and thus form a natural block of phonological processes. In fact, their relatedness has really nothing to do with the fact that they share a common environment but follows from an essential kinship of the phonetic processes involved. Thus they should be grouped together in a grammar even if they both were context free. To determine the natural groupings of rules was a goal of traditional historical linguistics which has been abandoned to a large extent in structuralism, at least in America. For example, *a* and *b* would have been considered *weakenings*. Probably phonology would profit by attempting to develop further and to make precise such concepts, which traditional grammars use to introduce an organization into their treatments of diachronic phonology.

## 4. Diachronic Evidence Concerning Phonological Levels

The psychological reality of levels of representation which emerge in different linguistic theories is subject to verification and falsification by diachronic evidence along the same lines. A question to be asked whenever some level of representation is proposed as linguistically relevant is whether this level functions in linguistic change. For example, it would be a striking and, to my mind, conclusive piece of evidence for the reality of autonomous ('taxonomic') phonemics if it could be shown that there were sound changes whose conditioning environment could be stated naturally only at precisely this level. It should be made clear just what such a demonstration would involve. It would involve showing both that the environmments of this sound change were not morphophonemic and (the crucial part) that they could not be reformulated in terms of the phonetic level without restating exactly the rules that relate the phonetic and phonemic level. Of course, it is always by definition possible to reformulate a phonemic environment in terms of phonetic representations, and what would have to be shown is therefore that such a restatement of the conditioning environment of a sound change would lose a significant generalization. A hypothetical example of what to look for would be a change in some Russian dialect which affected all voiced obstruents except [ǯ] and [ʒ], the two voiced obstruents in Russian which are not phonemic but always come about only by automatic voicing assimilation of /č/ and /c/. As far as I know, no one has ever presented any instance of this kind, and there is therefore no basis for the claim that the facts of sound change somehow support a level of autonomous phonemics. And as has been repeatedly argued (Halle 1962, Chomsky and Halle 1968, Postal 1968, Kiparsky 1965, 1967), the facts of sound change do provide clear evidence for a deeper level of representation in phonology.

The contention has often been made that the level of autonomous phonemics is relevant to sound change in a somewhat different way. The suggestion is that the direction of sound change is determined by tendencies toward a symmetry of phonological units. What is important for our present discussion is that these units are often held to be specifically autonomous phonemes. Much the same comments again apply: if the level in question were demonstrably the relevant one here, and the tendencies in question could really be shown to exist, then this would decisively refute those who deny its existence. But once again, the necessary proof has, to my knowledge, never been provided.

Moulton had studied the vowel systems of Swiss dialects with the purpose of testing these concepts of 'phonological space'. He maintained (1961) that Rule 4 — the lowering of *o* to *ɔ* before dentals, palatals, and *r*, whose relation to umlauting we discussed as an example of reordering — was caused by a drive towards symmetry through 'filling' the 'empty slot' in the systems which Moulton supposes that these dialects possessed before the lowering took place:

| (A) | i | ü | u | | (B) | i | ü | u |
|-----|---|---|---|---|-----|---|---|---|
|     | e | ö | o | |     | e | ö | o |
|     | ɛ |   |   | |     | ɛ |   |   |
|     | æ |   | a | |     |   |   | a |

But what is the justification for assuming that System *B* had this asymmetrical structure rather than the symmetrical structure, $C$, which one would have normally supposed it to have?

$(C)$  i  ü  u
    e  ö  o
     ε   a

Why did Moulton not assign $a$ to the back vowels in these dialects as he did in the $A$ dialects? Moulton has discussed the reason for his choice in another article (Moulton 1960: 174), where the justification given for the asymmetrical System $B$ is that these dialects underwent the lowering by Rule 4: 'The fact that the subsequent development of the vowel system of the North was parallel not to that of the West and Center but to that of the East confirms the belief that arrangement [$B$ above] represents linguistic reality more faithfully, and suggests that arrangement [$C$ above] would indeed be only a playful manipulation of symbols on paper.' In other words, these dialects had an asymmetrical system because they underwent lowering of $o$ to $ɔ$, and they underwent lowering of $o$ to $ɔ$ because they had an asymmetrical system!

In sum, one prediction to which such theories lead is that certain phonological changes should be determined by whether or not pairs of certain sounds are contrastive in some phonetic environment and hence that isoglosses formed by phonological changes should characteristically be coextensive with boundaries between different autonomous phonemic systems. Other predictions are certainly also entailed, and the cases I have mentioned by no means constitute a full or even representative illustration of the range of predictions made, nor of the kind of evidence that is available to test them. But they nevertheless show how this theory and related ones do have very specific consequences which can be tested fully on historical material. I would guess that when this is done it will turn out that real enough tendencies towards phonological symmetry exist, but that they have nothing to do with the autonomous phonemic level for which they are often claimed. Rather they are probably brought about by simplificatory phonological changes such as rule simplification and rule reordering, and the symmetry they result in is phonetic rather than phonemic symmetry. This at any rate is what the Swiss German dialect material recently investigated by Moulton suggests.

## 5. Diachronic Evidence Concerning Features and Underlying Representations

The particular Swiss German example that I have talked about also raises a nest of further problems unrelated to that of the reality of the autonomous phonemic level, but highly relevant to the general topic of the relevance of linguistic change to linguistic universals. It will have been noticed that phonemic System *A* above, with four distinctive vowel heights, is a clear counterexample to Jakobson's distinctive feature system, which allows only three phonemic degrees of vowel height to exist in a language. First of all, the four degrees clearly contrast in simple, underived words and cannot be predicted by any general rules from some system with only three heights in any way that would not be ad hoc. For example,

| | | | | | | | |
|---|---|---|---|---|---|---|---|
| ælf | 'eleven' | gɛld | 'money' | šelm | 'rogue' | bild | 'picture' |
| sæmǝl | 'stool' | swebǝl | 'sulphur' | šnebǝl | 'sty (in | šwibǝl | 'grip' |
| hæks | 'witch' | xrɛps | 'crayfish' | | the eye)' | blits | 'lightning' |
| hællǝr | 'small | šellǝ | 'bell' | nets | 'net' | willǝ | 'will' |
| | coin' | | | xellǝ | 'scoop' | | |

In addition these dialects have a phonemic *a* which is quite distinct from all of these front vowels. Evidently, then, Jakobson's features compact and diffuse (low and high) should be replaced by two other features which allow four distinctive degrees of vowel height. A natural one would be the following:

| | æ | ɛ | e | i |
|---|---|---|---|---|
| High | − | − | + | + |
| Mid | − | + | + | − |

Yet if we shift our point of view somewhat and regard impossible systems simply as the end points of increasing scales of markedness, the proposed change to allow four heights is a relatively minor one. In a sense, these dialects, particularly if the historical evidence is brought in, support Jacobson's thesis in the modified form that vowel systems with four heights are complex, that is, highly marked systems, in the technical sense. For historically, a four-height system of this kind had to arise in all High German dialects. However, everywhere, with the exception of some tiny Swiss areas in Appenzell and Toggenburg, the four heights have been reduced by three by mergers either of the two mid vowels or of the two low vowels. These mergers have taken place quite independently in numerous dialects and thus have the character of drift or simplification rather than of normal sound changes. What this seems to indicate is that systems of four vowel heights are unstable because of their complexity, a conclusion which is indicated in any case by the rarity of such systems in the languages of the world.

The particular way in which these four-height systems have merged to three in the various dialects is itself a small piece of historical support for the feature system which I have proposed. The other possible alternative of characterizing four vowel heights by two features would be this :

|        | æ | $\epsilon$ | e | i |
|--------|---|---|---|---|
| High   | − | − | + | + |
| Raised | − | + | − | + |

There would be no natural way of formulating the merger of mid vowels here since mid vowels do not make up a natural class under these features. On the other hand, this alternative suggests mergers such as *æ* and *e* or $\epsilon$ and *i* which certainly do not occur. Vowel shifts of the type $\bar{i} > æi$, which are common in many languages, would also be expressed more simply in the system I have proposed. However, an alternative which may be even preferable and should in any case not be counted out yet is that vowel height is not broken down into two binary dimensions at all but forms a single dimension expressed by a feature which in underlying representations can assume at most four values (and must assume at least two).

Against the analysis which posits four heights of vowels in these dialects one might try to carry the argument that this analysis is implausible because closely related dialects have only three heights, and one would expect closely related dialects to differ not in their underlying phonemic system, but only in the rules which relate phonemic representations to phonetic representations. This would be a complete non sequitur. It is an empirical observation that related dialects often have the same phonemic system, but it is not a theoretical condition on related dialects that this should be the case. To say otherwise would be to credit children with historical or dialectological knowledge which they cannot possibly possess. The fact that the children of each generation in learning their language take a fresh look at the facts means that there is reason for underlying representations to be transmitted only when the synchronic facts of the language warrant it. The argument is just as irrelevant, and for just the same reason, as it would be to maintain that language *L* must have rule *R* in its grammar because *R* was a sound change in *L*.

A more difficult objection is based on the fact that *æ* in these dialects is the productive umlaut of *a*. To account for morphological umlaut in a language like German it is necessary to set up some abstract conditioning environment which will be a property of certain endings, such as plural *-er*. Whether this is a feature [± umlaut] as proposed by Zwicky (1967) or some phonological property of underlying representations will not matter here. Whatever this abstract environment is, generative phonology at present allows − and indeed probably requires − the trick of making it an obligatory part of isolated words like *schön, plötzlich, Tür*, which have umlaut vowels that correspond to no back vowels in any related forms. These words are then entered with underlying back vowels which undergo obligatory umlauting by virtue of this property of their underlying representations. The effect is to do away altogether with umlaut vowels in the phonemic system. In our case, then, *æ* would never be treated as phonemic and there would be only three phonemic vowel heights to worry about.

It is again the historical evidence which shows that this trick is wrong and that words like *schön, plötzlich, Tür* must have phonemic umlaut vowels. To see this let us go back to the example of reordering involving Rules 3 and 4 in Northeastern Switzerland. It will be recalled that as a result of the reordering, derived *ö* as in plural *böda* became *ɔ̈* but phonemic *ö* as in *plötsli* was not changed. There would be no way of accounting for a change like this (by no means an atypical case) in a theory which asserted that *all* umlaut vowels are underlying back vowels, for then we would have no natural way of telling apart those that are really so derived and do undergo lowering from those which are only fictitiously so derived and do not undergo lowering. This linguistic change cannot be accounted for unless phonological theory is tightened up in some way to exclude tricks of such a kind. It is interesting to note that whatever exactly the right way to do this turns out to be, it will bring the underlying representations of generative phonology a step closer to Sapir's descriptive practice (McCawley 1967). And once this necessary move is made, the existence of systems with four vowel heights cannot be argued away.[5]

This last conclusion has the peculiar status of at present resting entirely on historical evidence, and of a fairly indirect kind at that. Whether or not we draw it depends on what we consider the subject matter of linguistics to be. We could not draw it if we regarded a grammar simply as a theory of the sentences of a language, and a linguistic theory as a theory of grammars. For this position would entail that linguistic change is no concern of linguistic theory, although it might of course be a pleasant bonus if linguistic theory could be usefully 'applied' to questions of linguistic change. But it would not cause us to demand of a linguistic theory that it must (in conjunction with a theory of linguistic change) provide an explanation of the linguistic regularities of diachrony. It is a very different matter if we regard a grammar as a theory of linguistic competence, and the field of linguistics as the study of universal grammar. On this view, which forms the topic of this conference and which I share, the facts of linguistic change assume a new relevance as empirical evidence on the nature of language. We must be prepared to allow them to bear on even purely synchronic questions and, for example, to let the fact that some phonological change is explainable by one linguistic theory but not by another carry weight in the choice between these two theories. The application of linguistic change to linguistic theory now becomes at least as important as the converse process.

The above rather scattered observations illustrate various types of inferences that can be made about grammatical form from the ways in which it shapes linguistic change. The reason I have dealt with phonological changes and not syntactic ones is partly that I know more about phonology, but also that the historical facts are here much easier to come by and the evidence they give is more needed in phonology than in syntax. I have been concerned not so much with establishing the virtues and faults of specific notations, levels, and so forth — much more evidence would be needed for that in almost every kind of problem dealt with above — as with making a case for the legitimacy and potential fruitfulness of certain general patterns of inference from linguistic change to the nature of grammar. In no case have the conclusions depended on very specific or controversial assumptions about linguistic change. The basic assumption from which these conclusions follow has been the very tame one that where grammar is involved in linguistic change it is involved in terms of its natural components and rules.

It is not so with another kind of inference from linguistic change to grammatical form to which I should now like to turn. This inference is based so heavily on the existence of grammatical simplification as a form of linguistic change that before proceeding to it I should like to outline the justification for assuming the existence of such a form of linguistic change.

## 6. Formal Justification for Simplification

The conclusion that such changes as simplification and reordering must exist does not and could not rest just on the fact that we observe related dialects to differ in the ordering of their rules, or to show minor differences in the details of essentially shared rules. That such differences are typical isoglosses is true but compatible with the position that addition of rules is the only form of phonological change. For as long as we look at dialects without knowledge of their historical origin we could explain any rule-ordering difference between them in a wave-theory fashion. For example, a spreading rule might be adopted at one position in the sequence of rules in one dialect and at some other position in another. There is another wave-theory effect which can cause pairs of rules to be differently ordered in different dialects. If Rule A spreads from West to East and Rule B spreads from East to West across some dialect area, then, if the two rules are critically ordered with respect to each other, the Western area will end up with the order A, B and the Eastern area with the order B, A. Undoubtedly these are both, in fact, quite common causes of ordering differences between dialects. Small differences in the form of rules can well occur in the course of their diffusion from one dialect to another. It has been observed that in such borrowing a narrowing down in the scope of rules often takes place. Thus the diphthongization of the long high vowels of Middle High German during its spread southward in Swiss territory was restricted to word-final position at a certain point before it stopped spreading altogether. Compare also the gradual curtailment of the High German consonant shift in the so-called Rhenish Fan.[6]

However, we find just the same types of minor differences in the form of rules and in their ordering when we compare successive stages of the same dialect rather than geographically adjacent dialects, and here the wave-theory and imperfect borrowing explanations are excluded. Furthermore, in such cases the form of rules almost always changes in the direction of greater simplicity. Can such changes be accounted for on the assumption that addition of rules is the only form of phonological change?

Consider the Finnish example cited in Section 2, in which the diphthongization rule was dialectally shifted down to follow loss of medial voiced continuants so as to apply to the long vowels which arose by this historically later rule (for example, *teγe > tee > tie*). Technically, it is not impossible to account for this change by means of added rules. There are even two ways of doing it. One is to assume that a rule of loss of medial voiced continuants, identical with the original one, was entered before diphthongization, causing the original one to become vacuous and to be dropped. The other is to assume that a diphthongization rule, identical with the original diphthongization rule, was entered *after* loss of medial voiced continuants. The optimal grammar for the resulting output would once again be the desired one. The unfortunate aspect of this is the arbitrariness of the choice between the two descriptions. It is hard to see how the distinction between them could correspond to any linguistic difference. The two distinct grammars containing an identical rule at two different points which are required as virtual intermediaries seem to be mere artifacts of a theory which excludes reordering as a mechanism of change and therefore must make an inappropriate extension of rule adding to account for a quite different kind of process.

The difficulties become considerable in such a case as the loss of word-final devoicing in Swiss German and Yiddish. We cannot, clearly, simply suppose that a late rule which made final obstruents voiced was added. Such a rule could not distinguish between morphophonemically voiced and voiceless stops and would wrongly turn into *bund* not only the *bunt* that is related to *bunde* but also the *bunt* that is related to *bunte*. In desperation we would take recourse to an ad hoc rule which somehow would provide morphophonemically voiced stops with a diacritic feature before they got devoiced and later would use this diacritic feature as an environment for revoicing, after which the diacritic feature could be deleted again. Obviously this bears not the faintest resemblance to what actually happened, and no one would want to salvage a theory at the price of such an absurd analysis.

Chomsky and Hally (1968) discuss a convention for handling exceptions to rules which might be used in this particular example. The idea is that grammars can contain rules of the form

$$X \rightarrow [- \text{next rule}]$$

where X is a specification of the special cases in which some rule must not apply. Then it would be possible to say that a rule

$$[\quad] \rightarrow [- \text{next rule}]$$

was placed directly before the devoicing of word-final obstruents, thus preventing everything from undergoing it. The inoperative devoicing rule would then simply not be incorporated into the grammars of the next generation.

The difference here is not merely notational. The exception-rule solution generalizes neither to the reordering example that was just cited nor to cases like the simplification of the umlaut rule from 2 to 3 which was mentioned earlier. Since what was deleted here was *part* of a rule and the Chomsky-Halle convention for handling exceptions does not allow items to be exceptions to parts of rules, the solution which the convention made possible in the previous case is not available here. The best we can do is to say that the change consists of two separate but simultaneous events: first, the rendering inapplicable of the old umlaut rule (2) by the placement of a Chomsky-Halle exception rule before it, and second, the entering of the new umlaut rule (3) in its stead. That is, we are forced to treat this event as a composite product of two simultaneous changes, one of which alone would have far more spectacular consequences than the two have together. This leaves us completely in the dark as to why so many dialects (quite independently of each other, as is clear from the geographical distribution) should have undergone such a complicated pair of changes.

We see that to account for such examples by added rules, we would be forced to relax the proposed restriction that a sound change is the addition of a rule to the grammar to the extent of allowing a single historical change to involve the addition of *two* rules. In that case all arguments like those in Section 3 about sound change as a criterion for rule natural- ness at once go out the window. And if this is done we also prepare a welcome for innumerable absurd descriptions of other changes. For example, in the case of the Finnish reordering of diphthongization and loss of medial voiced continuants (see Section 2 above) there are now two further alternatives which add to the general arbitrariness: the change might consist of simultaneously making diphthongization inapplicable and adding an exact replica of it after the loss of medial voiced continuants, or of simultaneously making loss of medial voiced continuants inapplicable and adding an exact replica of it before diphthongization.

Also, it is now just as easy to express the reverse change, that is, a change as a result of which the order

- *a.*   loss of medial voiced continuants
- *b.*   diphthongization

changes into

- *a.*   diphthongization
- *b.*   loss of medial voiced continuants

The effect of this would be that all *ie* diphthongs derived by way of *ee* from *eγe* would revert to their intermediate representation *ee*, while the *ie* diphthongs derived from basic *ee* would stay unchanged. There is no doubt that a theory of linguistic change should either completely exclude the possibility of such a change or at least reflect the obvious fact that it would be a far more complex and unlikely historical event than what actually happened. But the version to which the theory that rule addition is the only form of linguistic change has been driven at this point is completely incapable of doing so. As the brute necessity of somehow accommodating one set of data has forced it to be relaxed and extended more and more, it has lost the capacity of expressing the facts about sound change that originally motivated it.

## 7. Simplification and Language Acquisition

To avoid this hopeless mess, the concept of simplification would be necessary even if we were concerned merely with characterizing the possible ways in which successive stages of a language could differ (which would be enough for purposes of linguistic reconstruction). But we also would like to find an explanation for why languages can change in the ways that they do. In that case, the reasons for assuming that simplification is a form of linguistic change become more compelling still. We cannot, then, close our eyes to the fact that the kind of driftlike changes which rule addition fails to handle without the special acrobatics of which samples were performed in Section 6 result in just the kind of grammars that appear spontaneously as intermediate stages in the course of the child's language-learning process.

I am not thinking just of the fact that instances of morphological analogy (*oxes, bringed*) are as characteristic of child language as they are of historical change, although this is perhaps the most evident instance of the correspondence. The parallelism goes deeper than that. For example, there is in many languages a drift toward multiple negation, as in substandard English 'I don't see nothing nowhere'. Such multiple negation has developed in the Romance languages and elsewhere in Europe too. Jespersen tried to attribute this drift to some vague tendency toward redundancy which he thought governed the direction of linguistic change. But this can hardly be true, for in other languages, such as Finnish, no comparable drift toward multiple negation is observed. Then it cannot be true that multiple negation is simply a general target in the direction of which all languages develop. In fact I think it is true that multiple negation appears only in those languages that have the equivalent of Klima's (1964b) *neg*-incorporation rule which produces negative quantifiers such as in English *nobody*, *nothing* and French *rien*.[7] Surely this is related to the facts about the development of negation in child language found by Bellugi (cited from McNeill 1966). She discovered that at the point at which the child's sentences like

I didn't see something.
You don't want some supper.

give way to sentences with negative quantifiers like *nobody, nothing, no supper*, a period of multiple negation at first sets in. As the child first formulates his *neg*-incorporation rule, it has not the form of standard English but of substandard English (which he very well may never have heard); and instead of producing the 'normal' sentences like

I saw nothing.
Nobody likes me.

he at first comes out with

I didn't see nothing.
Nobody don't like me.

Thus some relationship between 'substandard' *neg*-incorporation and 'standard' *neg*-incorporation may be responsible for the fact that the former is the natural predecessor of the latter in the development of a child's linguistic system and also the natural result of the latter by linguistic change.

These facts begin to add up when we think of language acquisition as a process in which the child arrives at adult grammar gradually by attempting to match to the speech it hears a succession of hypotheses of an increasing order of complexity (in the linguistic sense of complexity) as these increasingly complex hypotheses become available to the child through maturational change. For phonology this was clearly shown by Jakobson's spectacular discovery that the child learns phonemes in a largely fixed order, which is determined not externally by the order or frequency with which they are heard, but internally by their relative linguistic complexity, as reflected also in the rules governing the possible phonemic systems of the languages of the world (Jakobson 1962). Thus the child first produces the maximally unmarked, unvoiced, unaspirated stops, even if these, as in English, happen not to occur (except in some special environments) and only then splits up this first stop series into two series. In phonology, then, the order in which a child incorporates a particular piece of data into his internalized grammar is determined not by frequency or order of presentation, but by the readiness of the child to assimilate the kind of structure that underlies it. If we assume that the order in which the syntactic rules of the child unfold is internally determined in the same way, we can think of the child's multiple negation as analogous to his unvoiced, unaspirated stop in the sense that both are necessary prior structures which can be discarded only after the full structure develops. This is reasonable in view of the fact that multiple negation is produced by a version of *neg*-incorporation which is in two respects simpler than the adult version of this transformation. In the first place, the adult rule not only adds a *neg* to the quantifier, but it also deletes the original *neg* after the tense; this additional operation of deletion is absent from the child's first version of the rule. Secondly, the adult rule adds a *neg* to just one single quantifier in the sentence, whereas the child spreads the *neg* over all the quantifiers that appear in the sentence, producing such specimens as the following:

I can't do nothing with no string.

Normally these oversimplified intermediate grammars which the child constructs on its way to adult language eventually give way to the full complexity of the adult system. The linguistic change of simplification takes place on those relatively rare occasions when some feature of these intermediate grammars survives into adulthood and becomes adopted by the speech community as a new linguistic norm. See Jakobson's remark (1962: 332):

Die Sprachveränderung is kein äusserer Beitrag, den die Kinder dem Sprachgebilde aufzwingen, sondern sie antizipieren dessen innerlich vorherbestimmte, sozusagen in der Luft schwebende Umwandlungen.

That such survival is possible is not quite so surprising when we consider the extreme imperviousness of children to adult correction of their speech, as illustrated for multiple negation by the following dialogue (McNeill 1966: 69):

Child: Nobody don't like me.
Mother: No, say 'nobody likes me'.
Child: Nobody don't like me.

(eight repetitions of this dialogue)

Mother: No, now listen carefully; say *'nobody likes me'.*
Child: Oh! Nobody don't likes me.

Thus we can relate the concepts of rule addition and simplification to adult and child language, respectively. The typical form of rule addition is the borrowing of rules among adults; simplification typically occurs in the learning of language by children. An interesting consequence of this is that isoglosses formed by the spread of rules over a speech territory should form large, coherent dialect areas, whereas those formed by simplification should be characteristically discontinuous because of independent development of the same change in several speech communities. The historically interesting isoglosses, therefore, should be based on the presence versus absence of rules, and not on differences in the form and order of shared rules. Indeed, this is what dialectologists have always implicitly assumed. The boundaries between the major dialect areas of Germany are drawn according to the rules they have, such as the consonant shifts. The isogloss between the two forms of the umlaut rule, 2 and 3 (that is, between *e* and *æ* as the productive umlaut of *a*), would form a useless patchwork of no historical significance. Nor would anyone suppose a historical relationship between Yiddish and Swiss German on the grounds that they share the loss of the word-final devoicing rule. Very schematically, the two types of isoglosses would look like this (shaded areas are the innovating ones):

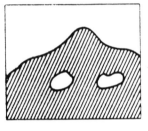

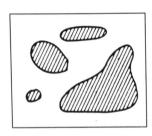

Spread of rule                    Simplification

## 8. Reordering as Simplification

Reordering resembles simplification both in the negative property that rule addition miserably fails to do justice to it and in the positive property of its driftlike character. I shall now claim that reordering is in fact a special case of simplification, and that the direction of reordering is predicted by general principles which assign certain types of order a higher value than others. If this can be established, then current phonological theory, which does not distinguish different kinds of linear order, is wrong and must be revised to account for this asymmetry.

To be convinced that reordering is a one-way affair, much as other simplification is, it is enough to examine the individual examples. For instance, many Swiss dialects have put the umlaut rule (3) after $o > \mathfrak{o}$ (Rule 4), but none of these have made the reverse switch, and we could not easily imagine it taking place. And a dialect of Finnish in which *tie* from *teγe > tee* becomes *tee* again but *vie* from *vee* retains the diphthong, that is, a dialect in which diphthongization reverts to its original position before the loss of medial voiced continuants (which I will now call $\gamma >$ $\emptyset$ for short) is inconceivable. The question is how this asymmetry, intuitively evident enough in each particular case, can be given a general characterization.

Of the various functional relationships that can hold between rules, two are of relevance here. One way in which two rules, $A$ and $B$, can be functionally related is that the application of $A$ creates representations to which $B$ is applicable. That is, the application of $A$ converts forms to which $B$ cannot apply into forms to which $B$ can apply; schematically:

$A$      $[\ \ ] > [\phi]$
$B.$      $[\phi] > [\ \ ]$

Such a relationship holds for example between $\gamma > \emptyset$ (*teγe > tee*) and diphthongization (*tee > tie*) in our Finnish example. If the rules are applied in that order, $\gamma > \emptyset$ supplies a set of new cases (namely those derived from *eγe*) to which diphthongization can apply. In such a situation, call $A$ a *feeding rule* relative to $B$ (for example, $\gamma > \emptyset$ is a feeding rule relative to diphthongization). Call this relationship between rules a *feeding relationship* (for example, $\gamma > \emptyset$ and diphthongization are in a feeding relationship) and the linear order in which the feeding rule precedes a *feeding order* (for example, 1. $\gamma > \emptyset$, 2. diphthongization is a feeding order). Then one of the principles that determine the direction of reordering is

I. Feeding order tends to be maximized.

Schematically:

$$A.\ [\Phi] > [\ ] \qquad \quad B.\ \ \ [\ ] > [\Phi]$$
$$B.\ [\ ] > [\Phi] \quad > \quad A.\ \ \ [\Phi] > [\ ]$$

A further example of I involves the several palatalizations in Slavic. By the so-called first palatalization, *k* and *g* became *č* and *ǯ* respectively, before front vowels and *y*, for example, *\*kĭto > čĭto* 'what', *\*givŭ > ǯivŭ* 'alive'.[8]

7.
$$\begin{bmatrix} +\ consonantal \\ -\ diffuse \end{bmatrix} \rightarrow \begin{bmatrix} -\ grave \\ +\ strident \end{bmatrix} / \underline{\quad\quad} \begin{bmatrix} -\ consonantal \\ -\ back \end{bmatrix}$$

But the resulting voiced affricate *ǯ* has become a continuant *ž* in all Slavic languages by the rule

8.
$$\begin{bmatrix} +\ voiced \\ -\ grave \\ +\ strident \end{bmatrix} \rightarrow [+\ continuant]$$

For example, *\*ǯivŭ > živŭ*.

Subsequently new front vowels came to stand after velars by the rule

9.    ai → ě

By the so-called second palatalization *k′* and *g′* (derived from *k* and *g* by an earlier rule) became *c* and *ǯ* before these new front vowels, for example, *\*k′ěna > cěna* 'price', *\*g′ělo > ǯělo* 'very':

10.
$$\begin{bmatrix} +\ obstruent \\ -\ grave \\ -\ strident \\ -\ diffuse \end{bmatrix} \rightarrow \begin{bmatrix} +\ strident \\ +\ diffuse \end{bmatrix}$$

The resulting affricate *ǯ*, unlike the earlier *ǯ*, is retained in Old Church Slavic and in modern Polish. The grammars of these languages have Rules 7-10 as phonological rules in an order that matches their relative chronology. But elsewhere in Slavic *ǯ* also has been replaced by its corresponding continuant, namely *z*, for example, *ǯělo > zělo*. These languages have the same four rules, but 8 must here follow 10, in order to apply to the affricate produced by the second palatalization as well. It is these two rules between which the feeding relationship obtains. Rule 10 is the feeding rule and the reordering establishes a feeding order between 10 and 8.

It should be noted that this relationship is a matter of the function and not of the form of the rules. In the Slavic example there is, as is often the case elsewhere too, a formal similarity between the related rules in that they mention some of the same features, and so on. But it would not be possible to define the correct relationship on the basis of the form of the rules. The two Finnish rules previously cited have very little in common, and the relationship is simply based on properties of the derivations the language has.

Another possible functional relationship between two rules is that *A* removes representations to which *B* would otherwise apply:

$A.\ [\ \ ] > [\sim \varphi]$
$B.\ [\varphi] > [\ \ ]$

Such a relationship holds for example between umlaut (*A*) and $o > \mathfrak{o}$ (*B*) in the example of Section 2. Thus the application of umlaut turns *o* into *ö*, a front vowel to which the lowering rule is no longer applicable. If the lowering rule comes first in the ordering, it applies, turning *o* into *ɔ*, and umlaut can then still apply. In the terms of the Indian grammatical tradition, umlaut is here the *nitya* or 'constant' rule. Call *A* a *bleeding rule* relative to *B*, the relationship between *A* and *B* a *bleeding relationship*, and the ordering in which *A* precedes *B* a *bleeding order*. The principle which underlies the asymmetry of order in this case is the following:

*A*. II. Bleeding order tends to be minimized.

$$A.\ [\ \ ] > [\sim \varphi] \qquad B.\ \ \ [\varphi] > [\ \ ] $$
$$B.\ [\varphi] > [\ \ ] \qquad > \qquad A.\ \ \ [\ \ ] > [\sim \varphi]$$

In this way the original order, in which umlaut preceded lowering, became switched around into the new order, in which the bleeding did not take place.

As another illustration of the effect of II, consider the relation of two rules pertaining to voiced obstruents in German. One of them, which is historically the older, is the devoicing of obstruents in word-final position (for example, *bund* > *bunt*, *tāg* > *tāk*). This is Rule 1, which has come up in the discussion several times already. The other, found only in a certain group of dialects (Schirmunski 1962: 302), is the spirantization of postvocalic voiced stops, for example, *tāgə* > *tāɣə*, *sāgt* > *sāɣt* (> *sāxt*). Originally, devoicing preceded postvocalic spirantization. Since, with this order, morphophonemic final voiced stops lost their voicing before spirantization applied, they remained stops and the contrast of *tāk:tāɣə* resulted. This bleeding order, in which word-final devoicing deprives spirantization of some of the voiced stops to which it would otherwise apply, is still retained in some Alsatian, Bavarian, and Middle German dialects. More frequently the reverse ordering is found, with final voiced stops undergoing first spirantization (*tāg* > *tāγ*) and then devoicing (*tāγ* > *tāx*). This order is widespread and especially common in the Low German dialects. We know that this order is a secondary development because some words like (*a*)*wek* (Standard German *weg*), where the voicing of the stop had no morphophonemic support, failed to spirantize even in the reordering dialects. This would be inexplicable unless we suppose that the devoicing was historically earlier even in these dialects in spite of the fact that it is synchronically later.

Another example can be cited from this same familiar area. A very widespread sound change in German dialects (Schirmunski 1962: 212) is the rounding of *ā* to *ɔ̄*. As *ǣ*, the umlaut of *ā*, is unaffected by this change, it brings about alternations between *ɔ̄* and *ǣ* such as *šwɔ̄n* 'swan': *šwǣn* 'pl.', *špɔ̄t* 'late': *špǣter* 'later'. Hence there is a bleeding order between the rules

   *a*. umlaut
   *b*. ā > ɔ̄

Many modern German dialects have just this system (see Rabeler 1911, and Hotzenköcherle 1934, for a Low German and Swiss German dialect, respectively). In others (for example, Wanner 1941) the system has changed in that the umlauted form of *ɔ̄* is *ɔ̄̈*, for example, *swɔ̄̈n*, *špɔ̄̈tər*. The grammatical difference is that umlaut now applies after rather than before the rounding of *ā*. As phonemic *ǣ* in words like *tsǣ* 'tough' and *lǣr* 'empty' stays unrounded (more proof of the correctness of the argument is in Section 5) it is clear that the possibility of a simplification of the rounding rule to all long compact vowels is excluded and we are again faced with a case of reordering, which conforms perfectly to Principle II.

There is a more general principle underlying the two reordering tendencies (I and II) which combines them under a single wider concept of fuller utilization and makes their nature intuitively much clearer:

   III. Rules tend to shift into the order which allows their fullest utilization in the grammar.

If I am right that such a principle determines the direction in which reordering proceeds, then it follows that the order toward which rules gravitate in this way is linguistically simpler than its opposite. It is hard to see what other explanation there could be for such a consistent tendency toward a specific kind of order in linguistic change. As a convenient designation for the order types which are shunned and preferred according to Principles I-III, I suggest *marked* and *unmarked* order, respectively. It may well be that marking conventions analogous to those which assign the unmarked feature values in segmental phonology are the appropriate device for reflecting the asymmetry of ordering relations as well.

## 9. Leveling and Extension

As further justification for my assertion that unidirectional reordering tendencies exist and that they obey Principles I-III, I want to adduce an unexpected parallelism which obtains between reordering, if so constrained, and rule simplification. We can begin with a distinction drawn in traditional and structural historical grammar between two types of analogy, one called *leveling* and the other called *polarization* or *extension*. By leveling was meant roughly that existing alternations are either curtailed or eliminated altogether, with the result that allomorphs of some morphemes become more similar to each other or merge completely. Thus the change of *bunt:bunde* to *bund:bunde* would have been regarded as a leveling of the alternation of voiced and voiceless stops in word-final position. The simplification of the umlaut rule (2) to its other version (3), which replaced *kraft:kreftig* by *kraft:kræftig* would have been regarded as a leveling of the height alternation in favor of the low vowel throughout the paradigm.

Polarization, or extension, on the other hand, refers to a type of analogical change in which existing alternations spread to new instances. Here linguistic contrasts come to be more fully implemented than before, whereas leveling has precisely the opposite effect. We would presumably be dealing with extension if, for example, the alternation of medial voicing and final voicelessness in obstruents as in *tāge:tāk, bunde:bunt*, instead of being eliminated altogether, had become extended beyond its original domain to the sonorants, as has in fact happened in Icelandic. The change of the limited Old English vowel shortening rule (6) to its present more general form (5) is another instance of extension.

This distinction, implicit in traditional historical studies, though rarely drawn systematically (but see Hoenigswald 1960: 63, 108), is a useful one, partly for reasons that have to do with linguistic reconstruction. Leveling will often be recoverable by historical reconstruction, because of the relic forms which reflect older linguistic stages that leveling leaves behind. Extension, however, will in general not be so recoverable because, with certain very interesting exceptions, it cannot leave relic forms behind. The difference between these two types of analogy can be defined in terms of the formal differences of two kinds of rule simplification in a very straightforward manner. Rules consist of two parts, a structural analysis, which specifies to what forms the rule applies, and a structural change, which says what happens to these forms. In the customary notation for phonological rules, the structural change is the part between the arrow and the slash and the structural analysis is everything else. Then any rule simplification which modifies the structural change of a rule (whether or not it also modifies the structural analysis) is a *leveling*, and any rule simplification which does not modify the structural change of a rule is an *extension*. Thus the loss of final devoicing (Rule 1) and the simplification of Rule 2 to Rule 3 affect the structural change of the rule and are hence levelings, but the change of the shortening rule in English did not affect its structural change and is hence an extension.

It is a fairly surprising fact that the two kinds of reorderings we have found, namely those governed by I and II, correspond pairwise to these two kinds of rule simplifications and in turn to the traditional distinction between extension and leveling. Reordering by II results in leveling and thus corresponds to simplification in the structural change of a rule. For example, the effect of placing umlaut after $o > \vartheta$ is that the height alternation in *bɔdaːbödə* and innumerable similar cases is leveled and the resulting forms, *bɔdaːbȫdə*, retain the low vowel throughout the paradigm. So, too, the reordering of spirantization and word-final devoicing results in the dropping of a two-feature alternation, *tak:taɣə* (with change of both voicing and continuance), in favor of a simpler one-feature alternation, *tax:taɣə* (with a continuant throughout the paradigm), that is, again in leveling. In their effect on surface forms and on the relation of surface forms, leveling by simplification in the structural change of rules and leveling by reordering in accordance with Principle II have similar effects in that they make more alike the different shapes in which morphemes appear. But they bring this effect about in different ways because leveling by rule simplification brings the forms closer to the base forms, whereas leveling by reordering takes forms farther away from their base forms. But both types share the property that they can leave behind relic forms which make the recovery of these processes by linguistic reconstruction a possibility. What guarantees us the earlier grammar in each of these cases are the forms like *weg* (in the case where the devoicing rule is lost and in the case in which it is reordered with spirantization), *plötsli* (in reordering of umlaut and $o > \vartheta$), and so on.

On the other hand, reordering by I results in extension (polarization) and so corresponds to simplification which affects only the structural analysis of rules. In the case of the Slavic palatalizations (see Section 8), for example, the voiced stop:voiced affricate alternation is polarized into a voiced stop:voiced continuant alternation. It is clear that in this case any forms which undergo the old form of the rules are also going to undergo them after the reordering, so that relic forms which would allow reconstruction of the change could not be created.

These relationships are summarized in the following table.

| Reordering | Corresponds to simplification of | Reconstructible by relic forms? | Surface effect |
|---|---|---|---|
| by I | Structural analysis only | No | Extension (polarization) |
| by II | Structural change | Yes | Leveling |

## Notes

1.     The reason is that abbreviatory conventions in the Indian grammatical tradition, originally an oral one, were not graphic devices such as braces, parentheses, or anything directly equivalent to them, but rather resembled the conjunction-reduction processes of natural language. In the following three sutras, for example, the bracketed words are omitted and understood as carried over from the previous sutra.

   6.1.77   *iko yaṇ aci* (high vowels become glides before vowels)
   6.1.78   *eco 'yavāyāvah [aci]* (e, o, . . . →ay, av, . . . before vowels)
   6.1.79   [*eco*] *vānto yi pratyaye (o, au →av, āv* before *y*)

It is hardly possible to collapse these three rules into one rule by any extensions of the conventions of generative grammar.

2.     The rule must be complicated somewhat to include secondary umlaut.

3.     The term *generalization* is sometimes confusing, and I will not use it here. It is applicable in the natural sense of the word only to simplification in the structural analysis of a rule; simplification in the structural change is hardly generalization in this same sense. Even regarding the structural analysis, it is hard for some people to get used to the idea that a rule applying to stops and to *f* is less general than one applying just to stops.

4.     Luick (1921, pp. 204, 353-353). In isolated words the Old English shortening also applied before geminates. But in these isolated words it led to restructuring, and since there was no shortening in *derived* words in Old English, the (synchronic) phonological rule of Old English was as stated. This rule covers all cases where there was actual alternation between long and short vowels in Old English.

5.     David Stampe points out to me that the naturalness condition he proposes at this same conference (cf. Stampe 1967, 1969) requires exactly the underlying representations which we have seen to be justified on historical grounds.

6.     E. Bach has pointed out to me that these examples are not certain. If, as he suggests, rules are never narrowed down in borrowing, the case for simplification becomes even stronger.

7.     Finnish has indefinite pronouns such as *kukaan, mikään*, corresponding to English *anybody, anything*, but a negative cannot be incorporated into them to form any equivalents of *nobody, nothing*.

8.     Other aspects of the Slavic palatalizations are dealt with by Halle and Lightner (ms.). My knowledge of the rules is based entirely on their work. I state the rule here with the Jakobsonian features rather than any of the recent alternative proposals which have greatly improved the system.

# Chapter 3

# Historical Linguistics

The first concern of the historical linguist is to understand how languages change. By a long series of historical processes the Proto-Indo-European parent language gradually split up into a number of separate languages such as Germanic, Celtic, Slavic, and these in turn evolved into their numerous modern descendants. The same processes of change are responsible for the diversity of dialects within English — and after some millennia they may well have resulted in a number of languages descended from English in just the same way that English, German, etc., are descended from Proto-Germanic. The nature of these processes stands as the question basic to all further work in historical linguistics.

One front on which this question is being attacked is the close analysis of the history of particular, preferably well-documented, languages, with the purpose of formulating on the basis of the changes there observed, the precisest possible characterization of the 'possible changes' that a language can undergo. This involves distinguishing types of change, such as *sound change* and *analogy*, and finding the conditions and limitations to which each one of these types is subject. Anyone working in historical linguistics soon gains a general feel for these conditions and limitations, without necessarily being able to formulate them in terms of the desired general principles. For example, [p] may change to [f], but hardly to [l], a sound change might be restricted to words of one syllable, but never, say, to words of three phonemes, or to palindromes. Things are not always so obvious, of course. Do sounds always change by just one phonetic property at a time? Can sound change be grammatically conditioned? What exactly are the conditions under which analogical change can become operative? Increased depth and precision in the historical study of languages depends on securing reliable answers to a large number of such questions. Some of them are also of great theoretical importance, as will be seen in the following pages.

Complementing this approach to the fundamental question of how languages change are investigations of the social context of speech, and of the child's acquisition of language. Variant forms and pronunciations may carry social connotations, of which the speaker may or may not be fully aware, and which may influence the course of linguistic change. And we shall not have a complete picture of change if we neglect the fact that language is not acquired ready-made, but must be created anew by each child in a tremendous intellectual achievement, most of which is accomplished between the second and fifth year of his life. It appears that certain types of change — especially so-called 'analogy' — may be traceable back to this continuous re-creation of language.

This short survey is concerned with the recent rethinking of the principles of historical linguistics which has been influenced more or less directly by generative grammar. Most of the discussion is based on Halle (1962), Postal (1968), Chomsky & Halle (1968), and Kiparsky (1968a). Such topics as comparative linguistics and internal reconstruction have had to be omitted for lack of space, although most of the conclusions reached in the discussion are very relevant to them.

## 1. Sound Change

The basic issue concerning sound change — and this is still a hornet's nest almost a hundred years after the famous Neogrammarian controversies — is best understood in terms of the distinction drawn in linguistics between *performance*, the production and perception of speech, and *competence*, the grammatical structure of language. Any sound change is obviously a change both in performance and in competence. When initial [k] and [g] were lost before [n] in seventeenth-century English, words like *knot, knife, gnaw, gnarled* came to be pronounced in a new way, and correspondingly, the grammar of English ceased to contain morphemes beginning with the clusters [kn], [gn]. We can distinguish performance and competence theories of sound change according to which of these two sides of sound change they hold to be primary.

Performance theories of sound change say that sound change arises outside the linguistic system, through modifications of pronunciation due to external factors impinging on performance. Concretely, the process is usually pictured as follows. Before any change had taken place in their grammar, many speakers began to pronounce weakly, and even to omit completely, the [k] and [g] in words like *knot, gnaw*. When this aberrant pronunciation became sufficiently common, it came to be regarded as standard usage, and the grammar itself was changed to incorporate it.

This notion of performance deviations leading to changes in competence might at first blush seem wholly absurd. Inept performances of a symphony do not change its score, and crimes, however frequent, cannot change the laws they violate. Then how could deviant performances caused by extra-linguistic circumstances lead to changes in the linguistic system? To this one might reply plausibly that laws and musical scores are learned as explicitly formulated norms, whereas grammars can only be abstracted from concrete speech material. Norms of the nonexplicit type, such as grammars, might well be constantly subject to revisions bringing them into line with actual performances. Performance theories of sound change postulate a kind of feedback mechanism by which a grammar is, as it were, constantly catching up with its own output.

An important question, which proponents of performance theories have been unable to answer quite satisfactorily, concerns the origin of the performance deviations which supposedly lie behind sound change. A constant tendency towards greater ease of articulation is most often held responsible. It is an undeniable and important fact that sound changes often proceed in the direction of greater ease of articulation — certainly far more often than could be attributed to chance. For example, the dropping of the outer consonant in a cluster (the first consonant of an initial cluster, and the last consonant of a final cluster), is incomparably more frequent than the insertion of such a consonant. Much of the phonological history of a language can be brought under various general processes of weakening, simplification and so on. Still, there are enough sound changes which cannot be understood in these terms at all to rule out a tendency towards greater ease of articulation as the *general* cause of sound change. In its place some linguists have proposed, still less plausibly, that sound change is simply the result of random vacillations. If this were the case, then the phonetic history of a sound, plotted on the phonetic co-ordinates, would have the character of a random drifting about in various directions; and it would furthermore be difficult to understand why sound changes should so often apply systematically to whole classes of sounds.

If in spite of these and other difficulties, performance theories once dominated the field, the reason was that they seemed to be strongly supported by the empirical findings of historical linguistics. These appeared to be not inconsistent with an interesting factual assumption about sound change: namely, that any sound change can be described in purely phonetic terms, without reference to the grammar of the language. A sound change, according to this assumption, replaces all cases of the sound sequence A (in a given phonetic environment) by another sound sequence B. Such grammatical factors as morphology and syntax could have no effect on this replacement. If sound change were in fact completely independent of grammatical structure, then performance theories would become worth looking for, since the best explanation for the independence of sound change from grammatical structure would be precisely that sound change originates outside grammatical structure, in speech performance.

However, the evidence from historical linguistics at present on the whole favors the opposite conclusion, that sound change *can* depend on grammatical structure, a conclusion which would render untenable any performance theory of sound change. The evidence is, unfortunately, difficult to assess, because we can rarely observe the actual process of sound change, but only the *fait accompli*, and the effect of grammatically conditioned sound changes, which would refute the performance theories, can be sometimes duplicated by various processes such as analogy, which performance theories must in any case allow for. Consider again English [kn], [gn]. When these clusters occurred in the middle of a word, they were not changed, e.g. *acknowledge, hackneyed, signature*. This condition cannot be expressed in purely phonetic terms, since *a knowledge* and *acknowledge* must have been normally pronounced alike, just as *a board* and *aboard* are normally pronounced alike today (and without this phonetic identity such words as *newt* could not have arisen through the wrong division of *an ewt*). The sound change 'knew' that the two identical stretches of sound *acknowledge* and *a knowledge* were grammatically different, and specifically that they contained one and two words, respectively. The notion of purely phonetic sound change could here be rescued only by the particularly unpalatable expedient of assuming that [k] and [g] were changed even in *acknowledge, hackney, signature*, etc., but were subsequently restored as spelling pronunciations. The question why they were not similarly reinstated on the basis of the spelling initially as in *knowledge, gnat* shows up the implausibility of the solution to which the performance theory in this case leads us.

Especially persuasive are examples of the interaction of morphology and sound change, as in the following case discussed by W. O'Neil (cf. Postal 1968: 263). The words *fell* and *tell* were in the earliest form of English pronounced *fællyan* and *tællyan*. In Old English (West Saxon) they are distinguished as *fiellan* and *tellan*. The explanation for the different treatment of the two words is revealing. Morphologically they are *fæll* + *yan* (with two [1]'s, seen also in *feallan* 'fall') and *tæl* + *yan* (with a single [1], seen also in *talu* 'tale'). In West Germanic, consonants were doubled before [y], so that both of the verbs came to be pronounced with two [1]'s. Now in Old English vowels were diphthongized before liquids followed by consonants, including sequences of two [1]'s. This so-called 'breaking' affected *fællyan* but not *tællyan* — evidently because breaking applied not to the phonetic form of the words, which were identical but for the irrelevant difference of the first consonant, but to the morphological form of the words, in which only *fællyan* had two [1]'s and therefore was subject to breaking, whereas *tællyan*, understood as *tæl* + *yan* had just one [1] and could not be affected by breaking. This shows that sound changes can distinguish between phonetically identical forms on the basis of grammatical differences, and that the view of sound change as a purely phonetic process, on which the defence of performance theories of sound changes rests, cannot be upheld.

Such facts instead argue for competence theories of sound change, that is, theories which maintain that sound change originates in competence and is irreducible to any prior, externally caused changes in performance. According to this view, sound change is change in the phonological part of the grammar. One or another form of this general view would at present probably be accepted by the majority of linguists. How the details are elaborated is in large measure a corollary of what conception of linguistic structure is accepted. A version of it which is very attractive in several respects has been formulated within the framework of generative grammar. Its essential point is that sound change involves the addition of new phonological rules to the grammar.

One great advantage of conceiving of sound changes in terms of new rules added to the phonological component of a grammar is that the types of changes and types of conditionings that occur also figure in the rules of a synchronic grammar. This means that a large part of the work towards characterizing the 'possible sound changes' is independently done in the form of a characterization of the 'possible phonological rules' that may figure in a phonological description. Our above example would be the addition of the rule which we can write

$$k, g \rightarrow \emptyset \, / \, \# \relbar n$$

'[k] and [g] are "rewritten" as zero ($\emptyset$) – i.e. are deleted – in the environment of word boundary (#) immediately preceding and [n] immediately following'. In general, any sound change corresponds to a possible phonological rule in grammar, although the converse is not true, for reasons connected with the notion of restructuring discussed later.

A second advantage of this view is that it enables the concept of *ordered rules* to be used in historical linguistics opening up wholly new possibilities of explaining historical phenomena. Implicit in saying that sound changes are added rules is the possibility that some sound changes might be added not just at the end of the existing sequence of rules, but before some of the rules in that sequence. The Old English example mentioned earlier shows that this possibility is not merely hypothetical. Prior to Old English 'breaking', the derivation of the forms *fællyan* and *tællyan* was as follows:

| Basic (morphological) form | fæll + yan | tael + yan |
| Application of consonant-doubling | | |
| rule | (no change) | tæll + yan |

After breaking, the forms, now distinguished as *fiellan* and *tellan*, were derived as follows:

| Basic (morphological) form | fæll + yan | tæl + yan |
| Application of breaking | fæall + yan | (not applicable) |

Application of consonant-doubling
    rule                                    (no change)        tæll + yan

with subsequent umlaut and loss of [y] bringing about the forms *fiellan,
tellan*. The breaking rule was therefore put into the grammar at a point in
the ordering before the consonant-doubling rule. If it had been placed
after consonant-doubling, there would have been breaking in both forms.

The possibility of placing new rules before existing ones raises an
interesting question: is it predictable where a rule is going to be placed in
the sequence of existing rules? This is one of the many unsolved problems
that lie at the very threshold of historical linguistics. At present all that
can be said is that the majority of sound changes are rules added to the
end of the existing sequence of phonological rules, in so far as the ordering
is fixed at all. Such sound changes are conditioned purely phonetically,
whereas rules added earlier in the sequence may be conditioned morphologically.

The significance of such examples was overlooked until relatively
recently, in part because such concepts as the ordering of rules, on which
these examples depend, were not generally recognized by linguists, and
in part also because the debate on the nature of sound change had become
deflected from the key question of whether sound change is always independent of grammar to some more subsidiary questions which in themselves are actually unable to decide between the performance and competence theories of sound change. One of these questions is whether
sound changes can have exceptions. It is apparent that they can, and that
while most sound changes are perfectly regular, the history of every
language has incompletely regular sound changes which have failed to
apply to particular words for no particular reason. But nothing much
seems to depend on this answer as far as the larger theoretical question
of performance versus competence theories is concerned, since neither of
the two theories is necessarily incompatible with either the possibility or
the impossibility of exceptions to sound changes.

A second question, likewise much debated, is whether sound change
(apart from certain special types of change such as metathesis) is necessarily gradual, or on the contrary necessarily proceeds in steps, or whether
perhaps both types occur. The evidence of dialect maps, which show both
sharply differentiated boundaries and, especially in the case of vowels,
gradual transitions between different pronunciations, would tend to
suggest that both gradual and nongradual sound change is possible. The
idea that sound change is the addition of new rules would also suggest precisely that, since a phonology has both rules applying to binary features
such as voiced-unvoiced, high-nonhigh, and rules specifying phonetic
detail by scalar features. But performance theories do not stand and fall

on this issue either, since they are not sufficiently clear about what external factors affecting performance they postulate.

## 2. The Role of Language Acquisition

Let us consider for a moment what it means to say that a child 'learns' its mother tongue. Obviously it is not given to the child as a finished product, but must be put together by the child from raw materials – the speech of the child's environment. For this the child must use some kind of innate blueprint giving it some general idea of what language is. Just how detailed this blueprint is is a matter of debate among linguists and psychologists. What is quite clear is that the child, unlike an adult learning a second language, cannot use explicit rules and exercises, and – at least in the critical pre-school years – benefits little from what adult guidance it may be offered. The child's acquisition of language is therefore an individual act of creation. Moreover, the child learns his mother tongue in complete ignorance of its history. The child is the synchronic linguist *par excellence*. On hearing [nayf] – i.e. the spoken form of the word *knife* – the child will have no reason whatever to postulate a basic form with initial [k] and to set up a rule deleting initial [k] before [n]. Synchrony gives no reason to do so, and history is irrelevant. For this reason a grammar, too, must be unprejudiced by historical considerations and built on the synchronic facts of the language alone.

It follows that rules which are added to grammars through sound change are retained in the language in so far as there is synchronic justification for them. For example, even the British speaker who pronounces no [r] in *star* has an [r] in the base form of this word if he pronounces [r] in *the star explodes*. His grammar has a rule which drops [r] in the context 'vowel——consonant or pause'. If there is no synchronic justification for retaining the rules in the grammar, the changes which they effect are simply incorporated in the base forms and the rules disappear from the language. What effect the written form of a word has on the base form of a literate speaker is a separate question. The frequent occurrence of spelling pronunciations, such as *falcon* pronounced with [l] in the United States, suggests that it is quite considerable.

A new rule may, then, remain productive in the grammar, or it may lead to *restructuring*. If it were not for restructuring, grammars would just keep growing more complicated as they accumulated rules through sound change, until they would no longer be fit for use in communication.

Recent investigations of child language by Ervin, Bellugi, Klima, McNeill and others show that the evolution of the child's grammar from one stage to another may itself be explained by means of the operation of a similar mechanism of addition of rules and their restructuring. One might have thought that the child would initially have great trouble with irregular forms and strong verbs. This is not so. The first speech of the child correctly reproduces many irregular forms such as *go/went*, and as a matter of fact strong verbs predominate there because of their greater frequency in the language and their general meanings. It is only as the child begins to learn rules that he begins to make mistakes. It is apparent that the child at first commits each inflected form to memory as a separate item, and later eliminates them from memory as he learns general rules for deriving them. Thus, as the child hits on the main rule for forming past tense forms in English, he not only is able to produce freely past forms like *walked, floated*, etc. but also tends to forget the correct irregular forms which he has previously used and regularizes them into *goed, hitted, drinked,* etc. These forms have then to be relearned as exceptions to the new rule. Later when the subregularities for strong verbs are learned, they too may erase correct forms. Thus, when *sang, drank,* etc. are learned, an earlier *brought* may for a time become *brang.*

The forms recorded from the speech of children are exactly the sort of 'analogical' forms that one might expect to see in the future development of English, and which have continuously encroached on the formerly much more complicated morphology of English. Child language is therefore the most likely source of analogical change. A good case can be made for the hypothesis that analogy as historical change arises through the retention into adult language of the over-generalizations that are, as we have just mentioned, a constant characteristic of child language.

Changes of this category are not limited to the simplification of inflectional morphology, but can also involve the simplification of phonological rules, and even their complete dropping from the grammar. There is, furthermore, a strong possibility that they may also result in sound changes. This possibility follows from the observation that the child's learning of the sounds of his language follows a fairly strict progression, which is similar in all children, from simpler to more complex kinds of sounds, in much the same way as his learning of morphology proceeds from the more general, basic rules (e.g. those for weak verbs) to more special rules (e.g. those for strong verbs). For example, children commonly learn the voiceless and voiced 'th-sounds', [θ] and [ð] , fairly late, and often replace them by [v] , [f] , pronouncing *mouth* as if it were written *mouf.* Suppose now that [θ] in some cases is not learned at all, and that this comes to be accepted usage. The result would be a sound change of the common type termed merger, that is, a falling together of different segment types, usually into the simpler of them — in this case, the merger of interdentals and labials into the labial series — a change which has in fact taken place in some dialects of English. If such a type of sound change could be established, we should have an explanation for the tendency noted earlier for sound change to take a direction towards greater simplicity. (I have assumed that [f] is relatively simple, or 'unmarked', by comparison with [θ]. That this is so would seem to follow also from the fact that [f] is far more common in the world's languages. Ultimately the explanation for such asymmetries must be provided by phonetic theory.)

It would seem, in any case, that the traditionally recognized change mechanism of proportional analogy which regards analogical forms as solutions to equations of the type *walk:walked* = *bring:x* (where *x* = *bringed*), is only a special case of a more general type of change which may be termed simplification, for which the notion of proportion is inappropriate. The characteristic property of these changes is that they simplify the grammar. Like the process called 'restructuring' above, they take place in language acquisition, Restructuring, however, differs from simplification in that it involves no actual change in the language, but merely the substitution, for an unnecessarily complex grammar arising through the addition of a new rule, of a simpler grammar which generates the same language.

The extent to which the process of simplification can cause change presumably depends on the degree of pressure towards linguistic conformity that prevails in the community, either directly, as for example through schooling in prescriptive grammar, or indirectly, as through the form of social organization. What is surprising is how often such changes do take place, and how sweeping they sometimes are. There are several circumstances which may partly help to explain this. It is well known that young children are largely impervious to adult correction of their speech. Furthermore children, in some societies at least, acquire the language of their older contemporaries to a much greater extent than their 'mother tongue'. There tend to be generations which, while not sharply demarcated, are nevertheless associated with typical linguistic characteristics. Furthermore it must be noted that features of child language can survive as variants alongside the adult patterns — cases are even on record where twins retained a form of baby talk as a secret language well into their teens.

## 3. General Conclusions

It has been suggested by critics of generative grammar (e.g. Hockett 1968) that it has become caught in the fatal trap of taking its theoretical entities such as rules, ordering, underlying base forms, etc., for real entities, whereas they actually, according to Hockett, are only tools to be used for analysing the real entities, such as phonemes and morphemes. It is as if, in Hockett's simile, a pathologist were to confuse his slides and microscopes with the bacteria under investigation.

Historical linguistics supports exactly the opposite conclusion in an especially direct way. We have seen that sound change and analogy is change in the grammatical system of a language, including precisely the rules and their order. If these real events, then, are changes in the rules and their order, then the rules and their order must be real entities, too.

Pushing further on these lines, we may say that historical linguistics is actually one of the best means at the linguist's disposal for investigating the detailed structure of grammars. Language change is for the linguist, to change the analogy a little, what earthquakes and volcanic eruptions are for the geologist, or supernovae for the astronomer. They add welcome new perspective in a field where the object of study is static and not readily amenable to experimental manipulation. Just as the careful analysis of earthquakes may reveal something about the earth's interior, so careful analysis of linguistic changes may reveal otherwise inaccessible aspects of linguistic structure. For example, the issue between performance and competence theories of sound change has wider implications and bears on the nature of phonology itself. Questions as to productivity of rules may be answered on the basis of whether they function in analogical change. The question whether two syntactic constructions are transformationally related may be answered in the affirmative when they are found to be singled out by some joint syntactic innovation which does not affect superficially similar cases. Similar reasoning can be applied in phonology.

But how does this fit in with the earlier point that the history of a language is irrelevant to its grammar? At first sight the use of historical evidence as just advocated might seem inconsistent with the very notion of synchronic linguistics. Actually there are two different, mutually consistent considerations here. One is that the description of a particular language is not to be based on the history of that language but on its synchronic structure. The other is that the general properties of linguistic change are part of the evidence on which our theory of language can be based, and the description of a particular language is carried out with reference to a general theory of language. Hence historical facts can become relevant to description via the theories of grammar and language change. There is no reason why some historical change observed in English, Greek or Nez Perce might not turn out to be evidence for a decision in linguistic theory which in turn may have consequences in the grammatical analysis of French, Papago, or Lower Umpqua.

At the turn of the century most linguists would have agreed with Hermann Paul (1886), that the scientific study of language was necessarily historical. Not long thereafter, under the influence of Saussure's posthumous lectures, general linguistics and historical linguistics began to diverge. Hjelmslev (1953) could actually propose that they were two wholly separate fields, and that historical linguistics should be consigned to some such discipline as sociology or perhaps general history. Today, when developments in linguistic theory have powerfully influenced historical linguistics, and historical linguistics is showing signs of being able to repay its debt, one would have to search hard to find an adherent of either one of these extreme positions. This pendulum may finally have come to a position of rest.

# Chapter 4

# Historical Linguistics*

Historical investigations in the framework of generative grammar have generally aimed at developing a theory of change which could hook up to the existing synchronic theory, so as to correctly characterize the possible forms of linguistic change, and the constraints to which they are subject. Much of the earlier work on this problem is summarized in King's book (1969). Since then, there has been much debate, for example, on the question of constraints on sound change: can rules be added to the middle of grammars (King 1971, Demers 1974)? Can the added rule be one that interchanges the values of a feature (Chomsky and Halle 1968, Matthews 1970)?

I will not try to cover this work here. I will limit myself to a parallel, and perhaps equally important line of research, which attempts to deepen our understanding of linguistic change by removing the obstacles that presently lie on the synchronic side. We cannot simply take the theory of grammar for granted and hold it constant while we 'apply' it to change. This is because many of the most central problems in historical linguistics, e.g., *when does restructuring take place?* or *what determines the direction of analogical change?* are really questions about language itself. However, the present state of linguistics is such that the synchronic theory is often rather indeterminate in exactly the respects that would be most relevant for historical linguistics. For this reason much progress in historical linguistics depends on sharpening the synchronic theory so that it will provide the right basis for diachronic explanation.

It is interesting that most work that has so far been carried out along these lines points to one general conclusion. This is that the function of the 'evaluation measure' in linguistic theory is carried out by a series of *substantive* conditions in addition to (not instead of) the *formal* condition of simplicity. Chomsky originally suggested that the language learner has two sorts of things available to him:

* This work was supported in part by the National Institutes of Mental Health (Grant MH-13390). A preliminary draft of this paper was read at a conference at the University of Maryland, 8-9 May, 1971.

(1)    formal devices for expressing rules
(2)    a way of picking the right analysis from the many analyses that these formal devices allow (an evaluation measure).

The usual claim (e.g. in Chomsky and Halle 1968) has been that the formal devices are very rich, and that the evaluation measure is very simple, viz. *pick the shortest description,* where length in phonology is defined in terms of the number of feature specifications in the grammatical description. It is especially the historical facts which show conclusively that this cannot be right, and that the 'evaluation' of grammars involves their substantive properties. I will discuss these substantive properties under three headings:

1.    Abstractness conditions
2.    Paradigm conditions
3.    Rule opacity.

## 1. Abstractness Conditions

The first modification of the theory that is suggested by historical facts is some constraint on abstractness. I discussed such a constraint in *How abstract is phonology?* (1968b), and it has been debated repeatedly in the recent literature. The type of theory that was proposed in the *Sound Pattern of English* (henceforth: SPE), and on the basis of which analysis of other languages than English were proposed in the sixties, led to a number of analyses that many people find implausible. For example: the analysis of *boy* in English as being underlying [œ̄] with an open, front, rounded vowel; the epsilon glide, i.e., the segment that is [-cns, -voc, -hi] that is claimed for the underlying forms of words like *tolerance*, or *menu*; or the distinction between the final vowels of *veto* and *motto* which in SPE is that between open *ɔ* and mid *o*. All of these posited forms do not correspond in any direct way to anything that is present on the surface in any allomorphs of the words or morphemes that are analysed as having these underlying segments. Similarly, in Lightner's analysis of Russian, a word like [šum] has the analysis /xeumos/ with several abstract segments. Considerable methodological importance is, in fact, given to these analyses in SPE.

In many of these cases, arguments have subsequently been given within the theory of SPE that refute or at least weaken the evidence for the analysis that posits such abstract segments (McCawley 1974, Harada and Imai 1970, Hoard 1972). Still, one might go on to ask whether there might not be some deeper, principled reason why these analyses are not right. Is there a *substantive* constraint limiting the relation between underlying and surface representations in some fashion? Such a constraint might say either that underlying representations which don't correspond directly to anything on the surface are HARD to learn for a child or, more strongly, that such representations are IMPOSSIBLE to learn. If such purely abstract segments in underlying representations are hard to learn, the theory will have to reflect this formally by making them expensive. There will be a clause in the evaluation measure that places a high cost on them. The other possibility, that they are impossible to learn, would require setting up some absolute constraint in the theory that excludes such analyses completely. In *How abstract is phonology?* I considered both of those versions without really saying which one I preferred, the reason being that I was not sure myself. Subsequently, there has been a lot of discussion of this proposal. Some modifications to it were suggested in Vetter (1968), Smith (1969), Davison (1971), and Piggott (1971). It was argued against in Hyman (1970a, b), Brame (1972a), Kisseberth (1969), Kim (1972). Campbell (1974) and Crothers (1971) have reviewed and countered some of this criticism, favoring some sort of constraint on abstraction. A view similar (in this respect) to mine was also proposed independently by Andersen (1969).

The evidence given in *How abstract is phonology?* consisted of *historical* facts. These facts seemed to indicate that the rules and underlying representations which are postulated in certain kinds of abstract analyses differ from other rules and underlying representations postulated in generative phonologies in not functioning in any linguistic changes, and that there is hence some reason to doubt their existence. The analysis I was specifically concerned with were those involving *absolute neutralization,* i.e., the context-free merger of an underlying phonological contrast on the phonetic surface. I concluded that absolute neutralization either contributes a great amount of linguistic complexity to a grammar (the *weak alternation condition*) or is excluded outright (the *strong alternation condition*). This amounts to saying that the present evaluation measure, which is based on formal simplicity, is giving the wrong answers in some cases and needs to be revised by incorporating some version of an abstractness condition.

What some of the replies to *How abstract is phonology?* showed was that there are languages in which the (strong) alternation condition leads to more complex analyses than would otherwise be possible. But showing that introducing the alternation condition can lead to more complex analyses cannot by itself refute the alternation condition, since the point at issue is precisely whether simplicity is the correct evaluation measure. The claim is that analyses involving absolute neutralization, however simple they may be, are still in some sense difficult or impossible for a child to learn; that simplicity is not the only criterion for evaluating a grammar and should be augmented by some substantive constraint on abstractness.

To avoid begging the question in investigations of this problem we must look for *external evidence* as to the correctness or incorrectness of specific analyses which are required or forbidden by the constraints at issue. The papers by Hyman (1970a, b) and Piggott (1971) went right to the heart of the matter. Hyman's papers are important in introducing another aspect of historical linguistics, viz. facts about borrowing, into discussion of phonological theory. However, as argued in Crothers (1971) and, in more detail, in Kiparsky (1973a), both the internal and the external arguments for Hyman's analysis are inconclusive. I should like to discuss Piggott's paper briefly here.

A major flaw in my paper was that it dealt mostly just with cases in which wholly abstract segments had been set up in order for ONE rule to have a phonological context. All the actual evidence given there pertains to such cases. True, the majority of cases in which wholly abstract segments had been used at that time were of this type, and it is these where the legitimacy of the device is most questionable. But obviously there exist cases in which wholly abstract segments are motivated by SEVERAL distinct phonological processes, e.g., in the Spanish vowel system (Harris 1969a); a clear example is Newman (1968). As pointed out especially by Brame (1972a) and Kisseberth (1969), who gave other such examples, the internal justification for abstract analyses is much stronger here. We might, accordingly, assume that wholly abstract segments are to be allowed when more than one rule refers to them crucially. From the viewpoint of language acquisition this would be very natural. We would expect, in general, the ease with which absolute neutralization is learned to go up with the amount of evidence which the phonological processes of the language provides for the neutralized distinction. In effect, this amounts to the weak alternation condition, viz. that absolute neutralization adds complexity to the grammar, but is not categorically excluded.

Since there is evidence for SOME constraint on absolute neutralization, it can be fairly said that the burden of proof falls at least in part on one who wishes to argue for a limitation on this constraint. At any rate, as noted above, internal justification is not enough, because the theory itself is at issue.

We have to find *external* evidence which shows that the abstract analyses posited in certain cases do have psychological reality. Of course, this cannot and need not be done in every single example. Once we have provided external justification in a few clear ones, we can provisionally adjust phonological theory so that it will require the abstract analyses in these cases. The resulting theory will then lead to specific predictions about what the correct analysis is in many other cases, where external empirical evidence may or may not be available to test the theory.

The beginnings of this external empirical justification have been provided by Piggott (1971). Piggott analyzes a series of phonetic mergers in the history of the Algonquian languages. The cases which Piggott investigates involve segments which before the merger behave differently with respect to at least one phonological rule. For example, Proto-Algonquian */θ/, which palatalized to */š/ before */i/, became */l/, thereby falling together with Proto-Algonquian */l/, which was not affected before */i/. Similarly, Proto-Algonquian */i/, which caused palatalization of certain preceding segments (including */θ/), merged with */e/, which did not cause palatalization before it. Some of these phonetic mergers subsequently resulted in morphophonemic mergers. Changes took place which eliminated the need for making a morphophonemic distinction between the *l* from */θ/ (which turned to š in the palatalizing environments) and the original *l* (which was not subject to change). The way this happened in some Algonquian languages was that all *l*'s, including those from */l/, started to become š in the palatalizing environments. In Delaware, the opposite happened: the *l*'s from θ became like the original *l*'s and stopped being palatalized to š.

|  | basic | in palatalizing environment | basic | in palatalizing environment |
|---|---|---|---|---|
| Proto-Algonquian | θ | š | l | l |
| After merger | l | š | l | l |
| Usual reanalysis | l | š | l | š |
| Delaware reanalysis | l | l | l | l |

We can interpret the reanalyses as the result of language learners failing to r·tain the underlying phonological distinction in their synchronic grammars, and instead setting up a rule *l* → š, which some *l*'s have to be marked as not undergoing. Subsequently, this mark is either removed from all *l*'s (i.e., all *l*'s become regular — the usual change) or the rule itself is eliminated (the Delaware change). I.e., *the reanalyses proceed from a non-abstract synchronic analysis of the merged segments.*

In other cases, such reanalysis does NOT take place. For example, modern Algonquian languages still show the distinction between original *i*, which causes palatalization, and *i* from */e/, which does not cause palatalization. Piggott now observes the following correlation: phonetic merger leads to reanalysis where the distinction is relevant to the operation of just one rule; phonetic merger does not lead to reanalysis where the distinction is relevant to the operation of several rules. For example, palatalization is the ONLY process that distinguishes original *l*, and *l* from */θ/. But the two *i*'s are distinguished by processes of vowel coalescence IN ADDITION TO the palatalization rule. If the abstract analysis is permissible in this latter kind of case, then the preconditions for reanalysis are not met there. We then have an explanation for why these cases do not in fact undergo reanalysis.

If this idea proves to be generally valid (and it is certainly consistent with the examples known to me), then my claim in *How abstract is phonology?*, that absolute neutralization is unstable, must be qualified. The instability seems to show up mainly just where the neutralized distinction is weakly embedded in the grammar, making a difference for only one rule. This suggests a version of the alternation condition which has the effect of ruling out absolute neutralization under these conditions, but which allows absolute neutralization where the internal evidence involves several phonological processes of the language. There is no need to emphasize the lack of solid evidence as to the exact nature of the alternation condition, and the tentative nature of conclusions even as vague as those suggested here.

Another constraint on the relation between underlying and surface phonological representations has recently been proposed by Hale (1973), on the basis of ample synchronic and historical evidence from various Polynesian and Australian languages. Hale considers the type of morphological situation illustrated by the following data from Maori:

| *verb* | *passive* | |
|--------|-----------|--|
| awhi | awhitia | 'to embrace' |
| hopu | hopukia | 'to catch' |
| aru | arumia | 'to follow' |
| tohu | tohuŋia | 'to point out' |
| mau | mauria | 'to carry' |
| wero | werohia | 'to stab' |
| patu | patua | 'to strike, kill' |
| kite | kitea | 'to see, find' |

If we wanted an 'A' on our exam, we would, of course, say that the underlying forms are /awhit/, /hopuk/, /maur/, etc., and that the suffix is /ia/. We would then have a rule that consonants are deleted word-finally, but stay otherwise. Another rule would say that /ia/ turns to *a* after stems ending in a vowel, e.g., /patu + ia/ → *patua*. More support for this analysis would be the fact that the gerundive ending /aŋa/ also is preceded by the consonant postulated for the stem, e.g., *awhitaŋa, hopukaŋa* etc.

If someone were to say that the underlying forms are /awhi/, /hopu/, /mau/ etc., and that there are large numbers of different passive suffixes, /tia/, /kia/, /ria/ etc., he'd flunk. What Hale shows is that Maori children learning their language flunk this 'exam' and in fact set up underlying forms in which stems all end in different vowels and there are large numbers of different passive endings. There is strong evidence that the 'clever' analysis is not psychologically correct. The psychologically correct grammar of Maori has /tia/ as the basic ending and /kia/, /ria/ etc., as a set of allomorphs used in verbs that have to be lexically marked as taking them. We have, in other words, a regular /tia/-conjugation and a number of subsidiary conjugations. In support of this analysis, Hale cites the following facts:

'(1) Stems which are basically nominal are often used verbally in spontaneous discourse; when they are so used, in the passive, they regularly take the ending /-tia/. (2) Derived causatives (formed with the prefix /whaka-/) take /-tia/ in the passive even if the basic verb stem takes another alternant when not in the causative. (3) There is a rule whereby certain adverbials are made to agree in voice with the verbs they modify; these adverbials take /-tia/ in the passive regardless of the shape of the passive ending which the verb itself takes. (4) Borrowings from English, including unassimilated consonant-final ones, take the ending /-tia/ in the passive. (5) Compound verbs derived by incorporating a noun from an adverbial phrase regularly form their passives in /-tia/. (6) In general, /tia/ can be used when the conventional passive termination for a given verb is not remembered. These facts are entirely consistent with the suggested reanalysis. Only with difficulty can they be made consistent with the phonological alternative in the synchronic description of Maori. The situation is similar in other Polynesian languages – the extreme case of regularization is exemplified by Hawaiian, which now has a single passive ending /-ʔia/ (from *-kia, presumably).'

These facts are inexplicable under the 'clever' analysis. For example, why should we have *mau ~ mauria* but causative *whakamau ~ whakamautia*? The analysis which sets up underlying /maur/ must say in addition that the causative prefix triggers a change of the stem-final consonant to *t* (and, presumably, in vowel-final stems, epenthesis of *t*). Under the 'stupid' analysis the causatives behave exactly as expected. The fact that we get *whakamautia* is just a special case of the general fact that derived words tend to be morphologically regular as compared to simple words. For example, causative verbs are weak in English and other Germanic languages, belong to the first *a*-conjugation in Sanskrit, etc.

Historically, there is no doubt at all that the consonants were indeed originally part of the stem, and were lost by the historical analog to the rule which the 'clever' analysis postulates as a synchronic process. This sound change has taken place in the other Polynesian languages, too. Interestingly enough, they seem to have undergone the same kind of change as Maori, with the consonant being reanalyzed as part of the ending. But the fact that the various languages each pick a different consonant for the basic ending shows that the reanalysis has taken place independently in each of the languages. This is very strong evidence in support of Hale's claim.

What we must do now is to change linguistic theory so that this 'wrong' solution will be the right solution. Hale notes that Polynesian languages have no final consonants on the surface, and ascribes the reanalysis to a tendency for the canonical shape of the underlying representations to mimic the canonical shape of surface representations. Hale considers stating this as an absolute constraint:

(A') An underlying phonological representation of stems is disallowed if it violates a universal (i.e., exceptionless within the language) surface canonical pattern.

but suggests that it may be more correct to regard it as a RELATIVE constraint:

(A)   *There is a tendency in the acquisition of a language for linguistic forms to be analyzed in a way which minimizes the necessity to postulate underlying phonological representations of morphemes which violate the universal surface canonical patterns of the language.*

This formulation brings out the relationship to the weak alternation condition very clearly. Just as the alternation condition says that underlying distinctions which do not directly correspond to surface distinctions are hard to learn, so Hale's principle says that underlying canonical forms which do not correspond to surface canonical forms are hard to learn. The motivation of both principles in the process of language acquisition is readily apparent.

### 2. Paradigm Conditions

Another type of substantive constraint that is needed to account for the historical facts has to do with the relation between the allomorphs in a paradigm (for more detailed discussion, see Kiparsky 1972; cf. also Miller 1973). The first of these is essentially the traditional notion of 'leveling' (see Harris 1970, 1973). A standard example of analogical change is the elimination of *s* in the inflection of certain Latin *s*-stems like *honōs ~ honor*. The stems that underwent this change were basically masculine and feminine polysyllables. In the oblique cases they were originally subject to the rule:

$$s \rightarrow r \ / \ V \ \underline{\hspace{2em}} \ V$$

The *s/r* alternation due to this rule was eliminated by generalizing *r* in the nominative:

|        |          |          |
|--------|----------|----------|
| N.     | honōs    | honor    |
| G.     | honōris  | honōris  |
| A.     | honōrem  | honōrem  |

(The shortening of *ō* to *o* is due to a general rule of Latin which says that vowels are shortened before consonants word-finally.) In my thesis (Kiparsky 1965) I said that the change was formally a reanalysis of the base form from /honōs/ to /honōr/. Thus the *s → r* rule would no longer be needed in this derivation, although it continues to operate where the change did not take place, i.e., in monosyllables (*flōs ∼ flōris*) and in neuters (*genus ∼ generis*).

What I forgot was that some of the changing stems retain *s* in derivatives, e.g., *honor ∼ honestus*. To account for this, some *ad hoc* measures must be taken. Two come to mind as possibilities: (1) The underlying form is indeed restructured with /r/, but there is a special minor rule that sends *r* to *s* in derivatives like *honestus*. This cannot be a general process in the language and must be restricted to a fairly small number of words. (2) We do not have a restructuring of the underlying form after all, and /s/ is retained. Instead, there is a special additional clause on the *s → r* rule, which states that the rule must be also applied in the nominative (even though no vowel follows the *s*) in masculine and feminine polysyllables. Either way we have a complication of the grammar. And yet we would like to say that this is basically the same type of change that generally involves optimalizing the grammar. How can we change the theory to make this a good thing to happen to a language, in spite of the formal complexity that results? The obvious way is to say that in the child's acquisition of language there is a cost attached to having alternations in a paradigm:

(B)  *Allomorphy tends to be minimized in a paradigm.*

The existence of some such principle as (B) is shown by the fact that it can, in cases such as this, override *formal* considerations of simplicity. There are others in which it does not. Given that there is some such substantive principle as (B), it becomes our task to delimit the relative force of this substantive principle and the formal principle of simplicity in cases such as this where there is conflict between them, so as to be able to predict which one will win out. Obviously we are not even close to being able to do this yet.

Principle (B) also solves some problems which arise in rule reordering. There are cases which do not fit the characterization of unmarked order in terms of the *feeding* and *bleeding relations* defined in Kiparsky (1968a). For example, in German the final devoicing rule

$$\textit{Devoicing:} \ [+ \text{obstr}] \ \rightarrow \ [- \text{voiced}] \ / — \begin{cases} + \text{C} \\ \# \end{cases}$$

is ordered both ways, depending on the dialect, with respect to the rule that drops *g* after *η*.

$$\textit{g-deletion:} \ g \rightarrow \phi \ / \ [+ \text{nasal}] \ \underline{\hspace{3em}}$$

Depending on the order, we get [laη] or [laηk] for /laηg/ as follows:

*Dialect group I*

|  | /laηg/ | /laηg + e/ |
|---|---|---|
| 1. Devoicing | laηk | — |
| 2. g-deletion | — | laηe |

*Dialect group II*

|  | /laηg/ | /laηg + e/ |
|---|---|---|
| 1. g-deletion | laη | laηe |
| 2. Devoicing | — | — |

Historically, *Group I* seems to represent the original order, from which *Group II* has changed by reordering (cf. Vennemann 1970, for a detailed discussion of these rules). However, the relation between the rules is one of *mutual bleeding*. Only one of the two rules can apply to any one input representation, and this is always whichever rule applies first. Yet this formally symmetrical ordering relation is not functionally symmetrical. The innovating order is in conformity with principle (B). This case of reordering therefore furnishes supporting evidence for minimization of allomorphy as an independent functional principle which is not reducible to formal properties of the generative system of a language.

A second paradigm constraint has to do with preservation of semantic information on the surface (Kiparsky 1972). For example, in Labov's data on Black English (Labov et al. 1968: 158), final *s* is deleted much more frequently in genitives and third person singulars than in plurals. This fact has echoes in historical linguistics. In German, *-e* drops optionally in the singular dative but not in the plural. In Middle High German, the rule was optional in both cases but was applied more frequently in the dative. In Middle English, *-n* dropped more frequently when it was a case marker than when it was a plural marker. It seems to be a general phenomenon, then, that plural endings are more resistant to deletion than case and agreement endings. One would like to relate this to the fact that plural is selected in the deep structure and has a direct semantic interpretation, whereas (surface) case and agreement are inserted by transformational rules and have no direct semantic interpretation. Loss of the plural distinction hence impedes meaning more than loss of other categories. A consideration of analogical change supports this point. When lost, plurals are more likely to be re-introduced by analogical change than are cases or agreement morphemes. We can then formulate the following principle:

(C) *Morphological material which is predictable on the surface tends to be more susceptible to loss than morphological material which is not predictable on the surface.*

In the light of this last point it is worth reconsidering the significance of the kinds of facts that Labov and his collaborators have been unearthing. They found that if you measure the frequencies with which optional rules are applied, you get very systematic results. The relationship between the frequencies in different cases is fairly constant. If one speaker deletes case more often than plural, that will be the case for any other speaker, or for the same speaker one day later. There is a real question as to how such facts are to be accounted for in linguistic theory. There are basically two ways one could see this done. Labov's proposal is to devise a new sort of linguistic rule, the *variable rule*, in which the frequencies of rule application, or at least something from which these frequencies can be deduced, are attached to the rule. This amounts to saying that the frequencies have to be learned by the child, and are simply part of the linguistic information you have to acquire when you learn your phonology. An alternative, which is suggested by the cross-linguistic validity of the factors that control the frequency of application, is the following: the frequencies are *not* learned by the child, but predictable from exactly the kinds of substantive constraints we have been considering here. This may well be too strong. There are intermediate possibilities, for example, that the child must learn the 'basic strength' of an optional rule, i.e., its overall frequency of application, whereas the variations in frequency of application in specific environments follow from general functional considerations such as those discussed here.

The paradigmatic factors interact with phonotactic factors that have to do with maximizing the naturalness of the output sequences. For example, when consonants are deleted optionally at the end of a word, they are dropped more frequently when the next word begins with a consonant, less frequently when it begins with a vowel, i.e., the frequencies of deletion are such as to favor CVCV sequences in the output.

In addition, such factors as style, social class and tempo play a role. It will be useful to distinguish these as *nongrammatical* conditioning factors from the *grammatical* factors, i.e., phonotactics and paradigm structure. The justification for making this distinction is that the grammatical factors play a role elsewhere in grammar, for example in characterizing the possible targets of phonological 'conspiracies'.

The alternative hypothesis, then, is:

(D)    *Grammatically conditioned variability in the application of optimal rules favors optimal outputs*

where optimality should be characterizable independently of any particular language in terms of paradigmatic and phonotactic properties of the output. For example, we would not expect to find a dialect of English in which plural -*s* drops MORE often than genitive or third singular -*s*. More generally, NO language should show a bias in favor of deleting a deep structure category rather than a transformationally introduced category. No language should drop final consonants more often when the next word begins with a vowel, or drop final vowels more often when the next word begins with a consonant, etc. So far the available facts seem to be compatible with this hypothesis.

More unclear is the question whether we can also predict the relative force of the different factors that jointly condition variability. For example, could two dialects differ in that paradigmatic factors were more important in one dialect but phonotactic factors were more important in the other? The answer may be no. There is some reason to believe that the strength of the factors is itself predictably variable. Conditioning by grammatical category becomes relatively more important in more formal speech (Labov et al. 1968). This suggests that the strength of the conditioning factors is dependent on the functional requirements of the speech situation.

The closest I have seen to a counterexample is the tensing and raising of /æ/ in New York, on which Labov (1972b) has reported (cf. Bailey 1970 for further discussion of this example). This happens before voiced nonnasal stops (*bad, bag, cab*), voiceless fricatives (*laugh, bath, pass, cast*), and front nasals (*man, ham, land*). The raising is to some extent variable in all environments. For speakers over about seventy, there is more raising before fricatives and voiced stops than before nasals (i.e., the vowel is higher on the average in *pass, bad* than in *man*); but for younger speakers the situation is reversed: there is more raising before nasals than before fricatives and voiced stops. In addition, there is some less clear fluctuation in the relative strength of the fricative and voiced stop conditions. Before concluding that there is a genuine reversal of the nasal constraint, one should bear in mind two additional facts which are probably involved: (1) The tensing before fricatives in *pass, last*, etc., is a historically older process which is clearly related to the British English development of [a:] in these words (Luick 1964: 704-9). It is evidently a separate rule from the other tensing. In the speech of seventy years ago this was the primary process of tensing which operated. (2) Presumably the increasingly strong raising before nasals parallels the increasing nasalization and concomitant lengthening and tensing of vowels before nasals in American English. Evidently, then, there is more going on here than a simple reversal in the strength of the conditioning factors. The raising of /æ/ actually involves several separate processes.

Hypothesis (D) leads to a reexamination of the theory of sound change. Labov's work on sound change indicates that it typically proceeds in two stages. The first is a stage in which the new rule is optional and the frequency of application in particular cases is governed by a complicated interaction of different grammatical paradigmatic and phonological and nongrammatical social and stylistic factors. In the second stage, the rule becomes obligatory in some cases, in which it was frequently applied at the previous, optional stage, and it becomes inapplicable in other cases, in which it was less frequently applied before. The conditioning now becomes relatively simple, generally with either paradigmatic, or phonological, or social, or stylistic factors being selected as the single conditioning factor of the rule. I suggest the following interpretation of this phenomenon: in the first stage, the rule is optional and is subject to the systematic and predictable variability of optional rules in general. The complex interaction of conditioning factors at this stage is not learned as part of the grammar of the language but follows from the nature of optional rules. In the second stage, the conditioning factors become part of the acquired grammar of the language. But the variability is too complex to learn as such. The changeover necessitates a *polarization* and *simplification* of the conditioning: some conditioning factors are eliminated and for the others the high and low frequencies get sorted out as respectively obligatory and inapplicable cases of the new rule.

Generally the conditioning factor that wins out is the phonological one. This gives the regular case of phonologically conditioned sound change. When the paradigmatic, social, and stylistic conditioning factors win out we get cases which Neogrammarian theory handles variously as 'analogy' or 'dialect mixture'. It has long been noted that sound changes can depend on grammatical categories. We can add that particular KINDS of grammatical categories are going to block sound changes from taking place. This strengthens the theory of sound change considerably by subjecting it to the same constraints that hold on rule variability. In the same way, lexical splits should reflect factors of style or emphasis. Examples of stylistic split are the split between lengthening in everyday words like *grass, glass, ass,* versus short vowel in special words like *crass, lass, gas;* the earlier dropping of *r* in everyday words like *ass, cuss, bust* versus the retention of *r* in special words like *parsley, hoarse* (note the doublets *cuss/curse, ass/arse, bust/burst*). The erudite/vulgar splits known from many languages belong here. Split of emphatic versus nonemphatic is e.g., the lengthening (reported by Ferguson 1971a for Philadelphia) of the affective words *mad, bad, glad,* versus *lad, add, ad, Brad, Tad, fad, cad,* with *sad* varying for the two Philadelphia speakers I have checked with. Closely related are also splits along major versus minor category such as the English voicing of $\theta$ to $\delta$ in pronouns.

Bhat's (1969) observations on Indian caste dialects are also naturally explicable in these terms. Bhat compared geographic and social (caste) dialect differentiation in Tulu, a Dravidian language. He noted that, whereas regional isoglosses are formed by both regular and sporadic sound changes, *all caste isoglosses are formed by regular sound changes.* Bhat proposes to explain this by the assumption that regular sound changes are carried out by children (who rarely associate with children of other castes) whereas sporadic sound changes take place in adult speakers (who do interact with members of other castes). However, probably a simpler way of explaining Bhat's observation is that polarization of speech differences between social classes is naturally a powerful factor in a society where the boundaries between the classes are drawn very sharply.

Further work will have to show whether this is the right approach. It remains to be seen, for example, whether this framework can account for the facts that have led Wang and his collaborators to postulate the 'diffusion' of sound changes through the vocabulary, for such cases of grammatical conditioning of sound change as that cited by Postal (1968) from Mohawk, and many others. And even if it does turn out to be the right approach, there is no doubt at all that it will have to be greatly enriched and elaborated before it is nearly adequate to account for the complexities of synchronic variability and diachronic change.

## 3. Rule Opacity and Reordering

The reordering conditions proposed in Kiparsky (1968a), that feeding order tends to be maximized, and bleeding order tends to be minimized, in most cases correctly predict the direction of reordering. The unmarked status of feeding order is not subject to any serious doubt. Still, a number of examples have turned up where these conditions are inadequate. There are three sorts of cases like this: (1) reordering contrary to the conditions; (2) reordering where the concepts of feeding and bleeding are inapplicable; (3) reordering in cases of 'mutual bleeding'. Some examples have been collected in Kenstowicz and Kisseberth (1973a).

In this section I will review the examples known to me where the previously proposed conditions do not work. We shall see that they reveal an inadequacy in the concept of bleeding order. I will tentatively suggest a reformulation of the conditions which accounts for the problematic cases as well as for those which the old conditions handle. This reformulation will make use of the concept of *rule opacity*, which I will argue has an important role to play elsewhere in linguistic theory as well.

I will begin with the syntactic example analyzed in Klima (1964a). Klima wrote this paper before it had been shown that reordering of rules is a primary form of linguistic change. His analysis is therefore formulated solely in terms of rule addition and subsequent restructuring. However, it is now easy to recognize that the historical process Klima describes is essentially a series of downward shifts in the order of case marking, which makes case in English dependent on increasingly superficial configurations. For example, the shift from *whom did you see?* to *who did you see?* is a shift from a grammar in which case marking applies before Wh-movement (i.e., to a representation of the form *you past see Wh + PRO*) to a grammar in which case marking applies after Wh-movement (i.e., to something like *Wh + PRO you past see*). From the drift-like progression of this reordering of case marking we can conclude that it constitutes a natural development in the grammar of English. This raises the question, what general principle lies behind the directionality of the drift. The ordering asymmetries of feeding and bleeding order (Kiparsky 1968a) do not help us here. If anything, Klima's analysis shows a drift towards LESS application of the case marking rule.

We can make an initial approximation to the required principle in the following way. Let us make a distinction between *reordering transformations*, which move constituents around, and *feature changing transformations*, which add some morphologically realized mark onto a constituent. Consider tentatively a principle which says:

(E') Feature changing transformations preferably follow reordering transformations.

This implies that the evaluation measure assigns a higher value to a grammar in which a feature changing rule follows a reordering rule than to the otherwise identical grammar in which the two rules apply in the reverse order. This should, if correct, have the usual consequences in terms of directionality of change, language acquisition (children should make mistakes in the direction of the preferred order but not in the other direction), and frequency in the world's languages.

The study by Hale (1970) of the ergative and passive in Australian languages gives some support of principle (E'). On the basis of a comparative diachronic analysis of several languages Hale tentatively concludes that the ordering:

Pronominalization
Passive

is unstable. He shows that languages having this order tend either to reorder the rules or to make the passive structure obligatory and basic. It is possible, as Hale suggests, to attribute the reordering to the antifeeding nature of the unstable order. However, perhaps a more natural way of looking at the change is that the drift is toward making pronominalization, a feature changing rule, follow the passive transformation.

There is a phonological analog to this type of asymmetry in the order of transformations. In recent papers, Kisseberth and Kenstowicz (1973a) and Kaye (1971) have discussed cases in which the unmarked order of phonological rules is not characterized by the bleeding or feeding relations. The examples of Kenstowicz and Kisseberth are of the following sort. In Yokuts, vowels are shortened in closed syllables:

$$V \rightarrow [\text{-long}] \ / \ \underline{\hspace{1cm}} \ C \begin{Bmatrix} \# \\ C \end{Bmatrix}$$

e.g., *do:s-ol* 'might report' but *dos-hin* 'reports'. This rule is critically ordered with respect to an epenthesis rule:

$$\phi \rightarrow i \ / \ C \ \underline{\hspace{1cm}} \ C \begin{Bmatrix} \# \\ C \end{Bmatrix}$$

which breaks up clusters and thereby turns closed syllables into open ones. Epenthesis bleeds shortening, but as Kenstowicz and Kisseberth note, the bleeding order:

1.  Epenthesis
2.  Shortening

in which the rules actually apply is quite natural, and the one in which one would expect them to apply. In at least some cases, then, bleeding order seems to be unmarked.

Kenstowicz and Kisseberth do not actually give evidence that bleeding order really is unmarked in such cases. However, there are cases of historical change which support their conjecture. Wayne O'Neil (personal communication) has noted that Faroese has two rules:

1.  Intervocalic spirantization
2.  Vowel syncope

which originally apply in the given order, e.g., *heidinir→heiðinir→heiðnir* 'heathen (pl.)', and have been reordered into a bleeding order:

1.   Vowel syncope
2.   Intervocalic spirantization

giving *heidnir*, where spirantization no longer applies.

Another possible example where diachronic evidence may point to the unmarked status of a bleeding order is discussed briefly in Hurford (1971). Cockney English drops initial *h*. According to Hurford, there is an older dialect which says *a 'ouse*, whereas younger speakers say *an 'ouse*. We might say, then, that the nonbleeding order:

1.   an → a / _____ #C
2.   h → φ / #_____

has changed into the bleeding order:

1.   h → φ / #_____
2.   an → a / _____ #C

There are a couple of ways out. In the first place, we might say that the second dialect actually has no underlying *h*, but that words formerly ending in *h* have been restructured with an initial vowel. Secondly, we might argue that the rule for the indefinite article reads:

a → an / _____ #V

in which case we no longer have a bleeding relationship. But it seems to me that these objections are really beside the point. Suppose that it is possible to motivate the underlying representations which Hurford assumes for the second dialect. Clearly this is a POSSIBLE analysis. The change from *a 'ouse* to *an 'ouse* should be predicted under this analysis as well as under the other possible analysis. That this is not the case is a flaw in the theory.

Kenstowicz and Kisseberth discuss two distinct ways in which the theory of phonology might be amended to characterize the markedness of ordering relations in the correct way. The first is that:

(E") Where one rule A stands in a bleeding relation with another rule B by virtue of A's altering a structure so that it no longer satisfies the environmental conditions of B, bleeding order is unmarked.

That is, a rule of the form:

K → L / M _____ N

is preferably bled (i.e., preceded) by a rule which destroys M or N (the environment), although it is preferably NOT bled (i.e., followed) by a rule which destroys K (the input proper).

However, they note that (E") does not take care of the following sort of case. In some Slavic languages there is a vowel copy rule of the form:

(C) V R C → 1 2 3 2 4
    1 2 3 4

This rule, known to be a dialectal innovation of East Slavic, has to apply before an old rule which accents the initial vowel of certain words, as shown by the following derivations:

|  | /vórn + u/ | /golv + u/ |
|---|---|---|
| vowel copy | vórón + u | golov + u |
| accent insertion | — | gólov + u |
| later rules | vorónu | gólovu |

It seems evident that this is indeed the expected ordering of vowel copy and accent insertion. But here bleeding order is completely irrelevant. Both rules will apply to underlying /golv-u/ in either order, but with different results.

In view of this example, Kenstowicz and Kisseberth suggest an alternative principle (E'''), in terms of the *substantive* effect of the rules. I formulate it here as follows:

(E''') Rules which affect syllabic structure (e.g., metathesis, epenthesis, deletion) preferably apply before rules that refer to syllabic structure (e.g., assimilation).

It is clear that Kenstowicz and Kisseberth are generally on the right track. However, neither (E") nor (E''') can be correct. This is shown by Kaye's Ojibwa example.

Kaye discusses the following two rules in Ojibwa:

*vowel coalescense*            aw + i → $\begin{cases} \bar{a} \ / \ \underline{\hspace{1cm}} k \\ \bar{o} \ / \ \underline{\hspace{1cm}} n \end{cases}$

*n-assimilation*                 n → k / \_\_ k

He presents evidence that certain Ojibwa dialects have gone from the above order to the reverse order. Underlying /nontaw + in + k/ has thereby changed from *nōntōkk* to *nōntākk*. Again, the bleeding (and feeding) relations are inapplicable, so that principle (E") cannot be invoked. However, principle (E'") also gives the wrong result, since this reordering puts an assimilation rule *before* a rule that changes syllable structure, whereas (E'") says that assimilation rules preferably go AFTER rules that change syllable structure.

In place of these principles, which are still somewhat unsatisfactory, I would like to put forward tentatively a principle which accounts for all the examples, including the syntactic ones. Define the concept *opacity of a rule* as follows:

> *DEFINITION.* A rule  A → B / C ＿＿＿＿ D
> is opaque to the extent that there are surface representations of the form
>   (i)  A in environment C ＿＿＿D
> or  (ii)  B in environment other than C＿＿＿ D

(The first of these two conditions has been referred to by structuralists as an alternation being 'non-automatic' and by Stampe (1969) as a rule being 'contradicted on the surface'.) Note that both cases can arise in several ways. For example, CAD might arise through a rule E → C / ＿＿＿＿ AD, or a rule E → A / C ＿＿＿＿ D. B might appear in environments other than C ＿＿＿＿ D either through some process that changes CBD to EBD, or through a process that introduces B in other environments, etc. Of course, exceptions add opacity to a rule according to the above definition. The definition can be extended to syntax in the obvious way. Opacity as here defined is a matter of degree, although I have no suggestions as to how to quantify it formally. I suspect that the concept will ultimately turn out to be more complicated than the above definition indicates.

Let us refer to the converse of opacity as *transparency*.

The hypothesis which I want to propose is that opacity of rules adds to the cost of a grammar; more concretely, that opacity is a property of rules that makes them, and the underlying forms to which they apply, harder to learn. In particular, I conjecture that transparent rules are learned first, and that the acquisition of phonological rules proceeds roughly in the order of increasing opacity.

As regards unmarked ordering, we can now derive, as a special case, the following principle:

(E)  *Rules tend to be ordered so as to become maximally transparent.*

This principle seems to cover the hitherto recalcitrant examples of ordering asymmetry, capturing what is correct about the three principles (E'), (E"), and (E'").

For example, in Yokuts the preferred, unmarked order is that in which shortening applies to the superficial, more phonetic representations reached after epenthesis, rather than the deeper, more abstract representations that the derivation shows before epenthesis. If shortening came before epenthesis, it would be a more opaque rule by *DEF.*, Case (ii). In Slavic, the rule 'accent the first vowel in words of the *golv* class' would be opaque if it preceded copying, since copying would introduce a stressed vowel on the second syllable of these words as well (*DEF.*, Case (ii)). In Ojibwa, the *awi → ō | _____n* rule is more opaque in the order that gives *nōntōkk* than in the innovating ordering that gives *nōntākk* (*DEF.*, Case (ii)). Similarly, in Klima's syntactic example the drift is towards making case marking an increasingly transparent process.

The reader will have noticed that these examples all involve Case (ii) of the definition of opacity. The same is true of the syntactic examples of Klima and Hale, and of the other examples discussed in the paper by Kenstowicz and Kisseberth. What about Case (i), then? *This is simply a characterization of nonfeeding order;* the consequence that feeding order tends to be maximized is given by including Case (i) in the definition of opacity.

For example, suppose we have the two rules:

1.    $\gamma \rightarrow \phi \ / \ V \ \underline{\hspace{2cm}} V$

2.    $\begin{bmatrix} V \\ - \text{low} \end{bmatrix} \rightarrow [+ \text{high}] \ / \ \underline{\hspace{2cm}} V$

Now the order given is the unmarked feeding order, in which we get derivations like *eγe → ee → ie*. This is also the order in which both rules are maximally transparent. Reversing the order would result in an output *ee* for the input *eγe*, making the vowel raising rule opaque by Case (i).

Our revised characterization of the ordering asymmetries now takes care of feeding order, one type of bleeding order, and certain cases where the concepts of feeding and bleeding are not applicable. Then what about cases of marked bleeding order of the type discussed in Kiparsky (1968a), namely those in which two rules potentially apply in the *same* segment? For example, in Swiss German there is a reordering from

|  |  | /bode + Sg./ | /bode + Pl./ |
|---|---|---|---|
| 1. | Umlaut (e.g., in env. ___ Pl.) | – | böde + Pl. |
| 2. | o → ɔ / ___ [+ coronal] | bɔde + Sg. | – |

|  |  | /bode + Sg./ | /bode + Pl./ |
|---|---|---|---|
| 1. | o → ɔ / ___ [+ coronal] | bɔde + Sg. | bɔde + Pl. |
| 2. | Umlaut (e.g., in env. ___ Pl.) | – | böde + Pl. |

But these are exactly the cases in which the *paradigm* condition that allomorphy tends to be minimized, which we have seen to be needed on independent grounds, will give the correct result! In the Swiss German example, the innovating order preserves the stem shape between singular and plural. A review of the examples given in Kiparsky (1968a), King (1969), and elsewhere, shows that the cases which have been cited as reordering from bleeding into nonbleeding order are all of this type.

The proposed reformulation seems necessary in order to account for the examples brought up by Kaye and by Kenstowicz and Kisseberth, and the syntactic cases discussed by Klima and Hale. It has at least as clear a functional basis in language acquisition as the notion of maximal applicability which it replaces. In addition, it has some important further advantages which I will now mention briefly.

The notion of rule transparency enables us to establish a profound relationship between the two historical phenomena of rule reordering and rule loss.

It has been pointed out by Stampe (1969) and Andersen (1969) (cf. also Darden 1970) that rules tend to be lost from grammars through historical change only under certain specific conditions. Basically, we can say that rules are susceptible to loss *if they are hard to learn.* And one of the major factors that makes rules hard to learn (though not the only one) is precisely *opacity* as defined above.

Consider the first condition that leads to opacity (Case (i) in the *DEFINITION*). A rule is opaque if representations of the sort which it eliminates exist on the surface. Loss under this condition is common (cf. the Algonquian example cited from Piggott (1971) in Section 1 of this paper). To give just one more case, a similar situation arose in early Iranian. The Iranian languages once had Bartholomae's Law, by which voiceless stops were subject to progressive assimilation of aspiration and voicing after voiced aspirates, e.g., /drugh + ta/ → *drugdha.* Voiced *unaspirated* stops did not cause progressive assimilation, and were themselves subject to regressive assimilation of voicing (with velars in addition being spirantized), e.g., /bhag + ta/ → *bhaxta.* Subsequently the voiced aspirates were deaspirated. The resulting situation is one in which some voiced stops (the old aspirates) cause progressive voicing assimilation, but others (the original unaspirated stops) do not, e.g., (assuming rephonemicization) /drug + ta/ → *drugda,* but /bag + ta/ → *baxta.* This stage essentially survives in older Avestan. In later Avestan, however, the now opaque progressive assimilation rule is simply lost, giving /drug + ta/ → *druxta* like /bag + ta/ → *baxta.* Bartholomae's Law is lost as a rule and survives only in isolated words in lexicalized form, e.g., in *azda* 'thus'. Other examples are given in Andersen (1969).

We would also expect the second type of opacity (Case (ii)) to lead to rule loss. There is not a great deal of evidence for this being so. But a tentative analysis by Erteschik (1971) is, if correct, exactly such a case. The Hebrew spirantization rule, apparently applicable originally to all stops, has been limited to *p, b,* and *k*. Erteschik suggests that *p, b,* and *k* were, at the time when the rule became restricted in this way, exactly the stops whose spirantized cognates were not phonemic, the system being:

| | | | |
|---|---|---|---|
| p | t | k | ʔ |
| b | d | g | |
| | s | | X |
| | z | r | |

In support of this conjecture she notes what happens when children learn spirantization in modern Hebrew. Here *X* has lost is pharyngealization, thereby merging with *x*, the spirantized form of *k*. This means that spirantization of *k* has become opaque with respect to Case (ii), since the output of spirantization of *k* now has another source in the grammar. Spirantization of *p, b,* on the other hand, remains transparent. According to Erteschik, children make mistakes with spirantizing velars (but not, apparently, with labials). For *lexabes* ~ *kvisa* she has observed children saying both *lexabes* ~ *xvisa* and *lekabes* ~ *kvisa*. That is, children find it harder to learn the opaque part of the modern Hebrew spirantization rule (and the underlying forms insofar as they are subject to this rule) than the transparent part of the same rule.

Stampe has suggested other factors which make a rule susceptible to loss, in particular the *unnatural* status of a rule. For example, certain natural processes of vowel lengthening or shortening may be unnatural as the corresponding tensing or laxing processes when the length opposition changes into a tenseness opposition in the course of historical change. Such rules might also be susceptible to loss. Therefore not all cases of loss will necessarily involve rules which are opaque in the sense defined here. Opacity will, however, be ONE of the factors that bring about the loss of rules from a grammar by historical change.

Rule opacity also plays a role in paradigm changes like those discussed above. Strictly speaking, Principle (B) is inadequate by itself to deal with an example like the change of *honōs* to *honor*. The *r* which is reintroduced in the nominative causes shortening of the preceding vowel by a general rule of Latin. As a result we have actually just traded in the *s/r* alternation of *honōs/honoris* for the *o/ō* alternation of *honor/honōris*. Still, everyone would grant that there is a real levelling here. It is obvious that the new paradigm in some sense shows 'less allomorphy' than the old one. But what exactly does this mean formally? I would like to suggest as the crucial difference that the shortening rule, which produces the *ō/o* alternation, is transparent with respect to Case (i), whereas the rhotacism rule, which produces the *s/r* alternation, is opaque with respect to Case (i). That is, there are no words ending in *-ōr* in Latin, but there are many words with intervocalic *s* (partly because of exceptions to the rule, e.g., *miser* 'miserable', *positus* 'put (pp.)', including loans like *basis, asinus* 'donkey', and partly because of *s* from other underlying sources, e.g., /cād + tus/ → *cāsus* 'fallen').

Finally, I should like to suggest that the concept of rule opacity may prove to be useful in *the theory of exceptions.* It is hard to find a clearcut division of phonological rules into those that may and those that cannot allow exceptions. However, it is possible to say that certain kinds of rules are much less likely to have exceptions than others. As a first approximation to the needed criterion I propose opacity. The more opaque a rule, the more likely it is to develop exceptions. More specifically, opacity by Case (i) leads to *input* exceptions, whereas opacity by Case (ii) leads to *environment* exceptions (see Kisseberth 1970d and Coats 1970 for these concepts). As an example of the first case, consider Finnish consonant gradation. This is a weakening affecting consonants in the environment

$$\underline{\hspace{2cm}} \text{VC} \begin{cases} \# \\ C \end{cases}$$

The rule applies to single stops and geminate stops in the following way:

| | | | |
|---|---|---|---|
| 1. *Weakening of simple stops* | t→d | (e.g., /maton/→*madon* 'worm's) | |
| | p→v | | |
| | k→φ, v | | |
| 2. *Degemination* | tt→t | (e.g., /matton/→*maton* 'carpet's') | |
| | pp→p | | |
| | kk→k | | |

Degemination has virtually no exceptions (only certain very foreign names might not be subjected to the rule, e.g., gen. *Giuseppen,* provided they are not assimilated in any way, including stress). On the other hand, the weakening of simple stops normally fails to apply in loans (*auton* 'car's', as well as in many native personal names (*Lempin,* 'Lempi's'), brand names (*Upon* 'of Upo'), slang and affective words (*räkän* 'of snot'), etc. It seems reasonable to correlate this with the fact that degemination is nearly completely transparent with respect to Case (i), whereas the weakening of simple stops is rather opaque with respect to that case. That is, the sorts of input representations that are destroyed by degemination exist on the surface only in the rare exceptions, and in a few cases where strong boundaries block the application of gradation, e.g., *Kekkosta* 'Kekkonen (partitive)' (Karttunen 1970). But the sorts of input representations destroyed by the weakening of single stops are quite frequent on the surface; indeed, they arise with every application of degemination. Thus, we might suppose that the weakening of simple stops, and the underlying forms subject to it, are harder to learn than the degemination rule, and the underlying forms subject to it. (This should be readily testable in child language.) The greater proneness of the weakening of simple stops to develop exceptions would, then, be a consequence of its greater opacity.

Examples of the second type (opacity by Case (ii) leading to environment exceptions) are commonplace. This case is simply the initial stage of the process of morphologization, by which rules lose their phonological conditioning and begin to be dependent on abstract features in the lexicon. The paradigm case is Germanic umlaut. The elimination of the conditioning $i$ and $j$ turned the umlaut rule opaque by Case (ii). At some point after this took place, umlaut started to be reanalyzed as a morphologically conditioned process.

# Chapter 5

# Explanation in Phonology*

## 1. Formal and Functional Explanation

The study of the formal properties of phonological systems has progressed to a point where it may be possible to return, with much greater precision and generality than could be achieved before, to traditional functionalist questions: how phonological structure is grounded in the requirements of speech performance, in the broad sense of perception, production, and acquisition. The interest and importance of these questions is obvious. However, the research paradigms of generative phonology have in several respects not been particularly conducive to their investigation.[1] Insufficient attention has been paid even to posing the relevant questions sufficiently clearly to allow empirical studies to get under way. Perhaps one reason for this is the sharp distinction which has developed in practice between work on linguistic competence and work on speech performance. More serious is the fact that many functional regularities differ in a basic way from the sort of phenomena that have been primarily investigated in generative grammar, and cannot be 'captured' by notational conventions and an evaluation measure based on simplicity. For example, we shall see below that recent attempts to reduce certain types of functional regularities to grammatical simplicity by means of derivational constraints fail for intrinsic reasons to provide an explanatory account of these regularities.

The questions which will be raised in this paper will be about the explanation rather than the description of phonological and morphological facts. The paper deals with the form and substance which functional explanations may have in these areas of linguistic structure. In spite of the fact that it continues a very traditional line of investigation, it is in many ways preliminary and speculative. The data used to illustrate and motivate the proposed generalizations comes from well-documented languages and should not be controversial, though its interpretation in a few cases may be.

* This work was supported in part by the National Institutes of Mental Health (Grant No. MH-13390-04). A version of this paper was read at a conference on the goals of Linguistic Theory at the University of Texas at Austin, October, 1969.

Let me begin by reviewing briefly the nature of explanation in phonology as it emerges from Chomsky and Halle (1968). The notational devices and the evaluation measure jointly characterize the notion 'linguistically significant generalization', in a way which is empirically testable through the investigation of linguistic universals, language acquisition, and linguistic change. As this explanatory paradigm is well known, I will simply give a short illustration of its functioning, and then proceed to point out some respects in which the paradigm breaks down. This will then lead into the general topic of functional conditions as a basis of explanation in phonology and morphology.

The examples which I will analyze come from a discussion of movable accent of the phonologically predictable type in Itkonen (1966). Itkonen cites the accentual systems of two Finno-Ugric languages, Eastern Cheremis and Komi. In certain dialects of Eastern Cheremis, and in Proto-Cheremis, vowels are divided into two groups: full and reduced vowels (what the feature correlates of this distinction are need not be settled here). On the basis of this distinction in the vowels, the accentuation of a word is predictable as follows:

1. [a] ... the accent falls on the syllable containing the last full vowel of the word. [b] If the word has only reduced vowels, the accent is usually on the first syllable (Itkonen 1966: 156).

In the Eastern Permyak dialect of Komi (which Itkonen assumes represents Proto-Permic in this respect) vowels are divided into heavy and light. The accentuation of a word is determined by the following rule, which is exactly the mirror image of the Cheremis rule:

2. [a] The accent normally falls on the syllable containing the first heavy vowel of the word. [b] If the word has only light vowels, the accent is on the last syllable (Itkonen 1966: 156).

For both Cheremis and Komi, a verbally formulated stress rule contains two separate statements: one for words which contain full (or heavy) vowels, and another for words which do not. No *intrinsic* connection between the [a] and [b] cases is shown. There is no reason, apparently, why 1[b] should read 'first syllable' and 2[b] 'last syllable', rather than vice versa.

Things are different if we work within a formal theory. Suppose that we write formally the Cheremis rule for words containing full vowels (case 1[a]). The simplest rule which puts the accent on the last full vowel is this:

$$V \rightarrow [+ \text{acc}] \ / \longrightarrow (C_0 \ \check{V} C_0)_0 \ \#$$

where V indicates any vowel, $\check{V}$ a reduced vowel, and C a consonant. The rule discounts any syllables with reduced vowels at the end of the word and stresses the last vowel of the remaining portion.[2] This rule generalizes to the special case of words with only reduced vowels. By the normal conventions of disjunctive ordering, it stresses the *first* syllable of such a word. That is the correct result.

The inverse case of Komi naturally works just as well. The simplest rule for accenting the first 'heavy' vowel of a word (case 1 [a] ) is the following:

$$V \rightarrow [+ \text{acc}] \ / \ \# (C_0 \ \check{V} C_0)_0 \ \underline{\hspace{2cm}}$$

where $\check{V}$ indicates a 'light' vowel. This rule gives the correct accentuation, on the final syllable, of words with only light vowels (2 [b] ).

What phonological theory says, then, is that the accentuation of words containing only reduced (or light) vowels does not have to be specifically learned, but can be inferred from the accentuation of words containing both types of vowels. The notational conventions of generative phonology, in our case the use of subscripts and the principle of disjunctive ordering, together with the evaluation measure, which selects the simplest formulation of the rule, jointly make a correct prediction about the accentuation of one type of word on the basis of the accentuation of the other. The value of an abstract formulation of the theory and of grammatical descriptions is shown by examples of this type, where the formalism leads to a conclusion which would not necessarily be anticipated on the basis of a merely verbal statement of the facts. It is in this sense that generative phonology goes beyond simply making traditional process phonology more precise, and yields a deeper understanding of the structure of phonological systems than previously was possible.

The bases of explanation in current generative phonology are the formal constraints given jointly by the notational conventions and the evaluation measure. These formal constraints may be *absolute* or *relative*. Absolute constraints are given by the form of the notation itself, which limits the class of possible grammars. For example, a rule could simply not be written within the current framework which would drop the middle segment in words of a certain class (in words with an even number of segments, say, the two middle segments). The theory correctly makes this linguistically impossible rule unstatable in an absolute sense. Relative constraints are given by the interplay of the notational devices and the evaluation measure. The explanation in the examples I have cited is based on such relative constraints. The theory does not claim that Cheremis words containing only reduced vowels *must* have initial stress. Rules for stressing such words elsewhere than on the initial syllable could be formulated; they would merely be more complex than the actual rule. The claim is rather that a certain natural projection will be made from the general case [a] to the special case [b], which will be abandoned only if contrary evidence is encountered.

What basis does this claim have in actual linguistic fact? Before answering this question, let us review in a general way the sorts of specific factual consequences which *could* be derived from it.

The claim relates most directly to language acquisition. It says that the child projects correctly according to certain abstract formal principles from one set of data, which he may reasonably be expected to encounter first, to the full system that includes special cases whose relation to the normal cases may superficially appear quite irregular. For example, if in some language with an accent system like that described by rules 1 or 2 the child has not encountered words stressed by 1[b] or 2[b], but forms such words on the basis of morphological rules he has learned, he should be able to stress them correctly. Such predictions are in principle quite testable, for example, by study of the 'mistakes' made by children, which permit conclusions to be drawn about the system of rules the child has formed, and experimentally by asking the child to make up new words, asking him to repeat words given to him with neutral stress. The formal principles in question are so general that many languages will provide significant empirical tests for them.

Implicit in these consequences for first language acquisition is another set of predicted consequences for language change, which provide a second major source of empirical evidence for linguistic theory. For example, the generally well-supported assumption that 'sound change' is the addition of phonological rules to grammar entails that historical stress shifts of the [a] type will normally involve, as a special case, stress shifts of the [b] type – in general, that 'sound change', far from being a purely physiological process, is subject to the same abstract formal constraints as the synchronic phonological rules of a grammar. Likewise, the assumption that 'analogical change' is the simplification of grammars (in the linguistic sense of simplicity, intended to be specified by the notational conventions of generative grammar) entails that stress sytems having subrule [a] will, if they do not have subrule [b], tend to acquire it. In more general terms, it is claimed that the notational conventions, to the extent that they correctly characterize the linguistic notion of 'simplicity', provide a characterization of the form and direction of generalization in linguistic change. And finally, we should expect the formal groupings of rules to result in entities whose unity is reflected in common changes – e.g. that [a] and [b] should be reordered or generalized in the same way (see Kiparsky 1968a for discussion).

A third reflection of these formal conditions has to do with linguistic universals, including implicational ones, and with facts about the relative 'naturalness' of various properties of rules and grammars. On the basis of the investigation of large numbers of languages one might be able to verify the claims which the formalism implicitly makes about what sort of rules should tend to co-occur. The fact that rule pairs such as the [a] and [b] cases of the stress rules mentioned above are expressible as subcases of a general process of stress assignment means that such rule pairs should be characteristic of languages in general. The more specific the formal relationship expressed by the formalism, the clearer the exclusion of an accidental relationship. Because of its greater accessibility, synchronic evidence predominates quantitatively in discussions of universal grammar, although it can be difficult to interpret when detailed questions are at issue.

The role of what I refer to as relative constraints is usually said to be that of selecting the right grammar from among the alternative grammars for a set of data. In terms of a less overschematized model of language acquisition, in which the process is not viewed as instantaneous, we can replace this interpretation by viewing the relative constraints as a ranking of grammars which determines the order in which the grammatical system of the child unfolds. That order has little to do with the order in which it encounters the 'primary linguistic data', but rather depends on the relative linguistic complexity of the grammatical structure underlying this data. This is shown, in phonology, by such observations as Jakobson's (1962) that the elements of phonological systems are acquired roughly in the order of increasing markedness. Especially striking is Jakobson's point that unmarked segments often occur early in language acquisition even when no models for them exist in the adult system. For example, stop systems of the English type, with, e.g., $[p^h]$ : [b], but not [p], appear in many children to develop out of initial stop systems with the maximally unmarked series (e.g., [p]), an analog in child language to the fact that languages with a single stop series (such as Finnish, Menomini, or Polynesian languages) in general have that maximally unmarked series.

This paradigm of formal explanation in generative grammar has certain limitations. In theory, the evaluation measure is supposed to operate *globally* on the whole phonology and lexicon (indeed, the whole grammar). If so, cases should arise where overall decisions of a sort that frequently arise in phonology — for example, between adding a segment to the inventory of phonemes and adding a phonological rule to the grammar — are made on the basis of simplicity. Decisions of this nature have in fact sometimes been made on formal simplicity considerations. However, it is important to note that in no case has the resulting analysis been shown to be correct on independent grounds. The cases in which the formal paradigm has been confirmed empirically (by either synchronic or diachronic evidence) are all instances of *local* decisions. Examples are cases of disjunctive ordering of the type illustrated above (Chomsky and Halle 1968), and the collapsing of rule pairs by the notational convention of braces (Kiparsky 1968a). The only interesting global consequence of the paradigm of formal explanation in generative grammar that has ever been proposed was the analysis of 'accidental gaps' in the lexicon. Halle (1962) suggested that the distinction between accidental gaps such as *blik* and systematic gaps such as *bnik* is automatically drawn by the notational devices in conjunction with the simplicity metric. Accidental gaps, according to this proposal, are those gaps whose exclusion by morpheme structure rules does not pay off because the needed rules cost more (in terms of numbers of feature specifications) than they save in the lexicon. However, this treatment of accidental gaps has been withdrawn by Chomsky and Halle (1968) in favor of one which, while more adequate in a descriptive sense, does not provide an explanatory account, and so provides no confirmation of the notational devices and the simplicity metric. The explanatory function of these, therefore, remains relatively small at present.

This circumstance is reflected in the nature of the issues in phonological theory debated in recent years. On the one hand, proposals concerning the notational conventions are characteristically introduced on the basis of arguments based on descriptive rather than explanatory adequacy. For example, in Anderson's work on rule ordering (1969) it is shown that certain facts in Icelandic and other languages cannot be stated unless the hitherto accepted constraints on ordering are relaxed in certain ways. On the other hand, proposals based on considerations of explanatory adequacy have been made, but these have generally taken the form of substantive rather than formal conditions on grammars, such as various constraints on abstractness of underlying representations, or on the naturalness of phonological rules (e.g., Stampe 1969).

In some respects, furthermore, the paradigm of formal explanation breaks down altogether even with respect to what appear to be purely formal generalizations. A case in point are the ordering asymmetries proposed in Kiparsky (1968a). The concepts of 'feeding' and 'bleeding' order were there defined in purely formal terms as relations between pairs of rules with respect to the derivations of the grammar. But the greater 'simplicity' of the unmarked order types cannot be reduced to brevity by means of any reasonable 'notational conventions'. Yet the evidence for these ordering relations, especially in the case of feeding order, is of the same nature and quality as that for the relative constraints which the formalism does capture. Stampe (1969) has shown that children can initially apply rules in their unmarked order contrary to what the adult grammar requires, whereas cases of children's deviation in favor of marked ordering are not on record. Given that children initially select the optimal hypothesis, this is what we would expect on the basis of the assumption of ordering asymmetry. For historical evidence, see Kiparsky (1968a) and King (1969). The point could also be established on synchronic grounds if, for example, Anderson (1969) is correct in claiming that unmarked ordering predominates in the phonological rules of languages, or in proposing that local ordering is to be constrained in terms of unmarked ordering. It is suggestive that such diverse representatives of 'traditional grammar' as Boas and Pāṇini seem to have viewed unmarked ordering (certainly the feeding subcase) as the norm from which deviations had to be indicated by special proviso.

The limitations of formal explanation are much more serious than even these facts indicate. In this paper I propose to review various types of regularities in phonology and morphology which are based on general conditions of a *functional* nature. To account for them we have to add to the theory substantive conditions which pertain not to the form of grammars (i.e., to the system of rules that generates a language) but to their output. These conditions, which are relative rather than absolute, appear to be of two general types, which we can term 'syntagmatic' and 'paradigmatic'. At the level with which we are dealing, these amount to phonological and morphological conditions, respectively.

Syntagmatic or phonological conditions put certain relative constraints on the phonotactic structure of the output. I will argue that the theory of derivational constraints and 'conspiracies' fails to provide an adequate explanatory account of these constraints on phonotactic structure, and that a notion of 'negative target' is needed for this purpose.

The paradigmatic or morphological conditions which I will propose are closely related to traditional ideas about analogy and sound change, some of which were unjustly rejected by Bloomfieldian structuralism (Bloomfield 1933). We have, on the one hand, *distinctness conditions*, which, as an initial approximation, state that there is a tendency for semantically relevant information to be retained in surface structure. Secondly, there are *leveling conditions*, which state that allomorphy in paradigms tends to get eliminated.

All these conditions are functional. Syntagmatic, phonotactic conditions can be related to the requirements of speech production. Retention of functional information in surface structure would appear to be motivated by the requirements of speech perception, and elimination of allomorphy in paradigms by language acquisition.

Let us make it clearer and more precise what is meant by a 'tendency' here, and how the existence of such tendencies is to be empirically justified.

One of the reasons why functionalism has generally failed to get off the ground is that it has been content with making vague statements to the effect that there exist certain 'tendencies'. It is necessary to give a precise interpretation to this claim before anything can be done with it. I would like to propose that a tendency for some condition A to be implemented is for a language meeting condition A to be more highly valued, other things being equal, than a language not meeting condition A.

From this interpretation it follows that functional conditions, if correct, can be justified in the same way as other aspects of linguistic theory, namely by showing that they explain facts about language acquisition, linguistic change, or linguistic universals. At the risk of repetition, I will mention some of the ways in which this in principle can be done. With reference to language acquisition, it means showing that functional conditions account for facts about child language not predicted by the present theory, i.e., that children's 'mistakes' and the grammatical systems which are revealed by these mistakes to have been acquired, have functionally characterizable properties which are not explained by the principles of projection embodied in the notational devices of standard generative grammar. The historical arguments will involve showing, for example, that functional conditions define the targets for those 'analogical changes' which cannot at present be characterized as grammatical simplifications. In that case, functional conditions will be justified by enabling a satisfactory theory of analogy to be formulated. Finally, it should be shown that there are 'linguistically significant generalizations' which cannot be expressed in an otherwise adequate formal framework, but which have a ready functional interpretation.

The beginnings of such a demonstration are found below. Only in one case will reference be made to language acquisition. The major part of the evidence comes from linguistic change and synchronic structure. I will try to show that an understanding of both sound change and analogy depends in essential ways on functional conditions. I hope to establish also that a great part of the phonological and morphological phenomena that constitute counterexamples to the claims of current phonological theory are explicable on a functional basis. Besides 'conspiracies' these include various types of ordering paradoxes that require derivational or trans-derivational constraints, and the systematically variable application of optional rules uncovered by Labov (Labov et al. 1968, Labov 1969).

## 2. *Conservation of Functional Distinctions*

In this section and in the following one I will argue that the morphology of a language is subject to overall paradigmatic conditions of a functional nature, which are reflected both in its synchronic structure and in the phonological and morphological changes it undergoes. This section deals with the realization of morphological categories in surface structure.

It has been clearly established by now that phonological processes, including even quite 'low-level' rules, and specifically also sound changes, can be subject to conditioning according to morphological categories. But such morphological conditioning seems to be limited in an interesting way by functional conditions. It characteristically originates as a blocking of rules in environments in which their free application would wipe out morphological distinctions on the surface. The same functional conditions seem to underlie certain cases of 'analogical change' which have as their target the retention of a morphological distinction. Especially notable is the fact that some specific kinds of morphological categories are, in many languages and at many points of time, consistently stabler than others, in that they both put up a stronger 'resistance' to phonological rules which eliminate their distinctive surface characteristic, and are more frequently restored by morphological change.

The strongest of the cases which will be discussed here constitute counterexamples to the present theory of generative phonology. On the synchronic level, they involve formally unnatural or even unstatable regularities, such as ordering paradoxes, 'conspiracy' phenomena, and optional rules with consistently variable frequencies of application. Diachronically, many of them originate as analogical changes which cannot be represented as simplifications. If we can show that these regularities can be stated and explained in functional rather than in formal terms, we shall have shown that functional constraints have to be included in linguistic theory.

A simple illustration of the sort of phenomenon that I will be concerned with here is found in those varieties of American English which have the rule that drops word-final -*t*, usually optionally. Where this -*t* is the past tense ending, some speakers drop it only when the present and past tense forms of the verb show a different stem vowel (Twaddell 1935: 79).[3] These speakers have *keep–kep', creep–crep', sweep–swep'* etc., but retain -*t* obligatorily in cases like *steep–steeped, heap–heaped* on the one hand, and *step–stepped* on the other.

Labov et al. (1968: 130) showed a similar distinction between *t*-deletion in these types of past tense forms in the speech of Black teenagers in New York City. Here the rule is generalized so as to apply even when no vowel change takes place. However, -*t* was deleted more frequently in the type *kept* than in the type *passed*. The percentages of deleted -*t* in cases like *kept* were 50 percent before consonants and 31 percent before vowels; the corresponding figures for *passed* were 38 percent and 14 percent.

The vowel of the stem cannot in the present theory of generative phonology serve to determine whether or not -*t* may be dropped. If -*t* is dropped before the vowel shortening rule applies, then *keep* and *steep* cannot be distinguished from each other; and if -*t* is dropped after the shortening rule applies, then *keep* and *step* cannot be distinguished. There is no single point in the derivation at which the crucial information, whether a vowel *change* has taken place, is available. There is another way to formulate the condition on the deletion of *-t*, however. The vowel change in past tense forms is due to the phonological rule which shortens vowels before two consonants, e.g., /kēp+t/→*kept*. According to a plausible analysis of Chomsky and Halle (1968), the shortening fails to apply in past tense forms like /stēp#t/ (*steeped*) because the ending is here separated from the stem by an internal word boundary, as is normal for inflectional and more productive derivational suffixes in English. In *kept*, they suggest, this internal word boundary is reduced to a simple morpheme boundary (+) by a readjustment rule. Therefore, it is possible to formulate *t*-deletion, in these dialects, as being dependent on this same distinction between the # and + boundaries. When a # boundary precedes, the rule is either completely blocked, or less frequently applied than when a + boundary precedes.

This description of the application of *t*-deletion in terms of different boundaries does not yet constitute an explanation. I contend, furthermore, that it does not even constitute the basis of the true explanation. The facts fit into a general, cross-linguistic pattern of phenomena only if we view *t*-deletion as being dependent on whether or not there is a vowel difference between the present and past forms of the verb. The rule is blocked (or, in some dialects, applied less frequently) when its application makes the past and present forms indistinguishable (*pass:passed*), but applies freely where this distinction is retained because of the vowel difference (*keep:kep'*).

Consider the rule of German which drops *e* in unstressed syllables. In nouns, the plural ending *-e* is not subject to deletion (*die Tore*), whereas the phonologically identical dative singular ending *-e* is optionally dropped (*dem Tor(e)*). In the standard language, plural *-e* does not drop even when the stem undergoes umlaut (*die Bäume*) and no homonymy between singular and plural would result. In some dialects, however, *e*-deletion is extended to plurals as well. In Mecklenburg (Nerger 1869: 173-77) *e*-deletion applies in plurals only where its operation does not result in singular-plural identity: namely, when *neither* umlaut *nor* lenition of the stem-final consonant (which in this dialect must precede *e*-deletion) is applicable to the plural form; e.g., *spēr:spēre* 'javelin(s)', but *gast:gest* 'guest(s)' (with umlaut), *brêf:brêv* 'letter(s)' (with lenition). It should be noted that this is not an absolute rule — Nerger notes exceptions in both directions — but a fairly clear general tendency. The complementarity between stem changes and *e*-deletion is important in standard German as well, though it plays no role in the plural (Vennemann 1968, Kiparsky 1973a).

The mere existence of such morphological conditioning in rules is not of course in itself enough to prove that functional factors are at work.

The first step toward the required proof is showing that substantive aspects of the morphological conditioning are constant from language to language. There could not be a functional explanation of the greater stability of plural *-e* compared to dative singular *-e* in German if it turned out that in the next language a plural ending was less stable than a phonologically identical dative ending. But on the other hand, it is difficult to see what other explanations there could be than functional ones if plural endings proved to be stabler in *every* language in which an asymmetry of this sort exists. I would like to propose, as a subhypothesis, that plural endings are in fact, other things being equal, universally stronger than case endings. This is not to say that these grammatical categories condition every rule, but rather that *if* a rule is conditioned by them, the relative strength of the conditioning categories is predictable.

If this is correct, it may be that we shall be able not only to distinguish generally between 'strong' categories, such as tense and number, and 'weak' categories, such as case, but to set up a hierarchy of categories according to their relative strength. We shall see that things are actually even more complicated, and that the strength of a category in a language may depend on other aspects of its grammar, though in a way which strongly confirms the functional interpretation here proposed. I now turn to various sorts of phonological phenomena which provide evidence for such a general hierarchy.

Labov's investigation of synchronically variable rules have yielded clear indications of morphological conditioning which, on a statistical plane, parallels the substance of that which we find in obligatory rules. For deletion of *-s* in the speech of black adolescents in New York City, Labov et al. (1968: 158ff.) found plural *s*-deletion to be much less frequent than deletion of the verb ending *-s* or genitive *-s*. The percentage of plural deletion always stayed below 30 percent, whereas that of the third singular always was over 50 percent, sometimes reaching close to 100 percent, with the genitive showing similar behavior.

Sound change gives converging evidence. Historical grammars generally state sound changes in terms of their beginning and end points. Any such macroscopic statement — e.g. 'final *-e* is dropped' — represents in several respects a considerable smoothing of the actual event it refers to. Statistics based on spellings in texts written at the time of a sound change show that changes can occur in some morphological categories before others. Further-more, they show that as the frequency with which the new rule applies grows larger with time, the *relative* frequencies for the categories tend to remain stable. And, significantly, the relative differentiation of categories is comparable to what we find in synchronic rules, whether variable or obligatory.

Consider the statistics compiled by Moore (1927) for the loss of Middle

English *-n*. The findings, for the fifteen separate texts which Moore examined, are summarized in Table 1 reproduced from Moore, where the frequencies indicate the proportion of *n*-deletion according to grammatical categories.

As Moore points out, there is a constant differentiation between the first three lines and the last two. In the former, *-n* is a case suffix, and is relatively often lost; in the latter, *-n* is a plural suffix, and is less often lost. The differentiation among the subcases of these two major groups shows no comparable systematicity. It is particularly striking that *every* text shows this same distinction, though some show it more strongly than others. (A reflex of the distinction is *-n* retained in *oxen, children.*)

A study by Lindgren (1953) on the loss of *-e* in Middle High German, carried out with similar statistical techniques, but on a much larger scale, gives similar results. Lindgren examined texts from many different dialects covering a period of several hundreds of years. The loss of *-e* turned out to be morphologically differentiated. This morphological differentiation is parallel to the Middle English case in that plural *-e* was dropped relatively rarely compared to phonologically identical instances of *-e* representing case.

All these examples involve quite low-level phonological processes. Indeed, in the case of variable rules the question arises whether the different frequencies with which the rules are applied in different cases are to be given in the grammar at all, or whether they are consequences of some general constraints on speech performance. I return to this question below. However, it is important to note that functional differentiation is not *only* found in low-level rules such as *e*-deletion. The relative strength of plurals, for example, plays an important role in purely morphological processes, and especially in so-called analogical change.

A general conclusion to be drawn from the historical morphology of many Indo-European languages is that, other things being equal, lost plural distinctions are more likely to be analogically restored than lost case distinctions. Consider the extension of the English *-s* plural (and, earlier, of *-n* plurals) and the spread of *-r*, *-en*, and *-s* and umlaut as new plural markers in German, which are scarcely paralleled by similar large-scale reinstatements of case endings, under ostensibly similar circumstances, with equally good 'proportional models' available. See Pandit (1961) for a Gujerati example; also see Jespersen (1949).

A reflection of this can be seen in a general property of Indo-European paradigms. Syncretism (i.e., homonymy) of case forms is very common between, e.g., dative and ablative, or ablative and genitive. But syncretism of number, tense, or mood is rare. There are few cases of a case form serving equally for singular and plural. Greek *-phi*, or the Finnish comitative, are exceptional examples of this.[4]

**Table 1**

| Function of -n | Grammatical Category | 1 | 2 | 3 | 4 | 5 | 6 | Texts 7 | 8 | 9 | 10 | 11 | 12 | 13 | 14 | 15 | Total |
|---|---|---|---|---|---|---|---|---|---|---|---|---|---|---|---|---|---|
| Case marker | Wk. noun, s ..... | .05 | .20 | .21 | .25 | .61 | .49 | .47 | .28 | .37 | .38 | .63 | .84 | .68 | .84 | .72 | .38 |
| | Wk. adj ....... | .36 | .26 | .14 | .14 | .50 | .51 | .28 | .48 | .50 | .53 | .67 | .63 | .83 | .86 | .50 | .50 |
| | St. adj. d. s. pl. .... | .20 | .18 | .36 | .49 | .24 | .19 | .29 | .69 | .64 | .79 | .59 | .72 | .92 | 1.00 | .88 | .43 |
| Plural marker | Wk. Noun, pl. .... | .01 | .06 | .14 | .21 | .07 | .04 | .26 | .00 | .07 | .00 | .00 | .00 | .25 | .08 | .28 | .11 |
| | St. noun, d. pl. .... | .04 | .13 | .18 | .14 | .02 | .14 | .24 | .14 | .14 | .02 | .14 | .05 | .71 | .07 | .36 | .15 |

Frequency of deletion of final *-n* in 15 Middle English texts.

The effect of such categorial polarization on morphological rules and analogical processes can be seen even more clearly in languages with complicated inflectional and derivational systems. I will cite a few cases in Sanskrit in which formally quite peculiar and unnatural conditions on rules are explicable as consequences of the functional factors here proposed.

The gerund of prefixed verbs in Sanskrit ends in *ya*, cf., *vi#bhaj+a+ti* 'hands out', *vi#bhaj+ya* 'having handed out'. When this form is derived from causative stems, the causative suffix *-ay-* in which these stems end is dropped in some verbs, e.g., *vi#bhāj+ay+a+ti* 'causes to hand out', *vi#bhāj+ya* 'having caused to hand out'. In others it is retained, e.g., *vi#kram+ay+a+ti* 'causes to step out', *vi#kram+ay+ya* 'having caused to step out'. Whether or not the causative suffix is retained is determined by the way in which the causative stem is formed from the simple stem. Most verbs lengthen the root vowel in causatives (*bhajati* → *bhājayati*), whereas others, a synchronically unpredictable class, retain it short (*kramati* → *kramayati*). Some verbs — mainly those ending in *-ā* — add *p* before the causative suffix *-ay-* (*gāyati* 'sings' → *gāpayati* 'causes to sing'). The conditions under which *-ay-* is retained are, in Whitney's formulation (1889: 385), the following: '[causative] stems showing in the root-syllable no difference from the root retain *ay* of the causative-sign in the gerund, to distinguish it from that belonging to the primary conjugation'. This rule is illustrated in the examples of simple and causative forms in table 2.

|  |  | Gerund | Causative | Caus. Ger. |
|---|---|---|---|---|
| **(1)** | | | | |
| vibhajati | 'hands out' | vibhajya | vibhājayati | vibhājya |
| avatarati | 'comes down' | avatīrya | avatārayati | avatārya |
| utpadyate | 'arises' | utpadya | utpādayati | utpādya |
| upavasati | 'fasts' | upoṣya | upavāsayati | upavāsya |
| ānayati | 'brings' | ānīya | ānāyayati | ānāyya |
| anujānāti | 'excuses' | anujñāya | anujñāpayati | anujñāpya |
| uttiṣṭhati | 'gets up' | utthāya | utthāpayati | utthāpya |
| abhijigharti | 'sprinkles' | abhighṛtya | abhighārayati | abhighārya |
| **(2)** | | | | |
| vikramati | 'steps out' | vikramya | vikramayati | vikramayya |
| avagacchati | 'understands' | avagamya | avagamayati | avagamayya |
| unnamate | 'rises' | unnamya | unnamayati | unnamayya |
| ujjvalati | 'flares up' | ujjvalya | ujjvalayati | ujjvalayya |
| **(3)** | | | | |
| prāpnoti | 'reaches' | prāpya | prāpayati | prāpayya[5] |
| (root *āp*) | | | | |

The deletion of the causative suffix *ay* in gerunds depends on the *relation* between the simple root and the causative form of the root: it takes place if they are phonologically distinct and fails if they are phonologically identical. In other words, the deletion is blocked where its application would eliminate the distinction between simple and causative forms.

Wackernagel and Debrunner (1954: 110) point out that many morphological rules in Sanskrit that introduce the common secondary derivational suffix *-a* in various meanings are restricted to words whose initial syllable does not have /ā/ as its nucleus. They ascribe this curious restriction to the fact that vṛddhi of the first syllable (essentially, insertion of long *ā*), which is the main morphological mark of this formation, would be vacuous in words of exactly this structure. For example, to denote authorship (Pāṇini 1962, 4.3.101 *tena proktam*) the suffix *-a* with vṛddhi is normally added, but names with *ā, ai, au* in the first syllable take *-īya* instead (Pāṇini 1962, 4.2.144 *vṛddhācchaḥ*). In designations of grammars and works on linguistic theory: *pātañjalam mahābhāṣyam* 'Patañjali's Big Commentary', but *pāṇinīyam vyākaraṇam* 'Pāṇini's grammar'. Likewise *candra* → *cāndra*, *jinendra* → *jainendra*, *apiśali* → *āpiśala*, but *vyāḍi* → *vyāḍīya*. Similarly in patronymic names (*bida* → *baida*, but *vāmadeva* → *vāmadevya*, with suffix *-ya*) and in metronymic names (*śikṣitā* → *śaikṣita*, but *vāsavadattā* → *vāsavadatteya*).

The distribution of *-a* is tied to potential ambiguity only in a general way. The suffix is avoided in stems with *ā, ai, au* not just when they end in *-a*, where truncation of the stem produces real homonymy between base form and derivative (and even here older Sanskrit often shows an accent difference which prevents homonymy), but also in the less frequent case when they end in *-i*, where no homonymy can arise. Furthermore, there are a few exceptional words which have *ā, ai, au* in the first syllable, end in *-a*, and still take the secondary suffix *-a* (Wackernagel and Debrunner 1954: 110 — to their examples add *kāśakṛtsna* → *kāśakṛtsna* 'written by [the linguist] *kāśakṛtsna*'). These facts make it difficult to exploit the overall regularity in the distribution of suffixes by a derivational constraint in the grammar.

The development of the aorist tense inflection in Sanskrit offers a striking illustration of the global effect which functional conditions can have on a paradigm. The active aorist endings were

|   | Singular | Dual | Plural |
|---|----------|------|--------|
| 1. | -am | -va | -ma |
| 2. | -s | -tam | -ta |
| 3. | -t | -tām | -us (-an) |

In the second and third person singular, the ending consists of a single obstruent. Since Sanskrit has a rule dropping word-final obstruents when preceded by a consonant, the 2.3.p.sg. endings were subject to loss by this rule whenever they were preceded by a consonant. This situation existed in two large groups of forms. It existed in verbs which took the suffix -*s*- after the root in the aorist. For example, the singular paradigm of *prā* 'fill' goes

1.    /a+prā+s+am/→ \*aprāsam (cf. ayāsam)
2.    /a+prā+s+s/→aprās
3.    /a+prā+s+t/→aprās

The situation also existed in verbs which did not take the aorist suffix -*s*-, if these verbs had roots ending in consonants. For example, the singular paradigm of *kr* 'do' in the *Rigveda* was:

1.    /a+kar+am/→akaram
2.    /a+kar+s/→akar
3.    /a+kar+t/→akar

When the root both ended in a consonant and took the aorist suffix -*s*-, both suffixes were deleted; e.g., the Rigvedic singular paradigm of *yaj* 'sacrifice' (with *a→ā* due to the suffix -*s*-):

1.    /a+yāj+s+am/→ayākṣam
2.    /a+yāj+s+s/→ayāj [ayāṭ]
3.    /a+yāj+s+t/→ayāj [ayāṭ]

Metrical considerations indicate that the loss of final obstruents by the rule in question took place during, or not long before, the composition of the *Rigveda*.[6] In later Vedic, and in classical Sanskrit, a series of morphological changes took place whose effect was to eliminate, in different ways, the ambiguity between the second and third persons singular introduced into the paradigms by the final obstruent deletion rule.

What appears to have been historically the first development (Narten 1964: 19) resulted in a rule deleting the *inner* (instead of the outer) obstruent(s) in a terminal cluster. This rule was almost completely[7] restricted to verb inflection, i.e., precisely to those cases in which it was functionally motivated. The new version of the obstruent deletion rule resulted in derivations such as

2p.    /a+yāj+s+s/→RV ayās (replacing ayāṭ)
3p.    /a+prā+s+t/→AV aprāt (replacing aprās)

This system did not stay long in the language either. Already in the Vedic period it too began to be replaced by what became the classical form of aorist inflection. This developed through two major innovations. The first of these was that -*ī*- became inserted after the aorist suffix when a single obstruent followed, i.e., in exactly those cases where the terminal cluster rule was potentially applicable to delete the ending. This inserted vowel broke up the cluster and caused the personal endings to be retained. The new paradigm of *yaj* was

1.  /a+yāj+s+am/→ayākṣam
2.  /a+yāj+s+s/→ayākṣīs (replacing ayāṭ, ayās)
3.  /a+yāj+s+t/→ayākṣīt (replacing ayāṭ, *ayāt)

The -*ī*- insertion rule was not applicable in the second large group of verbs in which the personal endings were originally subject to deletion by the terminal cluster rule, namely in those verbs which formed their aorists without the suffix -*s*-, but whose roots ended in consonants, e.g., *akar* 'you, he made'. What happened here was that for exactly these verbs, the aorist ceased to be formed without -*s*-. This resulted in the new paradigms:

1.  /a+kār+s+am/→akārṣam
2.  /a+kār+s+s/→akārṣīs (replacing akar)
3.  /a+kār+s+t/→akārṣīt (replacing akar)

where -*ī*- is inserted by the rule just mentioned. The *s*-less aorist was retained *only* in verbs with roots ending in a vowel, i.e., exactly where the terminal cluster simplification rule was not applicable to the personal endings, e.g., in *dā* 'give':

1.  /a+dā+am/→adām
2.  /a+dā+s/→adās
3.  /a+dā+t/→adāt

Deletion of the 2.sg. and 3.sg. endings also arose in the imperfect of the small and unproductive class of athematic verbs (which added their personal endings directly to the root) when the root ended in a consonant:

1.  /a+han+am/→ahanam
2.  /a+han+s/→ahan
3.  /a+han+t/→ahan

These imperfects are rare compared to the aorists discussed above. Changes paralleling those that took place in the aorist were not carried through consistently in the imperfect. However, there are examples showing both

inner obstruent deletion in terminal clusters (/a+śās+t/→*aśāt* 'he ordered')
and insertion of vowels breaking up the cluster. In the verb *as* 'be' the 3.sg.
imperfect is, in Vedic,

/a+as+t/→ās

and, by -*ī*- insertion,

/a+as+t/→āsīt

which becomes the standard classical form. The verb *ad* 'eat' inserts -*a*-
in precisely the 2.3.sg. imperfect forms, and conjugates without a vowel
everywhere else:

/a+ad+s/→ādas
/a+ad+t/→ādat

This complex of morphological changes is a historical 'conspiracy' whose
target is the retention of distinct person inflection in the second and third
singular of the past tense paradigms.

At this point the reader may sense a contradiction. Remember that
Labov's findings show the third singular -*s* to be a *weak* category, subject
to much more frequent deletion than plural -*s*. How does this fit in with
the above Sanskrit facts, which would seem to indicate that person is a
strong category? I think the answer lies in a distinction which has to be
drawn between languages like English, which must retain unstressed subject pronouns, and languages like Sanskrit, which can delete them. The
hypothesis which I would like to advance is that person inflection on the
verb is a strong category *only* in languages which delete unstressed subject
pronouns. What little evidence I have on the question confirms this hypothesis. In Estonian, a language in which unstressed subject pronouns can
be deleted, -*n* has been lost *except as a first person singular ending:* e.g.,
/kanta+n/ 'of the base' (Finnish *kannan*) → Est. *kanna*, but /kanta+n/ 'I
carry' (Finnish *kannan*) → Est. *kannan*. Kettunen (1962: 106) points out
that *n*-deletion was a variable rule in some early seventeenth-century texts,
where its application in part depended on phonological conditions (less
deletion before a following vowel). The present situation is the result of a
morphological polarization of this variable rule. On the other hand, languages in which unstressed subject pronouns are retained seem to show
no comparable resistance to the leveling of the person endings in the verb
paradigm (see Pandit 1961, for Gujerati).

Very tentatively, then, we can sum up the division of categories as
follows:

| Weak | Strong |
|------|--------|
| case | number |
| verb agreement (in languages | tense |
| with no pronoun deletion) | gender |
| | verb agreement (in languages |
| | with pronoun deletion) |

Evidently the weak categories are those which register information that is relatively redundant. Cases (at least grammatical cases, which our data consists of) are specified by transformations on the basis of the tree configuration at a late stage in the derivation of a sentence. Verb agreement is predictable in a similar way, and loses its redundancy only when the subject with which agreement takes place is deleted. On the other hand, number and tense are specified in the deep structure and are associated with largely fixed meanings of their own. Their status as strong categories is therefore not surprising. This is not true of gender, unfortunately. I have placed it on the strong side because of the German data, which indicate that feminine *-e* is highly resistant to loss. I am totally unable to suggest a reason for this behaviour. To that extent the functional basis of morphological conditioning of phonological processes remains unsubstantiated.

## 3. Paradigmatic Coherence

One of the stock examples of analogical change is the generalization of *r* throughout the inflectional paradigm of a class of Latin *s*-stems, e.g., *honōs → honor*. The oblique case forms of these nouns were subject to rhotacism, yielding an *s ~ r* alternation which was eliminated in the new paradigm:

| N. | honōs | honor |
|----|-------|-------|
| G. | honōris | honōris |
| A. | honōrem | honōrem |
| | . | . |
| | . | . |
| | . | . |
| | *Old Paradigm* | *New Paradigm* |

It looks like the base forms are changing here.[8] In the older system, the base forms were /hon+ōs/, /arb+ōs/, etc., and the *r* in the case forms apart from the nom.sg. were derived by the rhotacism rule

$$s \rightarrow r \:/\: V \underline{\hspace{2em}} V$$

In the newer system, the paradigm can be derived by starting from underlying /hon+ōr/. No stem change now takes place in the oblique cases. The shortening of *ō* to *o* in the nom.sg. *honor* is by a regular shortening of vowels before a certain class of consonants in word-final position.

But it is not quite so simple as that. Suppose that the change is correctly describable as a replacement of the old underlying form /honōs/ by a new underlying form /honōr/. Within the framework of the present theory, there is no reason to expect this replacement of underlying forms to take place at all. Adoption of the new base form /honōr/ in no way simplifies the grammar. The rhotacism rule, while inapplicable to /honōr/, must still be retained in the grammar, because it is needed for numerous other nouns which did not generalize the *r*, such as *genus ~ generis*, *ōs ~ ōris*, as well as for other *s ~ r* alternations, e.g., *es-t* 'is', *er-at* 'was'.

In fact, the situation is even worse for the present theory: the change actually *complicates* the grammar. A number of words which changed their nominative singular from *-ōs* to *or* continued to show *s* before derivational suffixes beginning with consonants. The most notable group of such derivatives are the adjectives in *-tus: honestus* 'honest' (from *honor*), *arbustus* 'wooded' (from *arbor* 'tree'), *angustus* 'tight' (from *angor* 'constriction'), *rōbustus* 'robust' (from *rōbur* 'oak'), *augustus* 'august' (from *augur* 'augur'). This suffix is not very productive, and there are some problems with the vowel of the stem (why *-e-* in *honestus*?). Nevertheless, it seems likely that the adjectives were felt to be synchronically related to the corresponding nouns. If that is the case, then we must draw one of two conclusions from them. The first possibility is that the underlying forms did not change after all, but retained their old form with *s*. The *-s-* in the adjectives then causes no difficulty, but to get *honor* and the other nominative singulars in *-or* we need an extra rule which changes *s* to *r* in these nouns (but not in *ōs, cinis* and many others). This might be done by extending rhotacism for certain nouns to the environment V____# or to the environment ____ + Case (which would include the nominative). In either case the grammar would become more complicated through this development. The second possibility is that the underlying form did indeed change from /honōs/ to /honōr/. Now the noun inflection is derived without a hitch, but we need some rule, otherwise unnecessary, which turns *r* to *s* before certain consonantal suffixes, so that derivatives like *honestus* will be correctly formed. This alternative also represents a complication of the grammar.

Present phonological theory therefore not only fails to characterize the change from *-ōs* to *-or* as a simplification of the grammar, but actually characterizes it as a complication. However, given the two paradigms, a practising historical linguist would correctly conclude that *honōs* is older than *honor*, even if he had no textual evidence for this fact. *Honōs* > *honor* is a possible change (given the rest of the data), but *honor > honōs* is an impossible or at least unlikely change. The reason for this asymmetry, given our assumption that analogical change results in a more highly valued grammar, must be that the grammar with *honor* is more highly valued than the grammar with *honōs*, in spite of the fact that current theory, in which simplicity is the only criterion for evaluating alternative grammars, leads us to the reverse conclusion.

The fact that analogical leveling sometimes takes place only within certain paradigms, and not in all allomorphs of a morpheme or class of morphemes, is commonplace in historical linguistics. See, for example, the discussion in Paul (1920: 206-7), where cases are given from German which are formally parallel to the Latin case just discussed. Thus, the German alternation between [x] before consonants and word boundary, and [h] before vowels (which drops intervocalically) has been retained in derivation (*sehen ~ Sicht, fliehen ~ Flucht*) but almost completely eliminated in inflection (*sieht, sah, flieht, floh*). This again represents the typical distribution of leveling in inflection versus retention in derivation.

But the consequences of this fact for phonological theory have not been seen. The notion of an inflectional paradigm plays no role in current generative phonology. Note especially that the postulation of special boundaries before inflectional endings is *not* an adequate descriptive solution to the problem which these examples raise, quite apart from its failure on the explanatory level. In the German example, inflection and derivation differ even where there are no endings (and therefore no different boundaries) involved at all: compare *schmähen* 'despise' ~ *Schmach* (derivation) with *sehen ~ sah* (inflection). Facts of this sort evidently require some sort of revision in the theory of generative phonology.

I suggest that we have here evidence for a second functional factor in phonology and morphology, which we may call *paradigm coherence*. This says that *allomorphy within a paradigm tends to be minimized*. We have seen a case in which this principle is implemented *at the cost of complicating the system of rules*. The result of the change in Latin was to generalize the *-r* form in the declension while breaking the phonological regularity in the distribution of *r* and *s*.

The effect of paradigm leveling is also produced by simplification of the structural analysis and by that type of reordering which eliminates a bleeding order (Kiparsky 1968a). What examples like the one given above indicate is that paradigm coherence is an independent factor, and not wholly reducible to formal properties of rules and relations between rules.

As a further argument in favor of the principle of paradigm coherence I should like to adduce a type of reordering which has the one-way character of the cases investigated in Kiparsky (1968a), but which escapes the generalizations there proposed. The usual conditions of maximizing feeding order and minimizing bleeding order are irrelevant here. What rather seems to determine the directionality of the reordering is paradigm coherence.

The clearest case I know involves two well-known rules in German phonology: the rule which devoices obstruents word-finally and before suffixes beginning in a consonant:

A.   $[+\text{obstr}] \rightarrow [-\text{voiced}] / \_\_\_\_ \begin{cases} +C \\ \# \end{cases}$

(e.g., Tag [tăk] ~ Tage [tăge])

and the rule which deletes [g] after a nasal (which can only be [ŋ]):

B.   $g \rightarrow \emptyset / [+\text{nasal}] \_\_\_\_$

German dialects differ in their treatment of words like *lang*. The pronunciation is [laŋk] in some dialects, and [laŋ] in others. This difference corresponds to a difference in the order of the devoicing and *g*-deletion rules, as can be seen in the following derivations:

Dialect Group I

|  | /laŋg/ | /laŋg+e/ |
|---|---|---|
| A. Devoicing | laŋg | — |
| B. g-deletion | — | laŋe |

Dialect Group II

|  | /laŋg/ | /laŋg+e/ |
|---|---|---|
| B. g-deletion | laŋ | laŋe |
| A. Devoicing | — | — |

It is fairly certain on historical grounds that dialect group I has the original ordering of rules, and that dialect group II has innovated by reordering the rules. The Middle High German spelling *lanc* indicates that the system of dialect group I prevailed at this time: see Vennemann (1970) for discussion of these rules.

The relationship between devoicing and *g*-deletion is the unusual one of *mutual bleeding*. Only one of the two rules can apply to an input representation. If *g*-deletion applies first to /laŋg/, it deprives devoicing of a chance to operate. If devoicing applies first, it in turn deprives *g*-deletion of a chance to operate. Whichever of the two rules is ordered first bleeds the other and is the only one that can apply in forms that meet the structural analysis of both rules. Under the usual ordering conditions, then, both orders, being bleeding orders, are equally marked and no directionality of reordering is provided for.

Perhaps it is possible to construct some more elaborate theory of ordering, which imposes an asymmetry of the right kind in cases of mutual bleeding, too. It would have to state that the unmarked order here is that order in which a whole paradigm is subject to the *same* rule (*g*-deletion in our example) rather than some forms being subject to one rule and others to a different rule. The surface consequence of making whole paradigms subject to the same rule or rules is of course normally going to be precisely the effect we have been talking about: minimization of allomorphy.

Nevertheless, formal conditions on ordering are not, I believe, the correct solution to the problem. The reason is that even if they could be formulated in such a way as to always specify that order which gives paradigm coherence (which they at present do not), they still would fail to relate the cases of leveling in which rule order is not involved at all. Again, a unified functional goal, namely paradigm coherence, is implemented in formally diverse ways.

Paradigm leveling is also the only explanation I can see for some of the facts that have been reported in the literature on child language. Kazazis (1969) describes a case in the Greek speech of his daughter Marina. In Greek, velars are palatalized to palatals before front vowels, yielding such paradigms as that of *exo* 'have':

Sg. 1. [éxo]
    2. [éxʻis]
    3. [éxʻi]
Pl. 1. [éxume]
    2. [éxʻete]
    3. [éxune]

During a short period in her linguistic development, Marina failed to apply the palatalization rule *in the verb paradigm*. Instead of [exʻete], she pronounced [exete] with a velar. Does this mean that she had not yet acquired the palatalization rule at this point? The answer is no: 'Marina was at that time perfectly capable of pronouncing palatal spirants, and she did so in environments where there was no obvious velar ~ palatal alternation, such as within a stem' (p. 385). The rule was suspended *only in paradigms*.

This is a clear case where the principles of projection which the present theory of generative phonology attributes to the child are making the wrong prediction. They let us expect either that the rule should be dropped (i.e., not learned) everywhere, with resulting elimination of the alternation between [xʻ] and [x] and that between the other palatalized ~ nonpalatalized consonant pairs, or else that it should be acquired and applied in its most general form. The child is rather applying the rule except where its application would produce paradigmatic alternations of velars and palatals. This is in good agreement with what we know to be the typical historical development of palatalized-nonpalatalized consonant alternations in Indo-European verb paradigms: they have been leveled out in Sanskrit, and in varying degrees in some Slavic languages. The general point that analogical change is optimalization of the grammar due to retention into adult speech of features of child language is not vitiated but rather strengthened by this example. What is wrong is simply the assumption that optimality is a function of length under the notational conventions of generative grammar. These have to be augmented, as such examples show, by an independent principle of paradigm regularity.

The elimination of distinctions associated with functionally important categories tends to be retarded in places where it results in merger (as in the dialects which allow *t*-deletion in *kept* but not in *heaped* because *t*-deletion in the latter results in ambiguity of tense – see section 2). If paradigm coherence is a target of linguistic change, we would expect conversely that the elimination of arbitrary distinctions should tend to be *accelerated* in places where it results in merger. There are some cases where this in fact happens. A good example is the elimination of the Verner's Law alternation in the Germanic languages.

The loss of free accent had turned the interchange between the reflexes of the Germanic voiced and voiceless continuants into a process governed by an arbitrary morphological categorization. The alternation was eliminated in all the Germanic languages, aside from a few residual cases. The interesting point about this process of elimination in verbs is that (at least in West Germanic) it depends on the type of ablaut to which the verb is subject. Generally the alternation is first eliminated where there is no associated vowel difference. In the past tense Old English retains it in *snāð ~ snidon* 'cut' (I class), *cēas ~ curon* 'chose' (II class), *cwæð ~ cwǣdon* 'spoke' (V), but not in *slō͡ʒ ~ slō͡ʒon* 'hit' (VI class). Similarly in Old High German (see Paul 1920: 203). Note that while rule simplification would account for the overall loss of the residue of Verner's Law, it would *not* account for the differences between the strong verb conjugations in this respect.

Recently James Harris (1973) has made a strong case for paradigmatic uniformity as a principle in the evaluation measure. The main part of his argumentation is based on historical facts. Accepting the assumption that a certain type of linguistic change results in more highly valued grammars, Harris goes on to show that several Spanish changes which we would regard as belonging to this type are not characterized as simplifications by the present theory of generative phonology. The common feature of these cases is that they establish paradigm uniformity. He concludes that 'paradigmatic relationships, or analogy if you like, play a role in the organization of grammars, both synchronically and diachronically, and therefore must be incorporated into linguistic theory.'

Two other recent articles provide more ammunition to support this position. Kisseberth (1970a) shows that in Klamath (Oregon) an *a* is inserted in the context C__CC just in case there was a vowel in this position at an earlier point in the derivation: 'A sequence $C_a C_b C_c$ takes an *a* between its first two consonants just in case that sequence derives from V* ($C_o$) $C_a V C_b C_c$. Insertion of *a* must not take place if a $C_a C_b C_c$ sequence is underlying or derived from V* ($C_o$) $C_a C_b C_c$'. Kisseberth is able to show clearly that the vowel must be deleted and missing from the representation at a certain stage in the derivation prior to the insertion rule. I return to this example later, noting here only that preservation of stem shape here leads to an ordering paradox, which leads Kisseberth to propose a derivational constraint.

The example is reminiscent of the well-known problem of zero grade in roots of the *CreC* and *CerC* type in Greek. The basic facts are as follows. In certain morphological environments, a zero-grade rule operates to delete *e* in verb roots, e.g., *léipō* 'leave' ~ aorist middle *elipómēn*. In the same environments, roots of the form *CreC* and *CerC* are reduced, not to *\*CrC*, but to *CraC* and *CarC*, e.g., *térpō* 'amuse' ~ *etarpómēn*, *trépō* 'turn' ~ *etrapómēn*. As a rule, the *a* goes on the same side of the *r* as the original *e*. The exceptions to this rule are almost all old Homeric forms, and are cases of *CerC* ~ *CraC*, such as *dérkomai* 'see' aor. *édrakon* (almost never *CreC* ~ *CarC*). This, together with the fact that in nouns, *CraC* is the rule (*pater+si → patrsi → patrasi*), suggests an older system with the following derivations:

|  | leip | derk | trep |
|---|---|---|---|
| zero grade | lip | drk | trp |
| $\emptyset \rightarrow a / Cr\_C$ | — | drak | trap |

The new system, where the type *derk* ~ *drak* disappears, and *terp* ~ *tarp* takes over, represents a formal complication of the rules in terms of the usual theory of generative phonology. We can either say that a new branch of the zero-grade rule was added, which changed *e → a* in the neighborhood of *r*, or retain a general zero-grade rule but have two branches of *a*-insertion, with verbs marked for which one they undergo. In the former case we lose the generality of the ablaut system, in the latter case the rules fail to reflect the fact that it is predictable where *a* gets inserted. Again, a paradigmatic leveling takes place at the price of a systemic complication.

Carstairs (1970) has shown paradigmatic regularities in the noun declension of ancient Greek which cannot be represented within the standard theory of generative phonology, and which again indicate the need for incorporating paradigmatic leveling into linguistic theory as a principle of the evaluation measure.

The common feature of these examples is the conflict between a paradigmatic condition and the simplicity of the phonological rules. The conflict was here resolved in favor of the paradigmatic condition. But this is clearly not always the case. In simplification of the structural analysis of a rule, and in reordering into a feeding order, the simplicity of the system of rules is often established at the expense of paradigmatic uniformity. The investigation of what determines the trading relation between the two sometimes conflicting principles is an enormously difficult task, but one which is necessary if the notion of paradigmatic conditions is to yield precise predictions about the direction of possible analogical change. It requires investigation into the structure of paradigms at a level which generative grammar at present may not be ready for.

### 4. Conspiracies and derivational constraints

There have been some attempts to account for facts of this sort within the formal paradigm of explanation. To my knowledge the earliest discussion is by Vennemann (1968), who on the basis of the complementarity of *e*-deletion and vowel change in dental stems in the German conjugation suggested that phonological rules may need to be given access to paradigmatic information. What he proposed has recently come to be termed a *derivational constraint*. The topic has been raised again independently in a series of articles on phonological problems in American Indian languages by Kisseberth (1970 a, b, c, d).

Kisseberth has argued that some of the kinds of phenomena discussed above require us to abandon certain formal constraints on phonological rules which have so far been assumed to be valid. Practically all versions of generative phonology say that the applicability of a rule to an item is determined just by whether that item has, through the ordered application of the earlier rules to the underlying form, acquired a representation which fits the structural analysis of the rule. Kisseberth proposes to relax this constraint in at least two respects.

(1) Phonological rules are to have access to the derivational history of their input, i.e., to be able to make crucial reference to earlier representations which a form has had in its derivation, for example, to the underlying representation. A case in point is Klamath, where a vowel must be reinserted in the place from which it has been deleted earlier in the derivation. Kisseberth (1970d) argues that the theory has to be changed (he leaves it open exactly how this is to be done) so as to enable the vowel insertion rule to 'look back' at an earlier stage in the derivation to determine whether the vowel is to be placed.

(2) A phonological rule can also be constrained by global phonotactic conditions of the language, which block the application of the rule in cases where its output would violate the phonotactic condition. On the basis of a reanalysis of Newman's and Kuroda's work on Yawelmani Yokuts, Kisseberth (1970a) describes that part of Yokuts phonology which has to do with consonant clustering. He shows that these rules form a 'conspiracy' to avoid clusters of three consonants (as well as #CC and CC# clusters). Some rules eliminate such clusters when they arise in morpheme combinations (there are no CCC clusters inside morphemes, this itself being part of the conspiracy), and others are prevented from applying in exactly the cases in which they would introduce CCC clusters if they did apply. For example, three-consonant clusters are broken up by an epenthesis rule:

$$\emptyset \rightarrow V / C \underline{\quad} C \begin{Bmatrix} \# \\ C \end{Bmatrix}$$

where V is *i*, in some cases *a*. An example of the latter type — avoidance of introducing three-consonant clusters — is the rule

$$\check{V} \rightarrow \emptyset / VC \underline{\quad} CV$$

which deletes short vowels between consonants *wherever a CCC cluster does not result*. Kisseberth's suggestion is that the grammar has a derivational constraint which blocks rules from creating CCC clusters. The vowel deletion rule can then be written in the somewhat simpler form

$$\check{V} \rightarrow \emptyset / C \underline{\quad} C$$

where the rest of the environment is predictable from the general derivational constraint. In this way the generality of the phonotactic constraint is reflected in the greater simplicity of some of the phonological rules in the language.

In traditional descriptive grammar, as exemplified in Whitney's *Sanskrit Grammar* (1889), or in the three volumes of Boas' *Handbook of American Indian Languages* (1911, 1922, 1938), the use of equivalent 'derivational constraints' of both types is common. For example, in his Takelma grammar Sapir (1922) distinguishes between 'organic' (= underlying) diphthongs and 'inorganic' (= derived) diphthongs. The former receive a rising accent under certain conditions, whereas the latter, like short vowels, can never receive a rising accent even when the conditions are otherwise met. For example, *bilàuk'* 'he jumped' has an inorganic *a*, as shown by *bilwà?s* 'jumper', whereas *gayaũ* 'he ate it' has an organic diphthong (and hence a rising accent) — cf. *gayawá?n* 'I ate it'. The accent rule, as stated by

Sapir, in effect 'looks back' at the underlying form of a diphthong to determine how it is accented. The 'inorganic *a*' is inserted by a rule whose formulation in Sapir's grammar (p. 28) illustrates his use of the second type of derivational constraint, where rules 'look forward' at their output. Sapir says that consonant combinations 'which are either quite impossible in Takelma phonetics, or at any rate are limited in their occurrence to certain grammatical forms' are 'limbered up' by the introduction of an 'inorganic' *a*. Elsewhere (pp. 36-41) he then lists the possible consonant clusters of Takelma. In order to apply the *a*-insertion rule correctly, we must refer to the list, and insert *a* into any clusters in the input form which are not contained in the list.

There is an important difference, however, between this type of example and those on which Kisseberth has based his arguments. Sapir's rules can be restated, without loss of generality, in the standard theory of generative phonology, or in any framework where phonetic forms are derived from underlying forms by a set of ordered rules, which cannot refer back to earlier stages of the derivation, or to global conditions on the output. The need for making reference to earlier stages in the derivation here, as often, disappears as soon as the rules are placed in the right order. Had Sapir in his earlier work operated with ordered rules (as in Sapir 1930), he would have been able to simply state the rules in the following order:

1.    Place rising pitch on long vowels and diphthongs.
2.    Insert inorganic *a*.

Given this order of application, we derive

|   |   | /bilwk'/ | /gayau/ |
|---|---|---|---|
| 1. | rising pitch | —— | gayaū |
| 2. | inorganic *a* | bilauk' | —— |

with the correct accentuation. And on the other hand, Sapir's statement of *a*-insertion in terms of blocking impossible clusters has an element of circularity. Since impossible clusters appear to be just those into which *a* is inserted, the statement that *a* is inserted to break up impossible clusters has no explanatory value. The cases which Kisseberth has brought out are not so simple. In them, the current theory of generative phonology fails to bring out important regularities. It is to enable these regularities to be expressed that Kisseberth has proposed the introduction of new formal devices into the theory.

Do derivational constraints represent an adequate solution to the problems raised by these examples, and do they extend to the other types of phenomena mentioned in sections 1-3 above? In proceeding to seek an answer to these questions, let us keep in mind that the function of the notational conventions, insofar as they place relative rather than absolute constraints on grammars, is strictly explanatory. Their role in the paradigm of formal explanation is to enable 'linguistically significant generalizations' to be expressed, and, just as importantly, to prevent 'spurious generalizations' from being expressed.

A review of the conspiracies which have been described yields the interesting result that their target configurations are chosen from a rather small set. The targets are generally negative. Phonotactic conspiracies function to avoid certain complex syllable types or complex prosodic configurations. Conspiracies against consonant clusters seem to be common: see Kisseberth (1970a — Yokuts), Kisseberth (1970c — Tonkawa), Kiparsky (1973a — Finnish, Sanskrit). Another type is the conspiracy against vowel sequences, a case of which has been noticed by Ross (1973) in English. A strong form of both operates in Japanese to give a *CVCV* syllable structure (Nishihara 1970). Miller (1970) has analyzed the diverse processes whereby $\bar{V}CC$ sequences are eliminated in Middle Indic (to either $\bar{V}C$ or $\breve{V}CC$). In prosody, a common type is the elimination of adjacent stresses in favor of an alternating stress pattern, as in Tunica (Kisseberth 1970b), and even in English and German (see above). A partial conspiracy involving liquid dissimilation has been pointed out in English by Ross (personal communication). It is manifested in the following ways: (1) In the morpheme structure constraint that allows morphemes like *flicker*, *trickle*, but prohibits **fricker*, **flickle* (in view of *brother*, etc., this constraint may be restricted to 'descriptive verbs', as proposed by Bloomfield). (2) in the dissimilation rule that turns the adjective-forming suffix *-al* (as in *autumnal*) into *-ar* after stems with *l* (e.g. *cellular*, *circular*). (3) In a constraint on the derivational morphology that prevents the nominalizing suffix *-al* from being added to verbs containing *l* (e.g., *betrayal*, *rehearsal*, *acquittal*, *dismissal*, *burial*, but never **applial*, **displayal*, **allowal*, **dispellal*, **recoilal*, **collectal*, etc.). Liquid dissimilation seems to be a fairly common rule, although I do not know another case in which it figures as the target of a conspiracy.

The very interesting cases in Korean discussed by Kim (1972) do not really represent a conspiracy in the same sense, but rather a deeper phonetic parallelism between apparently diverse phonological processes in the language, which phonetic theory as yet cannot satisfactorily express. I will also set aside cases in which some phonological rule mirrors a morpheme structure condition in its content. The most common type of case here is that of a sound change which both remains as a productive rule in the phonology and causes a corresponding change in the morpheme structure conditions. What synchronically is overlap between a phonological rule and a morpheme structure condition is historically a single phonological process which is reflected, through restructuring, in several places in the grammar. The existence of such cases is simply a consequence of how languages change, and does not pose a problem for linguistic theory. More interesting is the possibility that the phonological structure of the lexicon might itself delimit the sound changes a language undergoes. For some discussion of the relation between morpheme structure conditions and phonological rules, see Kiparsky (1973a).

Apart from these special cases, to which the term 'conspiracy' is not applicable in the same sense as to the others, and for which a different explanation must be given, it seems to be true that phonological conspiracies always function to avert configurations which must be characterized as complex or highly marked, in terms of universal grammar. We have already noted two points in support of this conclusion: (1) Only a restricted set of conspiracy targets is encountered; and (2) If some language has a conspiracy avoiding strings of the form A, then rules eliminating A will be frequent also in other languages, even outside of any conspiracies. In general, relative linguistic complexity can be established in the ways discussed in section 1, by utilizing the evidence of child language, linguistic change, and linguistic universals. For example, if it is universally true that a language that has CCC clusters necessarily also has CC clusters, but not vice versa, or that children learn CC clusters before they learn CCC clusters, then we can say that CCC clusters are linguistically more complex than CC clusters. In this way the hierarchical complexity relations established in a theory of natural phonology may provide an essential basis for an explanation of the phenomenon of conspiracies.

The second major type of target of conspiracies appears to be the sorts of paradigm conditions we already encountered in sections 2 and 3. This is true at least for category distinctness. An example is the conspiracy relating to the past tense verb endings in Sanskrit (section 2). One of the other examples discussed there − the overall incompatibility of *-a* with vacuous stem vr̥ddhi in secondary derivation − we now see to be, in effect, a conspiracy, since the incompatability is a global characteristic not reflected in any single rule. Another English example is the systematic stress relation between English nouns and verbs, which is not the result of any one stress rule, but of features of several rules which conspire to make any stress difference show up as a stress farther to the left on the noun than in the verb (Ross 1973). As in the Sanskrit case, the effect is to decrease cases of derivation which are phonetically null.

It will not be essential for the remainder of my argument that the targets I have proposed should prove to be correct in detail. The essential point is that the configurations that phonological conspiracies conspire against are limited by substantive constraints to configurations of the sort we would on general grounds hold to be linguistically complex, and that

the few morphological conspiracies which have been so far proposed seem
to implement general paradigmatic conditions of the sort which on other
linguistic grounds must be incorporated into linguistic theory.

Can this be reflected in a theory of derivational constraints? The
*explanatory* role of the formalism of derivational constraints in phonology
is to simplify the formulation of particular rules by eliminating from them
whatever elements are predictable by an overall constraint. In line with the
paradigm of formal explanation, this converts 'linguistically significant
generalizations' into simplifications of the grammar. However, a formal
notation cannot claim to provide an explanation until it not only is rich
enough to express the generalizations, but its expressive power is also
limited in such a way that the notation cannot be used to express generalizations that could not hold in real languages. In what follows I want to
show that derivational constraints of the sort that have been proposed, or
could be reasonably devised, have some intrinsic inadequacies in both
respects. I will first consider the ways in which derivational constraints are
an excessively strong device.

How can we limit the formalism to allow conspiracies against three-
consonant clusters, but not, for example, conspiracies against *CVCV*
... syllable structure, or against words beginning with single consonants,
or against medial clusters of the form 'sonorant + obstruent stop' (e.g.,
*rt, mp, nt*)? Evidently the difference between the kinds of conspiracies
that occur and the kinds of conspiracies that do not occur is not of form
but one of content. There is no way to place purely formal restrictions on
derivational constraints so as to limit its expressive power to those conspiracies which are 'natural.' Accordingly, it becomes necessary to impose
limitations of substance, rather than of form, on this type of derivational
constraint. We may have to say that conspiracies can only function to
reduce, not to increase the linguistic complexity of the output. This may
ultimately prove to be somewhat too strong. It is evident, however, that
*some* such naturalness constraints must be placed on the formalism.

In itself, the need for these substantive constraints still does not invali-
date the concept of derivational constraints in any way. There is no
reason why the use of a formal notation in grammars should not be
subject to substantive constraints. On the contrary, this is exactly what we
would expect. For example, it is clear that variables over feature specifications are necessary for assimilatory phenomena such as that expressed
by the common rule

$$[+\text{obstr}] \rightarrow [\alpha\text{voiced}] \: / \underline{\qquad} \begin{bmatrix} +\text{obstr} \\ \alpha\text{voiced} \end{bmatrix}$$

but that the use of variables has to be limited by substantive constraints, to
prevent the statement of absurd rules such as

$$[\text{+voiced}] \rightarrow [\alpha\text{obstr}] \ / \ \underline{\hspace{1.5em}} \ \begin{bmatrix} \text{+back} \\ \alpha\text{nasal} \end{bmatrix}$$

In the case of 'conspiracies', however, the question arises whether the facts which the formalism is supposed to explain cannot be in their entirety explained by the substantive constraints, which must in any case be part of any theory of phonology. The alternative approach which I have in mind is quite simply this: three-consonant clusters, adjacent stresses, and so on, are linguistically complex configurations, and rules eliminating or avoiding them are accordingly highly natural and occur frequently in the languages of the world. It is therefore only to be expected that there should be some languages in which several rules should eliminate or avoid these configurations, and that there should be languages in which no instances of these configurations appear on the surface. This is no more surprising than it is, in view of the fact that extraposition of sentences and heavy noun phrases is a common kind of transformational rule in languages of the world, that some languages (English may be one) have several such rules of extraposition, and that some languages have no surface structures with sentences flanked by constituents of a higher sentence.

What I am questioning, then, is whether there is any fundamental sort of difference between the cases in which just one or two rules reflect general phonological conditions of this type, and the cases in which several rules are involved, which would be termed a 'conspiracy'. I have so far challenged the explanatory value of introducing derivational constraints to incorporate conspiracies into the derivations in the phonological component, and advocated doing away with derivational constraints for this purpose by an Occam's Razor type of argument. Concrete empirical differences are clearly also involved: for example, is there any evidence for a true 'functional unity' of the rules in a conspiracy which would not simply be characterizable by their sharing a common target? Are there cases in which they are subject to parallel historical changes at some point in the development of a language? Are there cases in which apparently diverse changes in the rules of a language at some point of time can be shown to be consequences of the imposition of a single derivational constraint? Are there cases where the rules in a conspiracy have the same set of lexical exceptions? This would be strong evidence in favor of derivational constraints. However, I have not found any such cases.

From another direction, the proposal to solve the problem of conspiracies by means of derivational constraints is weakened by some formal difficulties.

Derivational constraints simplify only rules that *fail* to apply wherever their output would violate the phonotactic constraint. For instance, some of the environment of the vowel deletion rule in the Yawelmani Yokuts example (see above) can be eliminated. How is one to express as a simplification of the grammar the conspiratorial status of rules that actively eliminate strings which violate the phonotactic constraint? For example, no part of the vowel epenthesis rule which breaks up three-consonant clusters in Yawelmani Yokuts is redundant even given the general derivational constraint. But rules of the latter type are surely just as frequent participants in conspiracies as rules of the former type, which derivational constraints can at least begin to accommodate in a direct way. Kisseberth (1970b) has proposed a principle to meet this difficulty: 'A derivational constraint does not add to the complexity of grammar as a whole if the sequence which it prevents rules from creating is *identical* to the sequence to which some phonological rule applies'. For example, the derivational constraint which says that no rule can introduce CCC clusters is free in Yawelmani Yokuts because there exists the epenthesis rule which destroys CCC clusters. To account for the observation that morpheme structure conditions often conform to a conspiracy, Kisseberth (1970c) likewise suggests that 'constraints on sequences of segments in morphemes automatically constitute derivational constraints'. Suppose we take this to mean that derivational constraints that reflect morpheme structure constraints are also 'free'. Then the question still remains what happens in case a language has both a morpheme structure constraint which conforms to a conspiracy, and a rule which eliminates sequences which the conspiracy excludes? How would it be formally characterized as more highly valued than a language in which only one of these belonged to the conspiracy? And what about a case like Yawelmani Yokuts, where there is not only such a morpheme structure condition, but *several* rules which eliminate the CCC clusters which the conspiracy excludes, viz., consonant deletion rules in addition to the vowel epenthesis rule mentioned above. The approach of building conspiracies into the derivational process would have to find some way of formally reflecting as a grammatical simplification the fact that each of these rules belongs to the conspiracy.

Similar formal problems arise because of the fact that not only phonological rules, but also morphological rules can participate in a conspiracy, as in Ross' case of liquid dissimilation in English, where a constraint on derivational morphology interacts with a phonological rule and a morphological constraint. We might perhaps say, again, that a morphological rule is highly valued or 'free' if its output meets the condition of the conspiracy.

Worse yet, we have seen cases where a rule participates in a conspiracy not directly, but by feeding or bleeding appropriately another rule. For example, the insertion of -*ī*- between the aorist -*s*- and the 2.3.sg. personal endings -*s*, -*t* in Sanskrit contributes to the retention of the person endings only indirectly, by blocking the application of the terminal cluster simplification rules. We would therefore have to say something like this: a rule is highly valued (or 'free') if its application creates representations to which other rules are applicable in such a way as to implement the conspiracy.

Note also that to incorporate morphological (paradigmatic) conspiracies in the derivations of a grammar, derivational constraints are not always sufficient. And some still more powerful device — viz., 'transderivational' constraints — would be needed. The target of category distinctness is not a property of the output of the derivation, but a property of the relation between this output and other surface forms. A formal account would have to say that the application of rules can depend on whether or not the ultimate result of applying them, taking into account the effect of subsequent rules, bears a given relation to certain other surface forms. It would also have to provide a mechanism for formally simplifying a rule subject to such a constraint relative to one not subject to it. For example, in Sanskrit the limitation of the s-less aorist to roots ending in vowels should on this approach not have to be stated in the grammar, but would follow from a general derivational constraint. Likewise, the s-insertion rule would have to be stated as context-free. A formalism strong enough to accomplish this (none has ever been proposed) will not be easy to stop from running amok.

All this brings us to a conclusion which lies at the heart of the second major objection to derivational constraints as a solution to the problem of conspiracies in phonology: the formal devices by which a constraint on the output can be effected are highly heterogeneous. Therefore, factoring out those parts of the structural analyses of rules which are in the conspiracy is technically feasible only in a small part of the relevant rules. Adding a list of auxiliary principles to the evaluation measure to take care of the kinds of rules which escape this formal simplification misses the general point that *any* rule or condition in the grammar is a potential participant in a conspiracy. What is significant and narrowly constrained about conspiracies, in short, is their content and not the means by which they are brought about.

Nevertheless, this does not exclude the possibility that some form of derivational or even transderivational constraints may after all be needed in grammar. I am rather criticizing their adequacy as explanatory theories. It may well be the case that derivational constraints have to be introduced into the theory for descriptive adequacy. Facts such as King's (1970) observations on the elision of the copula in English, or the sort of ordering paradoxes illustrated in Kenstowicz and Kisseberth (1970) may well motivate some form of derivational constraints on purely descriptive grounds. It remains to be seen whether King's facts can be dealt with in a more interesting way as our understanding of the interaction of syntax with stress assignment and related phenomena grows (cf. Bresnan 1971), and it also remains to be seen how many ordering paradoxes have, like the Klamath case, a functional underpinning which explains them on principles independent of the formalism.

## 5. The Role of Functional Conditions in Linguistic Theory

We have looked at some types of phonological phenomena which have recently been adduced as counterexamples to the formalism of generative phonology: variable rules, conspiracies, and certain ordering paradoxes. Our conclusion was that most instances of these phenomena have a functional basis. We have distinguished three sorts of general conditions to which they can be reduced: distinctness of categories, paradigm coherence, and optimalization of phonotactic structure. From a formal point of view, these targets are reached in several ways:

(1) Conditions are placed on the structural analysis or on the ordering of a rule, which block the rule in just those cases in which its application would go counter to the target (e.g. English *t*-deletion), or triggering it in just those cases in which its application would secure its realization (e.g. Sanskrit *ī*-insertion).

(2) Other phonological or morphological rules are introduced in a 'conspiracy' to implement the target.

(3) The actual frequencies with which optional rules are applied are such as to favor surface structures conforming to the targets.

The targets are evidently rooted in the requirements placed on language by speech 'performance'. More specifically, it seems plausible to assume that category distinctness derives from perceptual requirements, and optimalizes language for the hearer by providing more clues to meaning in surface structure. Phonotactic conditions presumably optimalize language for the speaker by keeping down the need for executing complex articulatory movements. The status of paradigm coherence is less clear. Presumably it can be related to language acquisition, though the other aspects of speech performance may also play a role.

These performance-based targets are put into effect by mechanisms which are, in general, unquestionably part of grammar, i.e. linguistic competence. We could not exclude them from grammar in the way that certain functionally motivated but formally unstatable constraints in syntax, such as restrictions on self-embedding, or on scrambling up to ambiguity, can be taken out of grammar and accounted for within a theory of performance. This is so because the phonological rules in question are, for example, ordered with respect to other rules, can have lexical exceptions, and are subject to change in time. Though grounded in performance, they are not themselves performance conditions, but are language-specific and must therefore be learned as part of the grammar of the language.

There is, however, one case in which it is not so clear what to make of the facts. This is the case of optional rules applying with systematically variable frequencies depending on phonotactic and paradigmatic conditions. For example, one might ask whether the relative frequencies indicated in table 3 (after Labov et al. 1968: 130) were specified by the grammar of those whose speech they characterize.

Table 3

|  | | ___##C | ___##V |
|---|---|---|---|
| C | ___ (fist) | 90 | 50 |
| C+ | ___ (kept) | 50 | 31 |
| C# | ___ (passed) | 38 | 14 |
| V | ___ (red) | 22 | 04 |
| V+ | ___ (said) | 29 | 12 |
| V# | ___ (stayed) | 22 | 04 |

Per cent of *t*-deletion in certain environments.

Note carefully what the issue is here. In asking whether variable rule application falls outside of grammar I am *not* asking whether it should be shoved under some rug where linguists put things that do not interest them. On the contrary, it would be a gain for linguistics if the variable frequencies, or some aspect of them, could be predicted by a theory of speech performance, for then we would have been able to substitute a general explanation for a description of language-particular facts. My question is rather whether the variable frequencies are part of the statement of the grammatical rules, or whether they might be predictable, wholly or in part, by universal conditions. That is, the question is whether the child has to *learn* to drop -*t* according to such a table, or whether he does so for reasons which have nothing to do with the specifics of English phonology. Labov (1969) has claimed that these frequencies are part of linguistic competence, and has developed a formalism for expressing them in grammatical rules. The alternative hypothesis would be that they are the result of general functional conditions impinging on speech performance. In this example, the conditions would relate to phonotactics and distinctness. Both preceding and following consonants increase the frequency of deletion (avoidance of consonant clusters). On the other hand, deletion is less frequent where it would make the past and present tenses identical.

This possibility is at the moment remote, however. We are far from being able to propose functional explanations for all of the frequency relations that have been found in optional rules. Even in the above table, it remains unclear why there is more deletion in C___ than in C+___ but less deletion in V___ than in V+___. And this is not a unique query.

The sort of evidence from which we would conclude that variable frequencies of rule application are not specified in the grammar would be that the frequency relations vary systematically with the speech situation according to the change in functional factors involved. For example, the relative importance of the distinctness factor should rise with increasing difficulty of communication, as on a telephone, and rapid speech should lead to a greater importance of phonotactic factors. Some facts pointing in this direction are mentioned by Labov et al. (1968: 137).

Functional conditions, then, enter the linguistic system in a grammaticalized form. At that point they begin to interact and conflict not only with each other, but with formal generality in the usual generative phonological sense. We have seen examples of this interaction and conflict above. At present I do not see how to predict which condition wins in a conflict of this kind. Note that this still does not reduce the theory to anywhere near vacuity. A unique claim is still being made in cases where only one condition is applicable.

The great difficulty with functional explanations in linguistics (and partly in other fields as well) has always been finding the general theories without which functional explanations of specific phenomena can have no empirical substance. It is easy to point at a specific historical event or synchronic fact and suggest an *ad hoc* 'reason' for it. But however plausible such explanations may seem, they carry no force until backed up by general claims, which go beyond the case at hand, and which for that reason can be put to a test.

This difficulty was not always recognized explicitly by traditional proponents of functional explanations. Hence Bloomfield's scathing attacks on Horn and Havers were in a way perfectly justified:

> A teleologic 'explanation' can be given without difficulty for any and every happening. If we create a vacuum over one end of a U-shaped tube containing water (the principle of the pump), the water will rise at this end: Nature abhors a vacuum. But the water rises only to a height of 33 feet above the level of the water outside: well, Nature's horror of a vacuum goes only so far and, after that, is offset by the weight of the water. Teleology cuts off investigation by providing a ready-made answer to any question we may ask.
> (Bloomfield 1934: 35)

Proposing an empirically testable version of functionalism involves giving a general, cross-linguistic characterization of what the functional factors are, and how they impinge on linguistic structure. I have tried to begin this here. I have suggested a way in which the concept of a 'tendency', which lends functionalist discussions their characteristic unsatisfactory fuzziness, can be made more precise in terms of hierarchies of optimality, which predict specific consequences for linguistic change, language acquisition, and universal grammar. Enormous areas of vagueness obviously remain. But there is enough to show that the project is a worthwhile one.

## *Notes*

1.    In syntax, the problems have been raised by Bever (1970) and Bever and Langendoen (1971).
2.    The subscript notation is normally used on single segments only. However, there is no reason to restrict it so. If subscripts are not used, we have to use the star notation, and, since application for the star is defined as conjunctive, an extra rule is then needed to wipe out all except the rightmost or leftmost of the stresses which are assigned by the main rule. But this would not affect the point of the example, since the generalization from one word type to the other is still correctly made by the formalism.
3.    Twaddell mentions a functionalist explanation of this rule, but rejects it as 'psychologistic' and 'mentalistic'.
4.    See Bolling's postscript to Moore (1927).
5.    However, Pāṇini (1962, 6.4.57) allows optionally also *prāpya.*
6.    See Wackernagel (1896: 304-5).
7.    The only exceptions may be a couple of nouns like *puroḍās* 'sacrificial cake', from *puroḍāś+s.*
8.    This is what I proposed in my dissertation (Kiparsky 1965). James Harris several years ago called my attention to the difficulties which words like *honestus* pose for this solution.

*Chapter 6*

# How abstract is Phonology?*

## 1. Abstract and concrete morphophonemics

What is the form of morphophonemic representations? How far removed are they from the phonetic or phonemic surface? The whole gamut of possible answers to this question has been given in modern linguistics. Taking the abstractness of the proposed morphophonemic level as our criterion, we can at first distinguish broadly between three positions:

(1)    At the concrete end, we find the view that the morphophonemic representation should provide a direct record of all the actual forms in which the morpheme appears. The underlying form of a morpheme is nothing but a set of its allomorphs, or some representation from which that set can be immediately constructed. Examples are the item-and-arrangement model developed by American linguists in the forties, and the approach initially taken by the pioneers of the Prague school.

* This paper was written in 1968 and mimeographed copies of it have been sold by the Indiana University Linguistics Club. It is reproduced here more or less in its original form, except that I have added some new footnotes, which are distinguished from the old ones by asterisks at their heads. Some minor, largely stylistic changes have been made in the text, and the only major substantive change in the content is the omission of the argument at the end of § 4, which cannot be maintained now that Brame (1972b) has found a better analysis than the one on which my argument was based. I have not tried to bring it up to date, or to incorporate into it any discussion of the recent literature on the subject. Some of this will be found in sections 2 and 3 of Kiparsky (1973a). The reader is particularly asked to keep in mind that many of the authors cited here may have changed their minds on the subject since the paper was written.

    I would like to thank Ted Lightner, Bruce Rigsby, Bohdan Saciuk, Michael Silverstein, William S.-Y. Wang, and Arnold Zwicky, in addition to the people mentioned in note 1, for their helpful comments. I have not always been able to follow their suggestions, and needless to say, they must not be assumed to agree, or ever to have agreed, with any of the things I say here. I am grateful to the organizers and participants of the 1970 Tokyo Seminar in Linguistic Theory, where a version of this paper was read. Especially I would like to acknowledge the very great debt I owe to Osamu Fujimura.

    1.    This work was supported in part by the National Institutes of Health (Grant MH-13390-02). Wayles Browne, Morris Halle, George Lakoff, John Ritter, and John Ross have read an earlier draft of this paper, and it has benefited from their comments and criticisms.

(2)   The diametrically opposed view that morphophonemic representations have a purely classificatory function has been defended by Lamb (1966), Fudge (1967), and, apparently, Householder (1965). Morphophonemes here are 'completely abstract' elements; they have 'absolutely no properties which are even remotely phonic' (Fudge). They are represented by 'completely neutral labels' (Fudge) which should be 'constructed ad hoc for each language' (Householder); according to Lamb these 'labels are chosen for mnemonic convenience and are not part of the structure'. As Fudge puts it, 'phonologists ought to burn their phonetic boats and turn to a genuinely abstract framework'. The writings of Hjelmslev may be interpreted as setting forth a similar position.

(3)   The third alternative, taken by linguists such as Sapir, Jakobson (1948), and Chomsky and Halle (1968), in a sense combines the ideas underlying fully concrete morphophonemics and fully abstract morphophonemics. Adopting a term used by Lamb, we can call this general approach process morphophonemics. There are important differences between the various theories in this general class with respect to the role of distinctive features, types of ordering used, and abstractness of underlying representations. At present I am concerned with what is common to process theories: they regard morphophonemic representations as *abstract entities* (as do the theories of Fudge and Lamb) but ascribe to them an *intrinsic interpretation on the phonetic level* (as does item-and-arrangement theory or Trubetzkoy's 'morphonologie'). This conception of morphophonemics incorporates the main virtues of both of the others without the main faults of either. Like fully abstract morphophonemics, it recognizes that there is an underlying phonological pattern which is not necessarily identical to the phonetic pattern (e.g., superficial [η] may function like /ng/), which fully concrete morphophonemics is forced to deny. On the other hand, it recognizes that this pattern, while abstract, is not arbitrary, but in general related to the phonetic level ([η] is hardly likely to function as /ö/ or /p/ or /l/), a relationship which fully abstract morphophonemics throws overboard. Process morphophonemics is the only form of theory which tries to do justice to the fact that abstract morphophonemic patterning is to a large extent (but not wholly) determined by concrete phonetic form. What Postal (1968) has termed the Naturalness Condition is precisely this common characteristic of process morphophonemics.

It is worth reflecting on the fact that the morphophonemic theories which have been proposed and seriously defended in structural linguistics are actually all those which are *logically* conceivable, and not just those for which *linguistic* motivation has been discovered. Given that there are sounds (or phonemes) and that there are morphemes, there really are no other, greatly different, ways in which one could imagine them related than the three kinds of theories into which current opinion exhaustively seems to divide.

No wonder, then, that the defense of abstract morphophonemics and the objections to process morphophonemics offered, e.g., by Lamb (1966) are characteristically not linguistic but a priori, quasi-logical, and methodological. One such objection to process morphophonemics is that it involves an illegitimate intrusion from another field. Linguists, so the objection goes, have unwittingly slipped into looking for phonological properties in underlying forms on the analogy of the historical linguist's derivation of the phonetic forms of one chronological stage from the phonetic forms of another. Thus Lamb (1966: 551) asserts that the process formulation 'crept into morphophonemic description from diachronic linguistics'. One can hardly decide which is the more ludicrous idea – that Sapir, Jakobson, Halle, and Chomsky are unable to distinguish synchrony and diachrony, or that Pāṇini (300 B.C.) was tricked into process morphophonemics by some unknown ancient Indian historical or comparative linguist, a forgotten Brahman Brugmann.

Another objection is that process morphophonemics is somehow logically inconsistent and springs from a confusion of linguistic levels. It seems that underlying this objection is the not very clearly formulated idea that a linguistic level is necessarily a set of representations in some distinct alphabet of symbols. What apparently raises uneasiness is the fact that in generative phonology and in other process theories, morphophonemic forms are represented in a phonetic alphabet, which has led to the idea that the morphophonemic level is thereby not kept distinct from the phonetic level. The fallacy here lies in assuming that a level must be defined by the symbols which appear in its representations. There is no inconsistency or contradiction in representing morphophonemes by phonetic categories if the levels are formally defined by the structure of the grammar, rather than by a set of symbols. In a generative grammar, the morphophonemic representation is defined as the input to the phonological component, and the phonetic level is defined as the output of the phonological component. There is absolutely no confusion between the two.

A kindred uneasiness apparently prompts some linguists to reject ordered rules in phonology in favor of unordered realization rules. In a derivation by ordered rules there appear between the underlying and the phonetic level numerous intermediate representations, one after the application of every rule, which have no status as linguistic levels. One advocate of abstract morphophonemics has termed them 'pseudo-levels' (Fudge 1967: 6), and finds them objectionable, though without saying why.

The only even remotely linguistic argument put forward for fully abstract morphophonemics is that this makes it possible to 'maintain neutrality as between the auditory and the articulatory [elements]' (Fudge 1967: 3). But this is simply a red herring. First of all, every phonetic feature in Jakobson's and Halle's feature systems has both articulatory and acoustic correlates. Moreover, Chomsky and Halle (1968: 293-294) regard phonetic representations as representations of a speaker's or hearer's percepts, rather than as physical records of acoustic signals or articulatory motions. 'Neutrality' is therefore maintained. But in any case, the whole issue has to do with the nature of phonetics, and is quite independent of one or another approach to morphophonemics. In fact, Fudge's own treatment of it by means of rules relating vocal tract configurations to acoustic properties (1967: 13) does not depend on his acceptance of fully abstract morphophonemics at all.

Fudge mentions another argument for fully abstract morphophonemics. According to him, phonological features 'must be completely abstract . . . to facilitate the link-up with the abstract morphological elements' (1967: 3). He gives no examples of how this facilitation is supposed to be achieved, and does not reveal to the reader any details of his reasoning.

The disastrous consequences of fully abstract morphophonemics have been discussed in detail by Postal (1968). To the many failures of fully abstract morphophonemics which Postal notes there, we can add the fact that if morphophonemes are arbitrary, diacritic symbols, then no general, universal statements about the structure of underlying forms are possible. For example, vocalic morphophonemes universally have a typical distribution as syllabic nuclei which is different from the distribution of consonantal morphophonemes. In fully abstract morphophonemics there are no vocalic or consonantal morphophonemes, but only arbitrary diacritic symbols, chosen ad hoc for each language, which are in no way part of the structure. This makes the universal elements of morpheme structure undiscoverable and unformulable. The view that morphophonemes are fully abstract denies the fact that morphophonemic representations are subject to much the same universal constraints as phonetic representations. For example, segments which are unpronounceable presumably never need to be set up in underlying representations either.

The other extreme, fully concrete morphophonemics, is much less of an issue today, but still merits a comment. In general, any theory of morphophonemics which uses disjunctive underlying representations is motivated by the desire to make morphophonemic representations maximally concrete. Two rather different varieties of such theories exist, depending on whether they regard morphemes as composed of morphophonemes or not. Trubetzkoy's 'morpho(pho)nologie' illustrates the variety which does. Trubetzkoy's morphophonemes are disjunctive sets of phonemes, which he termed 'idées complexes'. The underlying form which he would assign to *president*, alternating with *presidential, presidency*, would have a final morphophoneme [*t, š, s*], and the actual forms would be derived by rules which resolved the disjunction by selecting an alternant in each environment. Trubetzkoy's device is really quite similar to the item-and-arrangement model developed independently in America in the forties. The disjunction in item-and-arrangement morphophonemics is simply represented at the level of allomorphs, so that the underlying form of *president* would be /prezident/ ~ /prezidenš/ ~ /prezidens/.

The criticisms which can be made against this type of morphophonemics have often been made, and I will only very briefly recapitulate them. Essentially, both varieties generalize to all morphophonemic alternations procedures which are at best suited to handle a particular type of exceptional case. Trubetzkoy's generally quite redundant procedure, in which the information about the alternation is given once in the underlying representation and once more in the rule of selection, can be employed to indicate exceptions to regular processes. If a certain morpheme does not undergo an alternation which it should undergo, its underlying form can easily be made to exclude this alternation. But this approach to morphophonemics unfortunately makes such an exception of everything to which it is applied. It takes the irregular cases as the norm, and ignores the fact that in the normal case we do not have to mark separately morphophonemes for the alternations they can undergo. It is totally unnecessary to specify for each German morpheme ending in *b, d, g* that it has a word-final alternant ending in *p, t, k*. This devoicing is a general fact about all final voiced stops and it is pointless to repeat it separately for every particular final stop, as Trubetzkoy's notation forces one to do. Similarly, while we might perhaps grant that even item-and-arrangement morphophonemics provides a reasonable way of handling one type of exception, in this case suppletion as in *go:went*, it at the same time reduces every instance of alternation to this same special type.

Trubetzkoy's morphophonemics also leads to paradoxical consequences in cases of metathesis, epenthesis and other rules which affect the segmental composition of representations to which they apply. Implicit in his theory is the false claim that there must be a one-to-one pairing of morphophonemic and phonemic segments preserved in every case.

What will hopefully speed up the resolution of the debate on the nature of morphophonemics is that it does not have to be confined to such abstract arguments. Morphophonemic forms are fortunately accessible to observation. Changes in phonological systems may reveal ordinarily hidden structure, as a tiger lurking on the edge of a jungle, his stripes blending in with the background, becomes visible the moment he begins to move. Suppose, for example, that the distinction between the morphophonemes /A/ and /B/ is neutralized as [A] by a rule P:

In this situation there are many ways in which P can change so as to undo the neutralization and make the distinction between A and B appear on the phonetic surface. The precise lines along which [A] splits up indicate what their morphophonemic representation probably was, or in some types of cases even what it must have been.

Much of the following discussion will attempt to exploit this type of evidence in order to clarify problems of phonological theory. I will first illustrate the general approach by analyzing an example and showing how it bears on the controversy between the three major types of morphophonemics just discussed.

In Russian the dentals *t, d, s* and the velars *k, g, x* become palatalized to *č, ž, š* by a process that is quite productive in the verb conjugation. (The inverted hat (haček) represents palatalization and the symbol ȝ stands for a dental affricate.) This process is represented in a generative phonology by two rules:

(1)    Palatalization (*t, d, s* and *k, g, x* become *č, ǯ, š*)
(2)    Spirantization (*ǯ* becomes *ž*)

The palatalization rule first converts the dental and velar stops and continuants into strident palatals. The resulting affricate *ǯ*, derived by palatalization from /d/ and /g/, must be further converted into a spirant *ž* by the second rule.

| Underlying form | t | d | s | k | g | x |
|---|---|---|---|---|---|---|
| Palatalization | č | ǯ | š | č | ǯ | š |
| Spirantization | — | ž | — | — | ž | — |

In Ukrainian and Belorussian this system has been changed.[1] Those [ž]'s which, from the synchronic point of view, were derived from underlying /d/, have become reaffricated to [ǯ]. But there was no change in the [ž]'s which synchronically were derived from /γ/ (the Ukrainian and Belorussian reflex of Slavic /g/) and likewise no change in those [ž]'s which occurred in nonderived, synchronically isolated forms, no matter whether they historically had /g/ or /d/ before palatalization took place. Contrast, for example, the retention of Ukr. *bižu* 'I run' (stem *beg- > biγ-*) with the change of Ukr. *syžu* 'I sit' to *syǯu* (stem *syd-*), and likewise with the retention of *meža* 'boundary'.

Of course the reason that only [ž] from /d/ but neither [ž] from /γ/ nor underlying /ž/ becomes a stop phonetically by this change is that only [ž] from /d/ is an underlying stop.[2] The change is in fact quite simply the loss of the spirantization rule. Prior to this loss phonetic [ž]'s were derived as follows:

|  | A | B | C |
|---|---|---|---|
| Underlying form | biɣ | syd | mež |
| Palatalization | biž | syǯ | — |
| Spirantization | — | syž | — |
| Final form | bižu | syžu | meža |

Since /ɣ/ is a continuant, and /d/ is a stop, the simplest form of the palatalization rule will convert /ɣ/ into a continuant [ž] and /d/ into a stop (affricate) [ǯ]. The loss of the spirantization rule simply causes this state of affairs, represented by the next-to-last line of the derivation, to emerge phonetically.

The essential point is that two aspects of this change are explained if we base our synchronic description on generative phonology: the form of the split, and its regularity.

The form of the split can be explained in the sense that it would be exceedingly difficult to state any other split between the three groups of [ž]'s represented by the three columns in the above diagram. The [ǯ] arose in column B. A two-way split would also have resulted had it arisen in A, or in C, or in A and B, A and C, or B and C. A minute's experimentation will show that had any of the other five imaginable developments occurred, it could not be related to any natural change in the grammar, where by natural change I mean the following frequently encountered types: addition of rules at, or near the end of, the phonological component; loss or simplification of rules; or change in order.[3]

The regularity of the split can be explained because there are three systematic underlying units involved, of which one receives a different realization by the split. Every instance of [ǯ] which is *clearly* derived from /d/ (these are found in the verb conjugation, and in the more productive derivatives) is changed in the same way because the change is in an abstract rule of the grammar.

How would these explanations fare under an item-and-arrangement theory of morphophonemics? There would not be a single, systematic change of the grammar at all. The underlying forms of a large number of morphemes simply undergo a simultaneous, identical modification. Both the fact that a particular definite set of morphemes changed, and the regularity with which the change occurred, are beyond explanation, because these theories of morphophonemics express no connection between an alternation in one morpheme and the same alternation in other morphemes. Any other split between A, B, and C, and worse yet, any random split within these categories, would be structurally indistinguishable from the change which actually occurred.

I am discussing a single example here, but it is a general and very important fact that morphophonemic analogy operates with all the regularity of the Neogrammarian's sound change. It is for this reason that any theory which treats it as a change in lists of morphemes, and this includes the proportional model of analogy, cannot account for it. The regularity can only be due to the fact that the change is in the morphophonemic system.

Let us now consider the theory that morphemes should be represented wholly by diacritic symbols with no phonetic significance. For example, we can burn our phonetic boats by representing /d/, /γ/, and /ž/ by the morphophonemes %, *, and 1/4, respectively. In the system prior to the change, there would be the following realization rules:

$$(1) \quad \text{a.} \qquad \% \rightarrow \left\{ \begin{array}{c} /ž/ \\ /d/ \end{array} \right\} \quad \begin{array}{c} \text{in the palatalizing environments} \\ \downarrow \end{array}$$

$$(2) \quad \text{a.} \qquad * \rightarrow \left\{ \begin{array}{c} /ž/ \\ /γ/ \end{array} \right\} \quad \begin{array}{c} \text{in the palatalizing environments} \\ \downarrow \end{array}$$

$$(3) \qquad 1/4 \rightarrow /ž/$$

The change can be stated as follows: change the righthand side of subrule (1a) from /ž/ to /ǯ/.

What had enabled us to explain the affrication of the [ž] derived from underlying /d/ was its underlying representation as a stop, which is required by generative phonology, and the resulting appearance of [ǯ] at an intermediate stage in the derivation. The theory under consideration, however, denies this specifically and asserts that morphophonemes have no phonological characterization, and that no intermediate representations can ever figure in derivations. The basis of the explanation is thereby gone. The change becomes an arbitrary one. There is no reason within this framework why any other realization rule should not have undergone this, or any other, arbitrary modification. A change of % to [p] or to [s] would, in terms of this theoretical framework, have been just as natural.

The force of this kind of argumentation rests not of course on this single example, but on the general character of this class of phonological change. In other words, fully abstract and fully concrete morphophonemics fail not just because they cannot explain a particular change in Slavic, but because they are an inadequate foundation for historical linguistics in general.

Now item-and-arrangement morphophonemics and fully abstract morphophohemics do not really need this kind of rather labored and complicated refutation by historical evidence. They are both amply refuted by more general considerations. But I have not given this example for its own sake only. I have given it in order to illustrate a method by which linguistic structure can be investigated through language change. It is an extremely delicate method which in subtler disputes may well be the only available, at our present state of knowledge. The method, briefly, is this: examine changes that depend on linguistic structure and see what kind of structure they presuppose.

In the rest of this paper I will assume the correctness of process morphophonemics and proceed to investigate problems which mirror the gross trichotomy of the three basic approaches on a smaller scale within process morphophonemics. Specifically, I will be concerned with delimiting the proper role of diacritic features in generative phonology.

## 2. The Alternation Condition

Let us term the merger of distinct representations *neutralization*. The present theory of generative grammar allows phonological distinctions which are never realized on the phonetic surface to appear in the lexical representations of morphemes. I will term this kind of neutralization, which takes place regardless of environment, *absolute neutralization*, in order to distinguish it from the more usual *contextual neutralization*, in which an underlying distinction is lost only in a specific environment and retained elsewhere.

Neutralization rules which are contextually restricted are necessarily involved in the treatment of phenomena like these:

(1) In many American dialects, words like *rider* and *writer* are homophonous. The distinction between /t/ and /d/ is neutralized medially before an unstressed syllable, but is retained elsewhere, as in *ride:write*.

(2) In German and Russian, the distinction between voiced and voiceless obstruents is neutralized in final position. For example, German *Bund* 'union' and *bunt* 'colorful' are both pronounced [bunt]; the distinction appears before endings, e.g. *Bunde:bunte*.

The context in which neutralization occurs can also be morphological:

(3) In Classical Greek, an ablaut rule turns *e* to *o* in certain morphological contexts. In these contexts the distinction between underlying /e/ and /o/ is neutralized, e.g., *témnō* 'cut' : *tomos* 'incision', *kóptō* 'beat, exhaust':*kópos* 'exhaustion'.

(4) For many speakers of German, umlauted /a/ is pronounced like /e/; e.g. the plurals of *Nacht* 'night' and *Recht* 'right' rhyme: *Nächte, Rechte*.

In these examples the neutralization rule merges a form A with an already existing form B. It can also happen that two forms A and B merge into a third form C.

(5)    In Russian, the dentals *t, d, s* and the velars *k, g, x* are both pala-talized to *č, ž, š*. The distinction between velars and dentals is neutralized under palatalization. E.g. *plákat':pláču* 'weep', *platít':plaču* 'pay'.

I take such contextual neutralization to be a linguistic fact which is beyond dispute. The dispute begins where generative phonology parts company with more traditional approaches by also permitting absolute neutralization. Absolute neutralization is a consequence of setting up underlying distinctions for the sole purpose of classifying segments into those that do and those that do not meet the structural analysis of a rule. In a commonly posited type of absolute neutralization identical segments are assigned different underlying representations because they function differently as environments of some rule. Suppose, for example, that a grammar contains the phonological rule

$$A \rightarrow B \text{ in the context } \underline{\qquad} C.$$

The language has, however, certain instances of C before which the change $A \rightarrow B$ does not take place, but which are in themselves indistinguishable from those C's before which the change does take place. In the present theory of generative phonology it is always possible to prevent any C from serving as the environment of the rule by representing it as an underlying D, where D is a representation not otherwise found in the language which differs minimally in some way from C. It is then merely necessary to incorporate a late rule $D \rightarrow C$ into the grammar. The obligatory, context-free conversion of virtual D to phonetic C is an instance of what is here termed absolute neutralization. It is the legitimacy of this device which will be questioned in the following sections.[4]

In languages such as Finnish, Hungarian, and Mongolian, suffixes undergo vowel harmony. Suffixes exhibiting the harmonic alternation are back after roots with back vowels and front after roots with front vowels. Assume that these suffixes have basic back vowels, and that the vowel harmony rule causes their fronting after roots with front vowels (this will be justified in § 5). Hungarian has the peculiarity that certain stems containing the neutral vowels *i* and *e* cause no fronting of suffixes. Such a case is *héj* 'rind, peel', e.g. *héj-am* 'my rind', which contrasts with *kés-em* 'my knife'. The problem which a phonological description faces is that vowel harmony is partly predictable phonologically, on the basis of the front or back quality of the stem vowel, but unpredictable when the root contains only neutral vowels. In such cases some generative analyses have represented words like *héj* with underlying unrounded back vowels, which are obligatorily fronted, undergoing absolute neutralization with the underlying front vowels of words like *kés*, after the rule of vowel harmony has applied. Then *héj* is phonemically /hə:j/, although neither [ə] nor any other unrounded back vowel ever appears phonetically in this word of Hungarian.

Along with such purely diacritic use of phonological features, generative phonology has also allowed the phonological use of diacritic features. By this I mean rules which have the form of phonological rules but operate on diacritic features. This opposite possibility has provided the second current type of solution to vowel harmony which at present prevails in generative phonology. In the Hungarian case, this kind of solution would set up a nonphonological diacritic feature instead of the phonological front-back distinction. Vowel harmony is treated by a quasi-phonological rule which distributes this diacritic feature from the root to the whole word, and a late rule then spells out the underlying vowels as front or back, depending on the diacritic feature with which they are associated. While the former solution recognized *no* neutral vowels in underlying representations, this solution recognizes *only* neutral vowels. Both attempt to rectify the asymmetry of the system by generalizing to all vowels the treatment which is appropriate to one class of vowels.

A third alternative, which I will defend here, is to represent vowel harmony as phonologically conditioned insofar as it is in fact phonologically conditioned, and to introduce diacritic features where harmonically distinct but phonetically identical neutral vowels must be distinguished. Specifically, the rule features available for representing exceptions to grammatical rules are the appropriate diacritic features to be used.[5] An exception to a rule is a linguistic unit which meets the structural analysis of this rule, but nevertheless does not undergo it. That linguistic rules can have exceptions, and that rule features of some kind are needed to mark linguistic units as exceptions, is generally agreed. It is therefore not necessary to assign exceptional items different phonological representations from regular ones. They can simply be designated in the lexicon as exceptions to the particular rules which they should, but do not, undergo. This can be done in the present case. Words like *héj* can be entered in the lexicon with the same phoneme /e:/ as words like *kés*, but marked as [ - Vowel Harmony]. This will cause the suffixes to retain their back vowels when used with this specially marked category of stem.

The decision between the three alternatives is an arbitrary one within the present theory of generative phonology.[6] The theory enforces no choice, because the evaluation measure assigns no relative weight to rule features versus phonological features. In practice, however, descriptions in the framework of generative phonology have in such cases (which are numerous) tended to choose the phonological feature over the rule feature. The explanation for this preference is partly the fact that the theory of rule features is a recent development in generative grammar. In some cases the decision to use a phonological feature, and even the choice of the particular feature used, may have been under illicit historical stimulation. The synchronic analysis which sets up unrounded back vowels in Hungarian presumably reflects exactly the historical sequence of events which gave rise to the present system. It is a very natural, though theoretically unjustified, desire to have synchronic descriptions reflect diachrony to the greatest possible extent. The greater the similarity between synchronic and historical grammar, the less work either of them involves for the linguist. It would be ideal if we could simply provide the arrowheads of historical grammars with shafts to get synchronic descriptions, and perform the converse operation on *The Sound Pattern of English* to get a history of English phonology. But unfortunately we cannot assume that synchronic grammars necessarily have a form which takes the hard work out of internal reconstruction. Children learning their native language do not have the interests of linguists at heart.

Though the choice between these alternatives is arbitrary within the present framework of generative phonology, it is not without tangible consequences. The purpose of this paper is to work out the consequences of each alternative and to test them against the empirical data. These consequences are both historical and synchronic. While it is invalid to argue for or against a particular phonological analysis on the grounds that it does, or does not, reflect historical developments, numerous kinds of valid and fruitful conclusions may still be drawn from diachrony to synchrony. In the case at hand what I regard as the most significant evidence is in fact diachronic, although the synchronic evidence plays a large role too.

On this basis I will propose that the theory of generative phonology must be modified to *exclude* the diacritic use of phonological features, and the phonological use of diacritic features. One of the effects of restricting phonology like this is to enter nonalternating forms in the lexicon in roughly their autonomous phonemic representation. That is, if a form appears in a constant shape, its underlying representation is that shape, except for what can be attributed to low-level, automatic phonetic processes. These can be defined as processes which do not cause neutralization of distinct representations. For example, the vowel shift of English, or the loss of final /g/ in *sing*, are low-level automatic phonetic processes, since the underlying form is in each case recoverable from the phonetic form. One thing which the condition I propose to be added to phonological theory should do, then, is to require that morphemes which are always phonetically identical must have the same underlying representations. This will exclude a large number of cases of absolute neutralization, though it is still not strong enough to exclude all, as the examples we shall discuss will make clear.

The other branch of the condition will have among its consequences that morphemes which are always phonetically distinct must have different underlying representations. This is sufficient to ensure that root markers cannot be set up to cut in half the number of vowels in languages with vowel harmony. It is likely that the correct condition is even stronger, and excludes the use of rule features as elements in the structural index or structural change of phonological rules, restricting them to the categorization of elements into regular and exceptional classes with respect to phonological rules, along the lines proposed for syntax by Lakoff (1965). Likewise it probably should exclude the assignment of rule features to particular morphemes or segments by means of readjustment rules. Although Chomsky and Halle (1968: 379) allow for this operation, it is not certain that it is ever necessary. The examples they give there seem unconvincing. One, involving vowel harmony in Nez Perce, will be reanalyzed in detail in § 5, where a purely phonological rule will be seen to handle the phenomenon in question in a better way. The other can be briefly discussed here.

In Russian, the suffix /isk/ normally loses its vowel, e.g. [s'ib'írskəy] 'Siberian', [r'ímskəy] 'Roman'. After palatals, however, the vowel normally stays, e.g. [gr'éč'iskəy] 'Greek', [manášiskəy] 'monastic'. Chomsky and Halle propose a readjustment rule which marks the vowel of the suffix /isk/ as an exception to the vowel deletion rule if it follows a velar or a palatal. Since the underlying stem in [gr'éč'iskəy] is something like /grek/, with a velar, the readjustment rule will mark the suffix /isk/ after it with the diacritic feature which prevents vowel deletion from applying to it. However, this solution runs into difficulties in the case of words which are exceptions to the palatalization rule. When underlying /k/ irregularly fails to become [č] before the suffix /isk/, the vowel is no longer an exception to the deletion rule and drops, e.g. [kar'ákskəy] 'Koryak'. Apparently, then, vowel deletion fails to take place only after palatals, and not after velars. But a readjustment rule cannot tell the difference between them, since they are both represented as velars at the point at which readjustment rules apply. Rather than trying to make the readjustment rule somehow distinguish between velars which are going to become palatalized and velars which are going to stay velars, it is better to state the condition on vowel dropping *after* palatalization applies, making the vowel-dropping rule itself inapplicable when the suffix /isk/ is preceded by a palatal, and doing away with any readjustment rule. This also enables us to understand the phonetic reason for the failure of the vowel to drop, cf. English *churches, bushes,* but *books.* Evidently sequences of strident consonants are hard to pronounce and tend to be avoided.

The two major areas of phonology in which diacritic features have been used as elements in phonological rules are the treatment of foreign words and the treatment of accentual phenomena. It is open to question whether either of these uses of diacritic features in phonological rules is necessary. The choice between using features like [± Foreign] to classify morphemes, restricting certain rules to apply only in the environment [+ Foreign] or [− Foreign], and using rule features to mark words as exceptions to specific rules, is no mere matter of arbitrary notational convenience. Features like [± Foreign] have seemed more appropriate because loanwords are characteristically exceptions not just to one rule, but to a large number of rules, and tend to fall into classes exhibiting similar behavior. These regularities can be mirrored also by redundancy rules of the form

$$[ - \text{Rule X}] \rightarrow [ - \text{Rule Y}] \ .$$

This latter alternative predicts that the vocabulary should exhibit, typically, a hierarchy of foreignness, with exceptions to one rule always being exceptions to another rule, but not vice versa. This appears, in fact, to be a far better approximation to the situations actually encountered in languages than the simple bipartition of the vocabulary suggested by the use of diacritic features like [± Foreign]. To the extent that there are loanwords of varying degrees of assimilation in languages, rather than just one or two homogeneous classes of loanwords, rule features receive empirical confirmation as the appropriate notational device.[7] As regards accentual systems, I hope to show in a forthcoming study that diacritic features such as those employed by Heeschen (1967) in his investigation of Lithuanian accentuation are also reformulable with rule features.[8]

The condition which has these effects will be called here the *alternation condition*. I will consider some problems which have to be solved before an exact formulation of the alternation condition is possible. Since the diacritic use of phonological features is far more tempting than the opposite abuse, and far more prevalent in actual practice, I will concentrate on it in what follows. I will examine, then, primarily cases of absolute neutralization, and compare them with the alternative analyses required by the alternation condition, returning to the other side of the question in a fuller discussion of vowel harmony in § 5.

Cases of this type were first brought out by Halle (1962) in what was the first discussion of the possibility of absolute neutralization in phonology. Halle cited certain Russian dialects with the following seven-vowel system:

| i | | u |
|---|---|---|
| e | | o |
| æ | a | ɔ |

In these dialects, low and mid vowels after palatalized consonants are subject to a process of reduction which depends on the height of the following accented vowel. The rule is:

(1)    V → i / ___[ + low ] (ɔ, a, æ)

(2)    V → a    otherwise

For example,

| Phonemic form | /s'ɔl ó/ | /s'ɔl ɔ́m/ |
|---|---|---|
| Phonetic form | [s'al ó] | [s'il ć m] |

According to Halle,

> [I]n some of these dialects, the distinction between compact /ɔ/ and /æ/ and non-compact /o/ and /e/ is lost, yet the vowels in pretonic position are treated as before; e.g., [s,ilɔ́m] but [s,alɔ́]. In such dialects, therefore, phonetically identical segments − [ɔ] − produce distinct results in the distribution of the pretonic vowel. If the distinction between these etymologically distinct yet phonetically identical vowels were to be eliminated from the representation of morphemes, the statement of the distribution of the pretonic vowel [rules (1) and (2)] would become hopelessly complex. Considerations of simplicity would dictate that the distinction between the respective segment types be maintained and that their phonetic coalescence be accounted for by adding to the end of the grammar the rule [ (e, o) → (æ,ɔ) ].

Nevertheless there is an alternative which allows the coalescence without paying the price of undue complexity: the vowel in the ending *-o* and others derived from former mid vowels can be represented as / ɔ, æ/ but marked as exceptions to the first part of the vowel reduction process. This will make them, correctly, produce *a*-quality in the preceding unstressed vowel by the second part of the vowel reduction process.

From a synchronic point of view, *k* is palatalized to *č* in Sanskrit before some *a*'s but not others. The difference is ultimately due to the fact that Sanskrit *a* is derived from both Indo-European *e*, before which palatalization occurred at a certain stage in the prehistory of Sanskrit, and from Indo-European *a* and *o*, before which palatalization did not take place. It has sometimes been proposed that in Sanskrit the palatalizing *a*'s are phonemically distinguished from the nonpalatalizing *a*'s as /e/:/a/, a distinction which is absolutely neutralized on the phonetic level as [a]. The alternative which I propose posits only a single phoneme /a/, the ones which do not cause palatalization being designated in the lexicon by the appropriate rule feature.

Several examples of absolute neutralization are proposed by Chomsky and Halle (1968) in their analysis of English. For example, words like *tolerance, eminence, relevance, competence* are there assumed to end in a phoneme /ɛ/, a glide of *e*-quality. Every occurrence of this phoneme is always deleted, that is /ɛ/ is always neutralized with zero. Another example in their analysis is the suffix in words like *aristocracy, synonymy, telegraphy, economy, industry*, which according to them is not /i/ but the glide /y/, which always merges phonetically with /i/. A third example is the contrast they set up between the final vowels of *veto* and *motto*. Though these vowels are always phonetically identical, Chomsky and Halle argue that they are phonemically distinct as /ɔ/ versus /o/.

Chomsky and Halle's reasons for these analyses are complicated, and will not be repeated here. My view is that each of these analyses is wrong, and has to be rejected even within the theory of phonology proposed by Chomsky and Halle. Reanalyses can be made in each of the three cases which handle the facts that led Chomsky and Halle to their solution, often in a simpler way, without involving absolute neutralization.[9] The situation is somewhat different than in the earlier examples, for the reanalyses do not simply amount to replacing the absolutely neutralized phonological feature by a rule feature, but to more extensive revisions in the phonological system.

Let us return for a moment to the Sanskrit example and consider whether *phonetic plausibility* might not justify distinguishing between palatalizing and nonpalatalizing *a* in Sanskrit by a morphophonemic distinction of /e/ versus /a/. Does this solution not allow us to *explain* the palatalization synchronically as being a phonologically motivated process in the synchronic structure of Sanskrit, rather than a process based on an arbitrary distinction between two kinds of *a*'s? I find this reasoning circular. If the only reason for setting up the contrast between the two kinds of *a*'s as /e/ versus /a/ is their different behavior with respect to palatalization, then that same contrast cannot be invoked to explain this different behavior with respect to palatalization (although it can of course be used, and is being used, to describe it). From a synchronic point of view it is inescapably arbitrary and unpredictable which *a*'s palatalize and which do not. No matter how we choose to represent the contrast, we cannot explain it synchronically. The two alternative solutions we are considering are fully equivalent in this respect.

But perhaps one could, while admitting the vacuity of the above kind of language-particular phonetic-plausibility argument, attempt to give it some substance by reformulating it as a universal claim. One could say, as a substantive universal in phonology, that palatalization rules cannot have *a* as their environment in any language, but only front vowels. If, then, we find in *any* language a palatalization process taking place before *a*, such a theory claims that this *a* must be represented as a front vowel at the point at which the palatalization rule applies in the derivation of each word. The problem is whether this claim has any consequences at all by which one could test its truth or falsity. I can think of two possible directions in which they might be found.

First, such a theory entails that in a situation in which identical segments must be distinguished because they behave differently with respect to some rule, it is always *possible* to find 'vacant slots' which allow the distinction to be set up so as to make the rules become phonetically natural. For example, in the Sanskrit type of situation the claim would be that an unused front vowel must be available to take care of the palatalizing *a*'s. I think that this consequence, while true, still does not save the theory from vacuity. It is in the nature of things that there will always be some possible combination of phonetic features which fulfills these requirements. Even if Sanskrit, for example, already had both /e/ and /æ/, the palatalizing *a*'s could still be set up as nasal, or retroflex, or rounded /e/'s or /æ/'s. And if all these were already taken for other purposes too, we could bring in more exotic features, and if necessary make use of one of the many hundred possible combinations of these features, to find a front vowel distinct from all other front vowels which is free to be the underlying form of palatalizing *a*. The palatalization rule can be made natural in any conceivable situation. We can never miss, and for that reason we can never find anything to explain thereby. And if we want to rule out bringing in other features to save the situation, we are right back at the alternation condition.

The other test of the claim that underlying representations must be adjusted to make the rules of a grammar natural might come from sound change. Let us assume that it is true that sound changes are always natural rules in some sense, for example, that velars may in sound changes be palatalized before front vowels, but not before *a*. If we further assume that the set of possible sound changes is identical to the set of possible phonological rules, then the palatalization rule in Sanskrit would have to apply before front vowels, and palatalizing *a* would have to be represented as a front vowel. However, the claim that the set of possible sound changes is the same as the set of possible phonological rules is clearly untenable, given any presently formulated phonological theory. The pages of any detailed phonological study are full of rules which one could not imagine as sound changes. Does anyone seriously wish to say that the main stress rule of English (Chomsky and Halle 1968) could be added as a sound change to some language? Rather, it seems more accurate to say that sound changes are a special set of very simple rules, and that more complicated rules, which could not be added as such to grammars, may still come to exist in grammars through phonological restructuring. If this is granted, then there is no way of excluding a priori the possibility that a rule palatalizing velars before *a* (actually, before unrounded vowels) in Sanskrit might not be just such a rule which has arisen through restructuring.

I conclude that there is nothing in the way of explanation that has to be given up with the solutions rejected by the alternation condition. In the following sections I will argue that a good deal is gained, with respect to these very considerations of phonetic naturalness and explanatory power, if the solutions which accord with the alternation condition are accepted.

## 3. The historical arguments

The core of my historical argument against absolute neutralization has roughly the following form:

(1)    From the assumption that absolute neutralization exists, certain predictions about change in phonological systems follow.

(2)    These predictions are false.

(3)    The theory of change cannot be adjusted in any general way to exclude these predictions.

(4)    Therefore absolute neutralization does not exist.

A comparison of absolute and contextual neutralization from a diachronic point of view reveals three profound differences between the two types: contextual neutralizations are *reversible, stable,* and *productive* whereas the alleged absolute neutralizations are *irreversible, unstable,* and *unproductive*.

The reversal of contextual neutralization represents one of the two main types of morphophonemic analogy, the type often called morphophonemic *leveling*.[10] Such reversal, resulting in leveling, can take place formally either by a simplification of the structural description (analysis) of a rule, by the elimination of a rule from the grammar, or finally by a reordering of rules from a 'bleeding' order of the form

1.    [    ]    >    $[\sim\phi]$

2.    $[\phi]$    >    [    ]

to a reverse, unmarked order of the form

1.    $[\phi]$    >    [    ]

2.    [    ]    >    $[\sim\phi]$

Reversal of contextual neutralization by the elimination of an entire morphophonemic rule from the grammar was already illustrated at the beginning with an example from Slavic. We found that some of the East Slavic languages had lost one of the rules of the palatalization system, the rule which turned voiced affricates into continuants. As a result, the previously submerged distinction between [ž]'s from different sources reappeared on the phonetic surface, not, of course, on etymological lines, but according to their synchronic morphophonemic derivation. Another example is the loss of the word-final devoicing rule in Yiddish. It is generally agreed among specialists that all Yiddish dialects once possessed the same rule which in Standard German neutralizes the distinction between voiced and voiceless obstruents in word-final position, and that this rule has been lost through morphophonemic leveling (Sapir 1915, Weinreich 1963).

An example of the reversal of contextual neutralization through the modification of a rule is the simplification of the umlaut rule in various dialects of German. This has undone the neutralization of basic *e* and *e* from *a* by turning the latter into *æ*. The vowels in *Nächte, hätte* have become *æ*, thereby diverging from the previously identical vowels in *Recht, Bett, Netz* and other words, which, while including many historically umlauted vowels (e.g. *Bett* < *\*badi-*, *Netz* < *\*nati-*), are synchronically analyzed with /e/ and retain the mid vowel. The change is formally the simplification of the umlaut rule from (roughly)

$$V \rightarrow \begin{bmatrix} - \text{ back} \\ - \text{ low} \end{bmatrix}$$

to

$$V \rightarrow [ - \text{ back} ]$$

An interesting case of reversal of contextual neutralization which is not a case of leveling, and also is not formally typical, is Brugmann's Law in Indo-Iranian. Indo-European *\*o* when ablauted from *e* becomes Indo-Iranian *ā* in open syllables, whereas basic Indo-European *\*o* turns up as short *a*. Cf. the causative of the verb meaning 'sit', Skt. *sādayati*, IE *\*sodeyeti* (Goth. *satjiþ*), from the root *\*sed*; perfect *jajāna*, IE *\*ǵeǵone* (Gk. γέγονε) from the root *\*ǵen*, versus basic IE *\*o* in *apas* 'work' (Lat. *opus*), *pati-* 'lord' (Lat. *potis*), *avi-* 'sheep' (Lat. *ovis*). Kuryłowicz (1956: 321) has suggested that the change responsible for Brugmann's Law was basically a generalization of an Indo-Iranian vowel-insertion rule

$$\emptyset \rightarrow a \qquad \text{before all syllabic segments except } a$$

which governed the inherited guna ablaut in Indo-Iranian, (e.g. /da-dr̥ś-a/ > *dadarśa*) to the form

$$\emptyset \rightarrow a \qquad \text{before all syllabic segments.}$$

This generalization resulted in a new ablaut *a → aa* ( *→ ā*) (e.g. /ja-jan-a/ → *jajāna*), with the restriction to open syllables following as a later development.

Reordering of rules is capable of producing the same type of change. This in itself is an important reason why reordering must be considered a special case of simplification, like the other changes which have similar results. For several examples, which will not be reproduced here, see Kiparsky (1968a).

The reversibility of contextual neutralization contrasts sharply with the irreversibility of the alleged cases of absolute neutralization. There is not a single case on record, to my knowledge, of analogical reversal of absolute neutralization, although given the present theory of generative phonology such a reversal is every bit as easy to express as the amply documented reversal of contextual neutralization. As far as the evidence indicates, absolute neutralization is totally irreversible.

For example, I do not know of a vowel harmony language in which harmonically distinct neutral vowels have split up phonetically.[11] The underlying /ɨ/ which figures in generative phonologies of Hungarian, Classical Mongolian and other languages never re-emerges phonetically, although such a change is easily stated as the elimination of the rule /ɨ/ → [i] which merges it with underlying /i/. For that matter, the change is also statable as easily in terms of analogical proportions. The issue is clearly independent of any particular theory of change and concerns only the nature of underlying representations.

Nor can we easily imagine the alleged /ɛ/ and /y/ glide suffixes of Chomsky and Halle making a dramatic appearance at the end of words like *tolerance* or *industry*. And the two *a*'s which have been claimed for Sanskrit have not resurfaced phonetically anywhere in modern India. If absolute neutralization really exists, why cannot it be undone like contextual neutralization? If, as I propose, it does not exist, that difficult question disappears.

The two types of neutralization also differ radically in *stability*. Contextual neutralization is quite stable historically. While analogical reversal is possible, as we have seen, there seems to be no particular pressure to adjust the system in this or any other way. The Slavic palatalizations, umlaut in German, word-final devoicing in German are rules which have been retained in a fairly stable form in a large number of dialects for over a thousand years. In general, points of contextual neutralization are not susceptible to change more than any others.

This can hardly be said of absolute neutralization. No sooner has a sound change introduced a putative absolute neutralization, than analogical change begins to bury it. The nonphonetic environment of the rule is soon discarded in favor of a transparent, phonetic or morphological environment. For example, Classical Mongolian is known to have had, as Hungarian still has today, words which contained only neutral vowels and which took back vowel suffixes. Yet today every neutral vowel word in Mongolian, without exception, takes front suffixes (Sanžeev 1959: 18). For example, *id-* 'eat' forms *idmeer* 'edible'; *\*idmaar* would be impossible. Why this change? Because the neutral vowel (*i*) is a front vowel, obviously. The alternation condition enables generative phonology to express this natural answer formally by forcing it to represent those neutral-vowel words which cause back vowel harmony as exceptional front vowel words rather than as regular back vowel words which happen to be fronted by a late rule. The rapid disappearance of these words shows that their characterization as exceptions is a completely correct consequence of the alternation condition.

Presumably the Russian dialects mentioned in § 2, in which phonetically identical low vowels must be divided (corresponding to their historical origin as mid or low vowels) into two classes which differ in the way they determine vowel reduction in the preceding syllable, represent a similarly unstable situation. They appear to be extremely rare. I would assume such a dialect, wherever it arises, will be short-lived, and the nonphonetic distinction between the two kinds of vowels will soon be eliminated. If this is the case, then a linguistic theory which represents such systems as normal and regular is an inadequate basis for historical linguistics, since it cannot explain their instability.

Morphological conditioning is an alternative resolution of the instability. As a result of analogical changes within Indic, the *k:c* alternation is governed to a great extent by new rules of Sanskrit which often refer to morphological categories, rather than the etymological quality of the following vowel. For example, the theme vowel in the Indo-European conjugation alternated between *e* and *o*: *\*pek^wō* 'I cook', *\*pek^weti* 'he cooks'. But instead of Sanskrit *\*pakāmi, pacati* we get *pacāmi, pacati*, with the palatal generalized throughout.

The third point concerns *productivity*. New words which enter a language, from whatever source, tend to fall into the regular classes of the vocabulary as far as possible. Whatever is exceptional about loanwords is normally due to unassimilated features of the source language, and not to any contributions by the borrowing language. The plural of *helix* may be the borrowed *helices*, but its native plural form may only be *helixes* and never *\*helixen* like *oxen*. We can thus conclude that stems with *i* and *e* which take endings with back vowels have an exceptional status in Hungarian from the fact that they constitute a closed class. Any new words with *i* and *e* that enter the language are assigned to the regular front-harmonic class, as I. Bátori has pointed out to me. Nothing explains this asymmetry unless the alternation condition is incorporated into phonological theory.

In sum, it appears that the alternation condition is required to account for some rather elementary facts about linguistic change. At least in the cases discussed above, phonological theory should not permit analyses involving absolute neutralization of underlying feature specifications which function only as diacritic marks. The rules which are presupposed in such constructions stand out from other rules by not functioning in any way in language change. The systems in which they would be set up are characteristically unstable, and the classes of morphemes involved are closed and unproductive. All this suggests that these putative systems do not exist at all, and that the situations in which they have been postulated should be treated with the alternative descriptive mechanisms which the theory of generative phonology makes available.

I will perhaps be accused of having begged the question. If these observations about the diachronic difference between absolute and contextual neutralization are true, someone might well say at this point, then they may as well be viewed as facts about diachrony and not necessarily be taken to indicate that synchronic phonological theory is in need of revision. That absolute neutralization is irreversible, that it is unstable, and that the classes of morphemes subject to it are closed and unproductive, might then be so many new generalizations to be incorporated into the theory of phonological change. Historical linguistics would be the richer for it and synchronic phonology could go on as before.

This plausible counterproposal must be rejected because the three generalizations are rather clearly related and due to the same underlying cause. By not seeking that cause in the constitution of language itself we waive the opportunity to explain any of them, for there is nothing in the nature of language change that could provide the basis for explaining them. Furthermore, the alternation condition, which underlies the theory of phonology on the basis of which these facts do admit of a general and unitary explanation, has yet other historical and synchronic consequences, which in many instances can be tested and verified.

## 4. The Strong Alternation Condition

In the preceding sections I examined situations in which absolute neutralization had been postulated in analyses of various languages. In some of these cases the analyses were incorrect, for reasons purely internal to the language in question, and alternative analyses not involving absolute neutralization were possible and necessary. When these cases were discarded, there remained a number of genuine cases where superficially identical phonological segments fell into two classes depending on their morphophonemic behavior. The two classes could in these situations be distinguished either by means of phonological features (entailing absolute neutralization) or by means of rule features. Whereas the theory of generative phonology at present allows an arbitrary choice between these two alternatives, it will, when amended by adding the alternation condition, enforce the use of rule features in every such case. I presented evidence, mainly consisting of facts about linguistic change, that the rule feature analyses enforced by the alternation condition are the correct analyses. That constitutes my first main argument for the alternation condition.

But not every logically conceivable case presents these two alternative solutions. That absolute neutralization was not really necessary, because rule features made available an equivalent solution, was a fact about the examples so far analyzed merely because the neutralized features were used in them as a more or less ad hoc device for handling exceptions. The question arises whether cases of absolute neutralization which do not lend themselves to reanalysis by means of rule features, or do so only at some exorbitant cost, ever occur in languages.

The answer to that question will determine precisely how the alternation condition must be formulated. One possibility is that the alternation condition categorically forbids absolute neutralization. The weaker alternative, to which we may well be ultimately driven, is that the alternation condition is a clause of the evaluation measure which says (among other things) that absolute neutralization is linguistically complex. In that form the alternation condition would, in any given case, balance out the generalizations gained by absolute neutralization against some fixed cost assigned to it in phonological theory. The relation of absolute neutralization between underlying and phonetic representations would still be excluded in cases such as those analyzed above, where rule features do just as well, but it would be allowed where this is not the case.

There do not appear to be many examples where reformulation with rule features is impossible, a fact which may be significant in itself. It is possible that the vowel systems of the Romance languages offer such examples. The disappearance of the Latin length distinction has left synchronic residues in the morphophonemics of the Romance languages. In Spanish, some *e*'s and *o*'s are diphthongized to *ye, we* under stress, but other, ostensibly identical *e*'s and *o*'s remain unchanged under the same conditions, e.g. *dormímos* 'we sleep', *duérmo* 'I sleep', but *comémos* 'we eat', *cómo* 'I eat'. The same, or partly the same, categorization of vowels that determines diphthongization in Spanish is also to some extent involved in determining the place of stress. The historical reason for this is that both stress and diphthongization were determined by Latin vowel length. Foley (1965) distinguished the two classes of vowels by means of the feature [± tense]. Since the feature of tenseness is in free variation on the surface in most dialects of Spanish, and in no dialect bears any relation to the underlying tenseness distinction posited by Foley, his solution involves a rule which obligatorily wipes out the underlying tenseness distinction in all cases. Harris (1969a) proposed an alternative which uses a diacritic feature [+ D] to distinguish the two kinds of *e*'s and *o*'s. In Harris' analysis this diacritic feature does not just categorize elements with respect to whether they do or do not undergo rules, but actually figures in phonological operations. The crucial question is whether Harris' analysis can be reformulated with rule features which do not figure in phonological operations so as to be compatible with the strong form of the alternation condition.

Another question is to what extent stress and susceptibility to diphthongization are still interdependent in a language such as modern Spanish. Harris shows that the situation is actually quite involved. First of all, verbs get stress on a fixed position regardless of what kinds of vowels are involved (1969a: 99). That leaves us with nouns and adjectives. Here there are also some difficulties. Harris (146) points out that the *we:o, ye:e* alternations in cases such as *Venezuéla: venezoláno, aguéro: agorár, tropiézo: tropezár* constitute a conflict between diphthongization and stress: the diphthongization indicates that the alternating nuclei are lax, but the place of stress indicates that they are tense. We may ask whether the interdependence between stress and susceptibility to diphthongization that still does exist in Spanish is perhaps only residual and to be explained historically rather than synchronically.

These questions must be answered before it can be decided whether Spanish refutes the strong version of the alternation condition.

It would speak for the strong version of the alternation condition if it would correctly predict the absence of plausible phonologies permitted by the present theory. This would demonstrate that the present theory is overly rich, and that the strong version of the alternation condition constitutes the desired impoverishment of the theory.[12]

## 5. Vowel harmony

The alternation condition, whatever its exact form, enforces an analysis of vowel harmony systems that is quite different from those that have been proposed up to now by generative phonologists. In this section I would like to return to the whole problem of vowel harmony, working out the relevant rules in detail for some languages, and presenting further evidence for the solution I propose.

It has always been taken for granted by generative phonologists that the rule which determines the vowel harmony in alternating suffixes also specifies the harmonic feature in the vowels of the root. In this way of doing things, vowels are unspecified in dictionary representations for the feature which is involved in the harmonic alternation. There has been controversy about only one point: how are roots categorized? Two proposals have been made. One, seen in Lightner (1965), Aoki (1966), Rice (1967), and Chomsky and Halle (1968), maintains that roots are provided with completely abstract markers on the basis of which every vowel in the root and in the affixes attached to it is simultaneously specified for the harmonizing feature by the vowel harmony rule. For example, the Finnish words *pouta* and *pöytä* would have the following underlying forms, where capital letters represent archiphonemes unmarked for the feature front:back.

/pOUtA/                            /pOUtA/
+GRAVE                            −GRAVE

A phonological rule applies to the vowels in these words, and the vowels in all their affixes, marking them with the phonological feature [+ back] if the associated root marker is + GRAVE, and with the phonological feature [− back] if the associated root marker is − GRAVE. The other analysis, which Zimmer (1967) proposed tentatively, and Bach (1968) more decisively, is that instead of the whole root being marked with a completely abstract diacritic, as in Lightner's solution, the first vowel of the stem is distinctive for the phonological feature which is involved in the harmony alternation, and that the remaining vowels of the stem, as well as the vowels of the affixes, are assigned the same phonological feature by a rule of progressive assimilation. In this analysis Finnish *pouta* and *pöytä* are no longer phonemically identical, as they were in Lightner's analysis. Their underlying representations are now

/poUtA/                            /pöUtA/

The whole problem of vowel harmony will have to be reconsidered in the light of the theory of markedness, which undoubtedly in some version will form a chapter of generative phonology (Chomsky and Halle 1968, Halle 1970).[13] The most important implication of this theory for the problem at hand is the form of dictionary representation which it requires. According to the theory of markedness, dictionary representations are fully specified for every phonological feature. Archiphonemes appear in the form of their fully specified, maximally unmarked representatives. For example, the nasal archiphoneme in *find*, whose place of articulation is predictable, is entered in the dictionary as a dental rather than as a nasal unspecified for place of articulation. Some rather compelling reasons, quite apart from markedness theory, require fully specified dictionary representations in any case. In the first place, this eliminates the distinctness paradoxes which bother the phonologist as long as unspecified features figure in dictionary representations (Stanley 1967). Secondly, Chomsky and Halle have pointed out that the conditions which determine the well-formedness of dictionary representations must refer to predictable phonological features. In English, the only clusters before which long nuclei are generally found in morphemes are dental clusters, e.g. *beast*, *wield*. In order to determine that *fiend, ground* but not *\*fiemb, \*groung* are possible morphemes, it is necessary to have the place of articulation specified in the dictionary and not by the nasal assimilation rule which operates in the phonology in words like *congress, compel, condone*.

In the case of vowel harmony, this means that every root vowel is fully specified in the dictionary as a front or back vowel, whereas the variable vowel archiphonemes of the endings ($a \sim ä, o \sim ö, u \sim ü$), whose surface form is always determined by vowel harmony, are represented in the dictionary in their unmarked forms *a, o, u*. Root morphemes in Finnish thus have an eight vowel system of six paired vowels *a, ä, o, ö, u, ü* and two neutral vowels, *i, e*, whereas endings only have a five-vowel system *i, e, a, o, u*. For example, the first *ä* in *jättää* 'leave' is in the root and is a phonemic *ä*, whereas the *-ää* in the ending is assimilated by vowel harmony from *-aa*, the form in which it appears after back-vowel roots, e.g. *ottaa* 'take'.

This rather specific consequence of markedness theory for the analysis of vowel harmony meets every empirical test that I can think of. A very interesting piece of historical confirmation comes from a number of Finnish dialects of Savo and Carelia, which diphthongize *aa > oa* and *ää > eä*, e.g. *maa > moa* 'land', *pää > peä* 'head'. The diphthongization also applies to endings, e.g. *ottaa > ottoa* 'take', where the first *a* of the ending is a stem-forming suffix (cf. *otto* 'taking', *ote* 'grip'), and the second is an inflectional ending. Front *-ää* in endings is similarly diphthongized, to *-eä*, e.g. *jättää > jätteä*. In some dialects, however, this *-eä* has been replaced by an analogical *-oä*, e.g. *jättoä*, though *-eä* is always retained in stems (Kettunen 1960: 11). If the endings are set up as basic back vowels, the change is seen to be the result of placing the diphthongization rule before the vowel harmony rule. The original derivation, with the historically 'correct' order

| base-form | jätt-aa[14] |
| vowel harmony | jätt-ää |
| diphthongization | jätt-eä |

is replaced by the 'analogical' derivation with the two rules in the opposite order

| base-form | jätt-aa |
| diphthongization | jätt-oa |
| vowel harmony | jätt-öä |

The analysis of the variable suffix vowels as underlying back vowels, as required by markedness theory, is the only analysis which enables this change to be formulated as a systematic change in the grammar. It is precisely the asymmetry between stem and suffix vowels inherent in this analysis on which the whole change depends. If, as in the other proposed solutions, stem and suffix vowels are both unspecified in the dictionary, and are specified for the feature of frontness simultaneously, there is at no time any systematic distinction between them which could trigger their divergence by the analogical change described above. Various complex means of stating the change no doubt remain, but none that explain it as a consequence of the phonologically different character of roots and endings.

The phonological theory on which I base these remarks requires that in addition to a vowel harmony rule, which assimilates affixes to stems, there be a morpheme structure condition which states that certain vowels cannot co-occur within roots, just as in English it requires that in addition to a morphophonemic nasal assimilation rule for cases like *combine, congress* there be a morpheme structure condition which states that nasal-stop sequences in roots must be homorganic. In English, as we saw, there is strong internal evidence that this duplication is correct. Let us now consider the situation in the case of vowel harmony. The systems proposed by generative phonologists for the treatment of vowel harmony have been motivated in large part by the desire to combine vowel harmony within roots and in affixes by the same rule. For example, in Finnish *pöytä+ä*, all vowels are simultaneously marked [− back] in Lightner's system, on the basis of the root marker of the stem, and all vowels except the first are so marked on the basis of the first vowel in Zimmer's and Bach's system. According to the theory of markedness, only the affix vowel is fronted by a phonological rule; the stem vowels are specified as front vowels in the lexicon, and a morpheme structure condition states that *pöytä* but not e.g. *\*poutä* or *\*pöuta* contains harmonically compatible vowels and is a possible morpheme of Finnish. Does not the joint treatment of root and affix harmony give the solutions developed by Lightner, Aoki, Rice, Chomsky, Halle, Zimmer and Bach a decisive advantage over the solution which I am proposing? The truth is rather that it makes their solutions unworkable. It is impossible to derive both root harmony and affix harmony by a single rule, because they have different sets of exceptions, and are therefore different processes. Finnish (as well as Turkish and Hungarian) contains a large number of loanwords which contain harmonically incompatible vowels, e.g. *afääri* 'affair', *olympialaiset* 'olympic games'. Obviously these words are exceptions to the stem harmony morpheme structure condition. Yet they all strictly observe the vowel harmony rule; their affixes undergo exactly the same rule as do those of native words: vowels are fronted if the last nonneutral stem vowel is a front vowel, e.g. *afääri-ä, olympialaisi-a, Skylla-a, Peugeot-a, Camus-tä*. Affix harmony, then, is a totally regular process, whereas root harmony is to some extent irregular and does not apply in the relatively unassimilated strata of borrowed vocabulary. This situation is not just an isolated quirk of Finnish alone. Turkish and Hungarian present the identical difficulty for any solution which attempts to combine root and affix harmony. The joint evidence of these languages is rather strong support for the treatment of vowel harmony which I am proposing and thus for the theory of markedness, of which it is a consequence.[15]

I have so far looked at vowel harmony in the light of the theory of markedness. The result, well supported by internal and historical considerations, was that in a language like Finnish there are two distinct structural manifestations of vowel harmony: (1) a morpheme structure condition which excludes the co-occurrence of vowels from the sets (*u, o, a*) and (*ü, ö, ä*) in morphemes, and (2) a phonological rule which makes the vowels of suffixes fronted if the last nonneutral vowel of the root is fronted. Formally, the phonological rule is:

$$\begin{bmatrix} V \\ + \text{ back} \end{bmatrix} \rightarrow [\alpha \text{ back}] \Bigg/ \begin{bmatrix} V \\ \alpha \text{ back} \end{bmatrix} \left( C_0 \begin{bmatrix} V \\ - \text{ round} \\ - \text{ low} \end{bmatrix}_0 C_0 \right)_0 \# X \underline{\quad}$$

(where X does not contain a word boundary, and # denotes the boundary between root and affixes). The rule is to be applied with the longest interpretation of the parenthetical expression which is possible; it applies disjunctively, in that the rule is not reapplied to shorter environments which also might meet the structural analysis of the rule. Some examples of how the rule applies are given below.

| $\begin{matrix} V \\ \alpha \text{ back} \end{matrix}$ | $\left( C_0 \begin{bmatrix} V \\ - \text{ round} \\ - \text{ low} \end{bmatrix}_0 C_0 \right)_0$ | | $\# X \underline{\quad}$ | |
|---|---|---|---|---|
| | o | tt | #a+ma+ttom+a+na | ottamattomana |
| kä | ä | nt | #ä+mä+ttöm+ä+nä | kääntämättömänä |
| k | o | rist | #a+va+nsa | koristavansa |
| | y | list | #ä+vä+nsä | ylistävänsä |
| olympial | a | is | #i+ssa+han | olympialaisissahan |
| manö | ö | vere | #i+ssä+hän | manöövereissähän |
| P | a | riisi | #ssa | Pariisissa |

We can now reconsider the status of the neutral vowels. This is an independent problem in the sense that the theory of markedness by itself leaves open both the solution which derives the neutral series of vowels from two distinct underlying series of vowels, and the solution in the spirit of the alternation condition which posits only a single series of neutral vowels on both the morphophonemic and the phonetic levels. But on the other hand, it is only the general approach to vowel harmony suggested by markedness theory which makes the solution required by the alternation condition feasible in the first place. To this extent it can be said that markedness theory and the alternation condition are not only compatible but mutually supporting.

In Finnish, the two vowels *i* and *e* co-occur freely with vowels from both harmonic sets (*ü, ö, ä* and *u, o, a*) in morphemes, e.g. *velka* 'debt', *selkä* 'back'. To mark the first vowel in the stem as distinctively front or back in the dictionary, as Bach and Zimmer would have it, would entail distinguishing between the two words by the following underlying representations:

/vəlkA/        /selkA/

The phoneme /ə/ and the other nonphonetic back unrounded vowel which this treatment requires, /ɨ/, are, after the application of the vowel harmony rule, collapsed phonetically with the front unrounded vowels *e* and *i*.

If underlying back unrounded vowels /ɨ/ and /ə/ are set up, as must be done if Bach's and Zimmer's solution is to be carried out, they not only have to be eliminated on the phonetic level by a special morphophonemic rule which converts them into [i] and [e], but they also have a peculiarly restricted distribution in underlying forms. Recall that words containing only neutral vowels always front their suffixes, e.g. *kive-ä, keli-ä, perkelet-tä, venet-tä, pii-tä, tie-tä*, but never *\*kive-a, \*keli-a, \*perkelet-ta*.[17] Translated into the Bach-Zimmer analysis, in which the harmonic character of the root is specified by distinctive frontness in its first vowel, this means that there are morphemes of the type /kivE , kelI/, but no morphemes of the type \*/kɨvE , \*kəlI/. When stated precisely, the general characterization of possible vowel combinations in roots is, in terms of this analysis, extremely odd. It must be formulated as follows: If the first (the fully specified) vowel phoneme in a root is /ɨ/ or /ə/, then the root must also contain *at least one instance* of either the archiphoneme /A/, or /O/, or /U/. This is necessary to rule out \*/kɨvE/, \*/kəlI/, \*/pərkElEh/, but to allow morphemes like /vəlkA/ *velka* 'debt', /pɨrU/ *piru* 'devil', /tɨkArI/ *tikari* 'dagger', /təlAkke/ *telakka* 'docks'. If I am right in believing that such morpheme structure conditions do not exist elsewhere in languages, then a phonological analysis which makes them necessary in this one unique case must fall under heavy suspicion.

But even if the distributional restrictions on the supposed phonemes /ɨ/ and /ə/ were of the most banal and most easily statable kind, they would still demonstrate the artificiality of any analysis which sets them up. For in any case they remain completely unrelated to the other peculiarity of /ɨ/ and /ə/: namely, that these supposed phonemes are always realized as the corresponding front vowels. The root marker analysis of Lightner entails a similar duplication. The ±GRAVE marker here never appears in words containing as their only vowels I and E. A second, formally unrelated fact is that *ɨ* and *ə*, when they arise from *I* and *E* by the operation of the vowel harmony rule on back vowel words like *velka, tikari*, are converted into the front vowels *i* and *e*. But these are complementary complications. The analysis I propose simultaneously eliminates both.

If all neutral vowels are set up as underlying /i/ and /e/, there are no special distributional restrictions at all on the neutral vowels. They have exactly the distribution of the other vowels. And the vowel harmony rule treats them as front vowels simply because they *are* front vowels. The rule was formulated above to cover the cases of roots, both foreign and native, containing at least some nonneutral vowel. For these, the rule is: endings are assimilated in frontness to the last nonneutral vowel of the root. It is a striking thing that the formal statement of this rule, given above, already covers the harmonic behavior of roots with *only* neutral vowels, in exactly the right way. This is ensured by the convention of disjunctive ordering. Neutral vowels, when not excluded from consideration by the parenthetical expression, will function as front vowels by the remainder of the structural analysis of the rule:

| | $\begin{matrix} V \\ \alpha \text{ back} \end{matrix}$ | $\left( C_0 \begin{bmatrix} V \\ -\text{round} \\ -\text{low} \end{bmatrix}_0 C_0 \right)_0$ | # X ___ | |
|---|---|---|---|---|
| k̯ | i | ve | # ä | kiveä |
| s | i | i | # tä+pä+hän | siitäpähän |
| h | e | lvetti | # ä+nsä | helvettiänsä |

This is an interesting case where the theory of disjunctive ordering interacts with the alternation condition and the theory of markedness to explain a complex set of data. The solution required by the alternation condition, which sets up no more morphophonemes than there are contrasting segment types, therefore not only receives historical support, of the type outlined earlier in this paper, but even purely synchronic support. The special morphophonemes /ɨ/ and /ə/, which are ruled out by the alternation condition, are not only unnecessary, but actually lead to considerable loss of generality in the phonological analysis.[17]

This synchronic evidence is all the more impressive for its convergence in numerous languages. I have only mentioned the Finno-Ugric and Altaic vowel harmony type. But vowel harmony of another type, involving the feature [tense] or [covered] (for the latter term, see Chomsky and Halle 1968: 314) is extremely common in Africa. Here it is the vowel *a* which typically is neutral in the harmony system. In languages such as Ịjǫ (Williamson 1965), Igbirra (Ladefoged 1964), Maasai (Tucker and Mpaayei 1955: 52), Nzema (Chinebuah 1963), and Twi (Fromkin 1965), nine vowels are distinguished in stems: two kinds of *i, e, u, o*, distinguished by the harmonic feature, and an unpaired *a*. In some languages — Nzema is an example — the vowel harmony rule introduces an allophonic harmonic pair for *a*, which never appears distinctively in stems. But it is never the case, to my knowledge, that a morphophonemic distinction needs to be made between two harmonically different *a*'s in stems, which is always neutralized on the phonetic level.

I now turn to the root marker analysis. Relevant to this is the question of velar assimilation in Classical Mongolian. In Lightner's argument for the root marker solution, this phenomenon was one of the main pieces of supporting evidence. Lightner maintained that the root marker solution permits the collapsing into a single rule of two phonological processes in Mongolian: vowel harmony and velar assimilation, by which velars assume front quality before front vowels and back quality before back vowels. Zimmer (1967) pointed out that this will not work, because velars are fronted before any *i*, regardless of whether it occurs in front-harmonic or back-harmonic words.[18] If velar assimilation was stated together with a vowel harmony rule of the kind proposed by Lightner, or one of the kind proposed by Zimmer and Bach, it would front velars only before those *i*'s that occur in front vowel words while making the velars before the other *i*'s incorrectly back in articulation. The only order of rules by which the correct results are reached in this solution is the following:

1. Vowel harmony
2. ɨ → i
3. Velar assimilation

The necessarily intervening rule 2 prevents the collapsing of vowel harmony and velar assimilation and thereby deprives Lightner's solution of the main virtue which he originally claimed for it. However, if the treatment of vowel harmony which I defend is adopted, and in particular, if no underlying /ɨ/ is set up in the morphophonemic inventory, this difficulty in combining vowel harmony with velar assimilation disappears. To the extent, then, that there are independent and good reasons to combine vowel harmony and velar assimilation in the same rule, there is additional support for my solution to vowel harmony, which is the only one in which they can be combined.

We would be justified in concluding that velar assimilation and vowel harmony in Mongolian are truly related processes if it were a general tendency for vowel harmony to be associated with related consonant harmony processes. There are in fact parallel cases in other languages. Esako and Diola-Fogny, two African languages with so-called 'tense-lax' vowel harmony, reportedly also have concomitant consonant harmony. Consonants have tense allophones in the presence of tense vowels (Sapir 1965:5; and see especially the phonetic description of Esako by Laver 1967). It is probably not a coincidence that consonants are susceptible to assimilation in exactly the same feature as vowels in these very different types of cases. I see in this both general confirmation of my analysis of vowel harmony as a form of true assimilation, and specific support for combining velar assimilation and vowel harmony in Mongolian. Then consonant assimilation, too, becomes a positive argument in favor of the analysis required by the alternation condition.

A general criticism of the root-marker theory, which was pointed out by Bach, is strong enough to refute it, even if there were no other considerations involved at all. What is the root marker GRAVE? Not a phonological feature, certainly — this is just what is expressly denied. It is an abstract feature attached to the stem, which Lightner likens to the feature [± animate]. This is not a good comparison. The feature [animate] is a syntactically and semantically justifiable feature which unlike GRAVE has a fixed universal interpretation in semantic theory. The unique thing about GRAVE is that it is always mapped directly onto the phonological feature [± back]. The oddity of this state of affairs is somewhat camouflaged by giving the abstract feature GRAVE the same name as the phonological feature [± grave] and distinguishing it only by the typographical trick of capitalization. This pun should not be permitted to blind us to the fact that the theory expresses no connection between the abstract feature GRAVE and the corresponding phonological feature, apart from the purely arbitrary one contained in the mapping rule of vowel harmony.

The root marker solution to vowel harmony is quite reminiscent of the general approach of fully abstract phonology. Fudge (1967), a representative of this line of thought, has in fact presented an analysis of the Hungarian vowel system which is formally similar to the root marker solution, without, however, attempting to give any actual evidence for it, apart from the general defense of abstractness which I discussed in § 1.

There remain some purely notational points brought up by Zimmer which lend apparent support to the root-marker solution. Zimmer mentions three of these. The first is that the vowel harmony rule mentions fewer features if its environment is a root marker than if its environment is the first or any specific vowel of the root. I find this a trifling objection, as does Zimmer, and will not discuss it here. It is pointless to define evaluation measures until we know what kinds of phonological descriptions we want them to select. The other two points raised by Zimmer are more serious.

One concerns languages which have both prefixes and suffixes, in which any vowel harmony rule except a root-marker rule would apparently have to be very complex, with the change taking place both before and after the root under conditions which would be essentially the mirror images of each other. But the problem of mirror-image rules exists even apart from vowel harmony and must be solved for the general case. It is in fact particularly characteristic of assimilatory processes. For example, Grassmann's Law in Greek, a regressive dissimilation of aspiration, is paralleled by a similar but progressive dissimilation which deaspirates suffixes after stems which contain aspirates: *khú-tlon* but *géne-thlon*. A notational convention for dealing with such phenomena has been worked out by Bach (1968), and has been generalized for syntax and semantics by Langacker (1969). Denoting reversal of the structural analysis by an asterisk, we can say that a rule of the form

$$A \rightarrow B \ / \ *\#c_1 c_2 \ldots c_n \underline{\quad\quad} d_1 d_2 \ldots d_n$$

is applicable both in the environment

$$c_1 c_2 \ldots c_n \underline{\quad\quad} d_1 d_2 \ldots d_n$$

and in the environment

$$d_n \ldots d_2 d_1 \underline{\quad\quad} c_n \ldots c_2 c_1$$

For example, in German, a nonprimary stress becomes a secondary stress either before a nonprimary stress followed by a primary stress (*hȁlbtȍt*, but *der hȁlbtȍte Mȁnn*) or after a nonprimary stress which is preceded by a primary stress (*Hȍchdȅutsch*, but *Ȁlthȍchdȅutsch*). For the expected stress sequence 1 2 3 we get 1 3 2, and for 3 2 1 we get 2 3 1. In Kiparsky (1966) this rule (rule Dii) was stated in the form

$$[ >1 \text{ stress}] \rightarrow [ \ 2 \text{ stress}] \ / < [ \ 1 \text{ stress}] \ X > \underline{\quad\quad} < Y \ [ \ 1 \text{ stress}] >$$

$$\text{where X, Y} = [- \text{stress}]_0^n \quad [+ \text{stress}] \quad [- \text{stress}]_0^n$$

with an ad hoc notation of angled brackets to indicate inclusive disjunction. With the mirror-image convention, the rule can be stated in the form

$$[1 \text{ stress}] \rightarrow [2 \text{ stress}] \ / \ *[1 \text{ stress}] \ [- \text{stress}]_0^n \ [+ \text{stress}] \ [- \text{stress}]_0^n \underline{\quad}$$

A second example is rule (Di) in the same article. Further examples will appear below. The mirror-image convention, then, which I will assume is correct, meets Zimmer's second objection, as Bach points out.

Zimmer's third point is that any vowel harmony rule which treats the process as assimilation seems to have to refer to 'the quite irrelevant matter of intervening consonants between vowels'. Here, too, the problem is real enough, but extends far beyond vowel harmony. With the present notation for rules it is generally true that rules referring to accented vowels must refer to the quite irrelevant intervening unstressed vowels, rules referring to vowels must mention irrelevant intervening consonants, and so on. Some convention is needed which allows rules performing a certain operation to allow phonological elements which are *irrelevant* to this process to occur freely interspersed in a string which meets their structural analysis. It is not clear how irrelevance in general is to be characterized. One could assume that segments to which the features mentioned in the structural change are inapplicable could freely intervene (although they could be specifically required to intervene by being mentioned in the rule, and specifically excluded by adding special conditions to the rule). Then, for example, consonants could be ignored in stress rules, because consonants cannot be stressed. Another convention which would have the same result in this case would be that elements of lower sonority than the ones specifically mentioned in the rule could be ignored. This would allow the German stress rule mentioned above to be stated as

$$[1 \text{ stress}] \rightarrow [2 \text{ stress}] \ / \ *[1 \text{ stress}] \ [+ \text{stress}] \underline{\quad}$$

which corresponds exactly to how one would informally state it anyway. There are, of course, other alternatives worth experimenting with. In any case, while Zimmer's third objection cannot be met at present, it is in no way specific to vowel harmony. I therefore consider insufficient the objections against treating vowel harmony as an assimilatory process.

The interesting vowel harmony system of Nez Perce has recently attracted a good deal of attention (Rigsby 1965, Aoki 1966, Chomsky and Halle 1968). The language has five vowels: *i, æ, a, o, u*. The vowels *a, o*, and some *i*'s, form one harmonic set, which Aoki terms *dominant*. The vowels *æ, u*, and the remaining *i*'s, form the other set, which Aoki terms *recessive*. The dominant and recessive vowels are grouped into harmonic pairs as follows:

| Dominant | Recessive |
|----------|-----------|
| a | æ |
| o | u |
| i | i |

Underlying forms of morphemes can contain either dominant or recessive vowels. The presence of even a single morpheme (root or affix) with an underlying dominant vowel in a word triggers vowel harmony in every morpheme of that word. By vowel harmony, recessive vowels turn into the corresponding dominant vowels, i.e. *æ* becomes *a* and *u* becomes *o*. A hypothetical example of the vowel harmony changes would be:

$$\#\ldots æ\ldots a\ldots u\ldots i\ldots\# \rightarrow \#\ldots a\ldots a\ldots o\ldots i\ldots\#$$

The neutral vowel *i*, with two harmonic values, makes this system comparable to that of Hungarian. The added twist, which Nez Perce shares, as far as I know, only with some Paleosiberian languages, is that the harmonic vowel changes do not take place in a single phonological feature.

As in the case of Finno-Ugric vowel harmony, previous morphophonemic solutions have tried to convert the asymmetry introduced by the neutral vowel into underlying symmetry in both possible ways. The fully abstract solution treats all vowels as if they were neutral vowels, and sets up three underlying vowels plus a diacritic feature. The fully concrete solution treats vowel harmony as if it were phonologically determined throughout, splitting the neutral vowel into two phonologically differentiated underlying segments, and so getting six underlying vowels. Both of these solutions conflict with the approach advocated in this paper, which requires that what is phonologically predictable should in fact be predicted phonologically, and what is not phonologically predictable should be treated by means of diacritic features. The alternation condition claims that the underlying vowels are the five actually contrasting ones /i æ a o u/, and that vowel harmony is phonologically conditioned except for /i/. In the following, I will outline each of these three alternatives, and show that the one which is compatible with the alternation condition is at least as natural as the others and even somewhat simpler, for whatever that is worth.

*Solution 1.* The fully abstract solution was proposed by Aoki (1966) and worked out in detail by Chomsky and Halle (1968: 377), whose version I give here. They propose an underlying three-vowel system /i u a/, and a categorization of all morphemes into two harmonic classes by some diacritic feature such as [± dominant] (in their treatment the feature is called [± H], but I shall continue using Aoki's term 'dominant' to avoid confusing the reader). They propose a readjustment rule which distributes the feature [+ dominant] to all segments of a word which contains any [+ dominant] morpheme in it:

$$[+\ \text{segment}] \rightarrow [+\ \text{dominant}]\ /\ \begin{Bmatrix}\#\ X\ [+\ \text{dominant}]\ Y\ \_\_\_\_\\ \_\_\_\_\ Z\ [+\ \text{dominant}]\ W\ \#\end{Bmatrix}$$

With the mirror-image convention Chomsky and Halle's rule must be stated in the form:

$$[+ \text{segment}] \rightarrow [+ \text{dominant}] \quad /^* \ \# \ X \ [+ \text{dominant}] \ Y \ \underline{\quad}$$

The vowel harmony rule now turns *a* to *æ* in [- dominant] words, and *u* to *o* in [+ dominant] words:

$$
V \rightarrow
\begin{cases}
[-\text{back}] & / & \begin{bmatrix} \underline{\qquad} \\ +\text{low} \\ -\text{dominant} \end{bmatrix} \\[2em]
[-\text{high}] & / & \begin{bmatrix} \underline{\qquad} \\ +\text{back} \\ +\text{dominant} \end{bmatrix}
\end{cases}
$$

*Solution 2.* The corresponding fully concrete solution would set up six underlying vowels. Just how dominant and recessive *i* are to be phonologically distinguished is somewhat arbitrary synchronically. The simplest solution, and, as I will argue, the one which reflects the history, is to set up dominant *i* as mid back unrounded /ə/:[19]

| Dominant | Recessive |
|----------|-----------|
| a | æ |
| o | u |
|   | i |

No readjustment rule is needed, and the vowel harmony rule can be stated, using the mirror-image convention, as follows:

$$
V \rightarrow
\begin{bmatrix} +\text{back} \\ -\text{high} \end{bmatrix}
\quad /^* \#
\begin{bmatrix} X & +\text{back} \\ & -\text{high} \end{bmatrix}
Y \underline{\quad}
$$

A later neutralization rule, however, must still turn /ə/, which appears in underlying representations, and of which additional instances result from the application of the above vowel harmony rule, into phonetic [i]:

$$
\begin{bmatrix} -\text{low} \\ -\text{round} \end{bmatrix}
\rightarrow
\begin{bmatrix} -\text{back} \\ +\text{high} \end{bmatrix}
$$

*Solution 3.* If the five-vowel system /i æ a o u/, to which I am committed by the alternation condition, is taken as basic, not only the readjustment rule required in the fully abstract solution, but also the neutralization rule /ə/ → [i] required in the fully concrete solution, can now be eliminated from the phonology, and the whole process of vowel harmony can be accounted for by the single rule

$$\begin{bmatrix} \alpha \text{ back} \\ \alpha \text{ high} \end{bmatrix} \rightarrow \begin{bmatrix} + \text{ back} \\ - \text{ high} \end{bmatrix} /^* \text{ \# } X \begin{bmatrix} \alpha \text{ back} \\ - \alpha \text{ high} \end{bmatrix} Y \underline{\quad}$$

where the mirror-image convention is used as before. This rule turns *u* to *o* and *æ* to *a* in words containing *i, a,* and *o*. Morphemes with [- dominant] *i*-vowels can be marked as not undergoing this rule, so that the rule will only be sensitive to [+ dominant] *i*-vowels. This solution owes its simplicity to the fact that it handles the vowel changes in the most direct possible way, without either setting up diacritic features where an equivalent phonetic contrast exists, or setting up underlying phonological distinctions which have to be undone where there is no phonetic contrast.

Now the question arises whether the Nez Perce system is historically older or younger than the three-vowel system of the related Sahaptin language, which has no vowel harmony. The correspondences between the Nez Perce and Sahaptin vowels are the following:

| Nez Perce | i | æ | a | o | u |
|---|---|---|---|---|---|
| Sahaptin | i | | a | | u |

On the face of it, one could either suppose that the Nez Perce harmonic pairs had merged to give the Sahaptin system, or that Nez Perce had somehow developed out of an original three-vowel system. The alternation condition gives an unequivocal answer to this historical problem: Nez Perce is conservative relative to Sahaptin. The opposite assumption would involve split by reversal of absolute neutralization, a change which, as we saw in § 3, does not appear to occur in languages. We shall see that there is excellent confirmation for the conclusion that vowel harmony is an old feature of Sahaptian (the family of which Nez Perce and Sahaptin are the only surviving representatives).

In fact, we can reconstruct for Proto-Sahaptian a more complete system of vowel harmony than the Nez Perce one, in which what corresponds to dominant *i* in Nez Perce contrasted as ə with its recessive harmonic counterpart *i*. The Proto-Sahaptian system was, then, that of Solution 2 above, minus the neutralization rule ə → *i*. The evidence for this is threefold:

(1) *Phonetic plausibility:* the reconstructed system gives a rationale for what otherwise seems like a phonetically arbitrary system of harmonic alternations. The system will be seen to be one of velar harmony.

(2) *Sahaptin palatalization:* Rigsby and Silverstein have found that velars undergo palatalization in Sahaptin before the counterparts of Nez Perce *æ* and recessive *i*, but not before *u, o, a,* and dominant *i* (= our ə). In terms of my reconstruction, this means palatalization before *æ* and *i*, but not before *u, o, a,* and ə: in other words, palatalization *before front vowels.*

(3) *The Chukchi-Kamchadal parallel:* a group of languages spoken in the

easternmost part of Siberia show a system of vowel harmony of just the form I reconstruct for Proto-Sahaptian, not only as regards the vowel alternations, but also as regards the dominant-recessive pairing and the fact that harmony is caused by both roots and affixes. The similarity is too great to be a coincidence.

(1) *Phonetic plausibility.* The harmonic alternations which, according to my proposal, obtained in Proto-Sahaptian can be diagrammed as follows:[20]

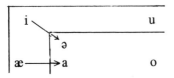

We can distinguish two main kinds of vowel harmony according to whether the harmony affects *manner of articulation* (rounding, tenseness, nasalization) or *place of articulation*. The two previously known kinds of place harmony are what we may call, in Jakobson's terms, *vertical harmony* (front-back alternations, as in the Finno-Ugric languages) and *horizontal harmony* (high-low alternations, as in Gilyak[21]). The Sahaptian-Chukchi type is a third type, *diagonal harmony*. The system is not arbitrary as has been thought. Rather, it shows the horizontal and vertical dimensions interacting. Germanic umlaut is comparable as a kind of diagonal harmony going in the opposite direction and conditioned by suffixes:

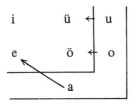

The Sahaptian-Chukchi type of vowel harmony is attraction towards *a*, home plate on the vowel diamond as it were, and umlaut is attraction towards *i*.

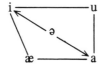

Examples of *u*-umlaut also exist, as in Germanic. Though it is clear what the fourth possibility, *æ*-umlaut, would look like, it does not appear to occur in languages. Perhaps this is not an accidental gap.

(2) *Sahaptin palatalization.* Rigsby and Silverstein (1969) have discovered the important fact that although Sahaptin has only three contrasting vowels, *i, a, u,* it has palatalization of velars in an environment which etymologically corresponds to Nez Perce *æ* and recessive *i.* In Sahaptin, the situation is synchronically as follows. The velars *k* and *k'* are palatalized to *c* and *c',* respectively, before the unrounded vowels *i* and *a* (a consonant may optionally intervene). But the palatalization does not take place *in any morpheme* of a word that contains at least one of a certain class of morphemes, synchronically arbitrary in Sahaptin, but etymologically as a rule corresponding to the dominant morphemes of Nez Perce. The simplest and most direct solution, and at the same time the one which is compatible with the alternation condition, sets up a three-vowel system /i a u/ and handles palatalization by the rule:

$$\begin{bmatrix} C \\ + \text{high} \end{bmatrix} \rightarrow [\text{- back}] \ / \ \underline{\quad} \ (C) \begin{bmatrix} V \\ - \text{rounded} \end{bmatrix} /^* \ \# \ X \ \underline{\quad}$$

The morphemes which do not undergo palatalization, and whose appearance in a word also stops palatalization from taking place anywhere in that word, are marked as exceptions to palatalization. The formulation of the rule given above ensures that any such morpheme, wherever it appears in the word, will always be included in the structural analysis of the rule, and so block the rule from applying anywhere in that word.

The Palouse dialect of Sahaptin, which is geographically close to Nez Perce, possesses, according to Rigsby and Silverstein, both the Sahaptin palatalization and the five-vowel system of Nez Perce with its vowel harmony. This dialect will therefore have both the vowel harmony rule given earlier, and a palatalization rule. The palatalization rule of Palouse is somewhat different from that of the other Sahaptin dialects, as palatalization is in part phonologically predictable in Palouse, because of the richer vowel system which this dialect preserves:

$$\begin{bmatrix} C \\ + \text{high} \end{bmatrix} \rightarrow [\text{- back}] \ / \underline{\quad} (C) \begin{bmatrix} V \\ - \text{rounded} \end{bmatrix} /^* \ X \begin{bmatrix} \alpha \ \text{back} \\ -\alpha \ \text{high} \end{bmatrix} Y \underline{\quad}$$

For Palouse, furthermore, the generalization appears to hold that the recessive *i*'s block palatalization. This can be stated by a lexical redundancy rule which links the exceptions to the vowel harmony rule and the exceptions to the palatalization rule in the following dependency:

$$[ \alpha \text{ palatalization}] \rightarrow [ -\alpha \text{ vowel harmony}]$$

Historically, Sahaptin palatalization is clear evidence that vowel harmony was more complete in Proto-Sahaptin than it is in any of the attested dialects. That dominant *i* does not cause palatalization, whereas recessive *i* does, indicates that they were once phonetically distinct. Furthermore, it allows us to deduce what the phonetic distinction was. Palatalization took place before *\*æ*, but not before *\*u \*o \*a* — before front vowels, as is normal. Recessive *\*i* also caused palatalization, as expected. Its dominant counterpart did not; therefore it was not a front vowel. And my analysis of vowel harmony in fact makes it a retracted *\*ə*.

(3) *The Chukchi-Kamchadal parallel.* The Chukchi-Kamchadal family of Paleosiberian languages (Skorik 1968a), spoken in a large area from the Bering Straits to the middle of the Kamchatka Peninsula, and so facing Alaska directly across the Bering Sea, has vowel harmony systems directly comparable to the Sahaptian one.[22] Chukchi (Skorik 1961) has three recessive vowels, *e, i, u*, and three dominant vowels, *a, E, o*. In addition, there is a neutral vowel *ə*. Recessive *e* and dominant *E* appear to be phonetically distinct. Recessive *e* is simply a mid front vowel, but I cannot make out for sure the nature of *E*, which is why I capitalize it here. Skorik (1961: 23) describes it as somewhat lower and more back than *e* and says 'like Russian *exo*, only lower'; according to Bogoras (1922: 643), it is 'the open *e* of *hell*, but long'. Presumably Bogoras picked a word in final -*l* in order to indicate the velarization of the vowel. Bogoras describes vowel harmony ('ablaut') as follows (646): 'When, in composition, weak vowels and strong vowels [i.e. recessive vowels and dominant vowels] come together in the same word, the former are changed by the ablaut into strong vowels.' The harmonic pairs are the following:

| Dominant | Recessive |
| --- | --- |
| a | e |
| o | u |
| E | i |

The change of recessive into dominant vowels takes place in the entire word when it contains even a single morpheme with a dominant vowel. This is, then, almost identical with the Proto-Sahaptian system as I propose to reconstruct it. The only differences concern phonetic detail: the recessive counterpart to *a* is lower in Nez Perce than in Chukchi (*æ* versus *e*), and dominant *E* in Chukchi appears to be a somewhat retracted, lowered [ɛ] instead of the *\*ə* which I reconstruct for Proto-Sahaptian. The neutral vowel *ə* of Chukchi is of transparently late origin (Bogoras 1922: 649-650).

A similar, but more restricted system is found in Koryak (Bogoras 1922: 671; Zhukova 1968a) and, somewhat modified and applying still more restrictedly, in Kamchadal (Bolodin and Zhukova 1968). It has been lost completely in Alyutor (Zhukova 1968b) and Koryak (Skorik 1968b). These two languages have, as a result of the loss of vowel harmony, ended up with a three-vowel system /i a u/ — exactly as happened in Sahaptin.

The reconstruction of Proto-Sahaptian vowel harmony proposed above is supported by its near-identity with the actually attested Chukchi-Kamchadal vowel harmony regardless of how we explain that near-identity. At the very least there is a typological parallel to show the naturalness of the reconstructed system. But it cannot be accidental that the Sahaptian languages are spoken in the Northwestern United States, and the Chukchi-Kamchadal languages are spoken in the Northeastern Soviet Union. In view of the well-known cultural contacts across the Bering Sea one could assume a historical identity between the two vowel harmony systems. The existence of standard types of vowel harmony in Africa (covered or tense as the alternating feature) and in Eurasia (fronting of vowels) shows that diffusion of vowel harmony rules frequently occurs even among unrelated languages. The same can have taken place between Chukchi-Kamchadal and Sahaptian. This particular case of diffusion must be fairly recent, because of the relative transparency and detailed similarity of the systems on both continents.

## 6. Conclusions

Vowel harmony systems are of special interest, because many of their apparently quite strange features can be explained by the complex interaction of several rich and detailed phonological universals. Neither markedness, nor the alternation condition, nor disjunctive ordering, were set up with vowel harmony in mind. Yet they jointly lead to just the right solutions in many different kinds of cases. Unless some version of the alternation condition regulates the relation between morphophonemic and phonetic representation, there is no basis, in the present theory of generative phonology, for choosing any one of the several possible kinds of analyses of vowel harmony. The alternation condition determines a specific choice in each case, and insofar as we can tell from both synchronic and historical evidence, it is the right choice.

The alternation condition embodies a claim about *the importance of phonetics in phonology*. It leads to underlying forms which are closely tailored to their phonetic realizations. Quite analogously, recent work in syntax is showing the importance of semantics in syntax, and is leading to deep structure representations which are close to semantic representations. It is only to be expected that progress in linguistics should consist of reducing the abstract part of language, the part consisting of the various theoretical constructs which must be set up to mediate between the concrete levels of phonetics and meaning, the only aspects of language which can be directly observed.

The desirability of this result, however, cannot alone justify it. We have seen that in many cases, the alternation condition leads to significant synchronic generalizations. The superficial, relatively concrete analyses enforced by the alternation condition are often the ones which turn out to have the greatest generality and explanatory value. Vowel harmony systems are probably the clearest illustration of the merits of hugging the phonetic ground in morphophonemic description in the specific respect that I have proposed; in other cases, while no particular gains in generality are made, the alternation condition eliminates an area of arbitrariness inherent in the present theory of generative phonology. There appear to be no cases where much generality is lost because of the alternation condition. But even if there were such cases, the historical evidence which supports this condition strikes me as sufficiently strong to establish it even in the face of all synchronic considerations.

## Notes

1.     *I am very grateful to Bohdan Saciuk for pointing out to me that some scholars consider the Ukranian [ǯ] forms to be old, rather than innovations, and for referring me to an article by N.J. Mirčuk (1964), containing dialect material, and references (85) to other treatments of the question.

     In any case, the phenomenon of rule loss, with the attendant split of phonological segments, is by now well documented. I would venture to suggest that questions like that of Ukrainian [ǯ] can be fruitfully studied by comparing typologically parallel developments in other languages. For example, Pavle Ivić, in a lecture entitled "Sound laws and the distinctive power of phonological patterns", given at the Linguistic Institute at the Ohio State University, 1970, presented an analogous case of rule loss in Western Serbo-Croatian dialects (see also Ivić (1958: 152, 194-195, 256-257)). In Serbo-Croatian, the dentals *t, d* are palatalized in certain environments, and the voiced *d'* is further turned to *j* (i.e. the palatal glide). Thus, the passive participles of *platiti* 'pay' and *osuditi* 'condemn' are *plaćen* and *osujen*. In the dialects in question, the *j* that is derived from *d > d'* reverts to *d'* (*đ* in the usual spelling). Thus, we might set up

|  | plat + i + en | osud + i + en |
|---|---|---|
|  | plat'en | osud'en |
| palatalization |  |  |
| d' → j | —— | osujen |

and characterize the innovating dialects with *osud'en* as having lost the rule *d' → j*. Interestingly, the *j* again remains in isolated words like *meja* 'boundary', presumably for the same reason that *z* remains in the cognate Ukrainian *meža*, namely, that the consonant, though historically derived by palatalization from *d*, has become lexicalized where it does not alternate with *d* in a paradigm.

2.     Former /g/ appears as [γ] in Ukrainian, and there is no reason to give it an underlying form that differs from this constant phonetic form, as far as I know. The

justification for analyzing isolated instances of [ž], where no [γ] or [d] appears in related forms, as morphophonemic /ž/, will become clear in the course of this discussion.

3. That all these are natural changes has been argued in Kiparsky (1968a).

4. Another attempt to remedy the deficiencies of current generative phonology is the naturalness condition proposed by David Stampe (1967). It has a rather different effect from the one I develop here.

5. Cf. Lakoff (1965) and Chomsky and Halle (1968) for discussion of the treatment of exceptions.

6. It is nonarbitrary in the present theory only when it happens that several segments in the same morpheme must be categorized differently as to whether they do or do not undergo some phonological process.

7. *An objection to this idea was raised by J. Harris (1969b: 223-226). This objection was that it is sometimes necessary to say that morphemes are exceptional in that they do not *trigger* a process (and not that they fail to undergo it). However, Kisseberth (1970d), and Coats (1970) have independently suggested that it is necessary to distinguish two ways in which a morpheme can be marked as an exception: either as an input to the rule or as an environment. If this proposal is accepted, Harris' point no longer holds. Cf. Bechert (1971).

8. *This study, 'The inflectional accent in Indo-European', is now in press in *Language* [see Kiparsky (1973c) of the bibliography of this volume].

9. *Briefly, the only real work done by /ε/ in SPE disappears if we say that words like *tolerance, eminence* end in -*i*, which is deleted in certain lexical items by a rule which applies after the *t → s* rule. Words like *economy, synonymy* are marked as not subject to the rule. It is now possible to say that the many doublets of the type *eminence/eminency, competence/competency* have the same morphological structure, and are differentiated only by whether the final vowel is marked in the lexicon as being subject to deletion. Surely this is preferable to the SPE analysis, which implies that such doublets involve a massive alternation between two derivational suffixes /i/ and /ε/, one of which is composed of a phoneme which occurs nowhere else in the language and is always deleted even in the one place where it supposedly does occur. (At one point (199), Chomsky and Halle also suggest -/ε/ at the end of words like *residue*, but as they themselves note, the only effect which this supposed /ε/ has, that of converting *u* to *ɨ* (*yūw*), can be obtained equally well by making the minimal change in the *u → ɨ* rule of allowing it to apply in the context ___ # as well as ___V).

The final segment in *aristocracy, synonymy, economy, telegraphy, industry* can likewise be analyzed straightforwardly as /i/. Chomsky and Halle (1968: 129) give two reasons for their underlying /y/. The first is that the suffix would be wrongly deleted if it were just /i/, by the rule which drops what Chomsky and Halle claim is a final *i* in words like *bile, reptile, president* (on the strength of derivatives like *bilious, reptilian, presidential*). But this latter assumption is dubious now that Hale has shown that in closely parallel situations in Polynesian and Australian languages, the segment which corresponds to the *i* in the English examples is demonstrably not analyzed as part of the stem, but as part of the suffix (Hale 1973). Thus, *bile* and similar words probably do not end in underlying /i/ at all, and there is no rule deleting final /i/ (other than the already mentioned one which applies *after t → s*). The second argument for /y/ is that /y/ is needed in order to prevent words like *industry* from receiving penultimate stress as e.g. *attorney, inferno* do. But the same result can just as well be obtained in a more direct way by allowing an optional suffix +*i* to stand in the environment of the stress assignment rule. Thus, there is no good reason not to set up just /i/.

As for the contrast between *veto* and *motto*, it is surely not to be traced to an underlying difference between /ɔ/ and /o/ in the second syllable. According to this proposal, *Otto*, rhyming with *motto*, should have /o/ as the second vowel, which is inconsistent with the lengthened [ōw] (not ūw]) in *Ottonian*. More important, there is no relationship between the alleged /ɔ/ : /õ/ contrast and the phonetic difference it is supposed to explain. I suggest rather than the stress difference is due to the fact that the initial syllable is strong in *veto* (likewise *Plato, Nato* etc.) and weak in *motto, ghetto* and similar typically flapped words. Thus the contrast is really the same as that between the secondary stress in *Arab* versus lack of stress in *scarab* that Fidelholtz has discussed in some well-known unpublished work. The contrast between *prĕsĕntàtion* and *prĕsĕntàtion* is derived by Chomsky and Halle in yet a different way (1968: 161). It is not the length of the first syllable which is determined by the stress of the following vowel, itself supposedly derived by the trick of varying the constituent structure arbitrarily, but rather the stress of the second syllable which depends on the length of the first, by an extension of Fidelholtz's rule to polysyllabic words. The length of the first vowel is the primary variable, and represents simply the common free variation of length in open syllables of Latinate words (*eliminate* ~ *Eliminate*, etc.). The *veto/motto* contrast thus falls in with other rhythmic principles of English phonology.

10.    I have discussed morphophonemic analogy and some of the following specific examples of it at greater length in Kiparsky (1968a).

11.    The ultimate outcome of such a split can sometimes come about in other ways. For example, Itkonen (1945) has proposed that back unrounded /ə/ in Vote and Estonian is not inherited from Balto-Finnic, as was generally believed, but is an innovation. The development, as he sketches it, is perfectly compatible with my claim of the irreversibility of absolute neutralization. According to Itkonen, Balto-Finnic had essentially the vowel system of modern Finnish. The vowel ə arose in Vote and Estonian by assimilation in words containing back vowels, e.g. *\*mela* (Finnish *mela* 'oar') > *məla*. This new back vowel ə was then suffixed to neutral vowel roots which took other back vowel suffixes. Neither the sound change which gives ə, nor the analogical extension of ə, contradicts my position. An alternative theory (Kettunen 1960: 114) sets up original Balto-Finnic back unrounded vowels ə, and assumes that they merged with *i* and *e* in Finnish. Cf. Rapola (1966) for a summary and discussion.

The reversal of absolute neutralization proposed by Halle (1962a) has now been analyzed differently by him (Chomsky and Halle 1968).

12.    *See section 3 of Kiparsky (1973a) for further discussion.

13.    A rather different interpretation of the Prague concept of markedness in a theory of generative phonology was given by Stampe (1967).

14.    Actually this is not the base form but an intermediate representation, to which certain rules, irrelevant for present purposes, have already applied.

15.    *According to a rule of October 11, 1945 by the Language Committee of the Finnish Society of Literature, *y* in foreign words is a neutral vowel like *i* and *e*. In practice, however, this ruling is not generally observed. Mauri Levomäki has recently shown that although there is a certain amount of vacillation in mixed harmonic words, *y* is clearly not treated as a neutral vowel on a par with *i, e*, but rather functions as a true harmonic front vowel (Levomäki 1973).

16.    Certain derivatives, such as those in *-uus*, can have back vowel suffixes even when the root contains neutral vowels, e.g. *pit-uus* 'length', *pien-uus* 'smallness' (*pitkä* 'long', *pieni* 'small'). One way of accounting for them would be a readjustment rule which drops the boundary between root and affix. They would thus be treated like single morphemes with respect to vowel harmony.

17.   *For additional analysis of Finnish vowel harmony, see section 3.3 of Kiparsky (1973a).

18.   Cf. Poppe (1960: 16-17):

> Das hintere, tiefe, velar-hinterlinguale *q kam im Altmongolischen vor allen hinteren Vokalen einschliesslich des *i* vor. Im Mittelmongolischen begannen *i* und *i zusammenzufallen und schliesslich ergab *i* ein *i*, so dass der Unterschied zwischen diesen beiden Vokalen nicht mehr spürbar wurde. Dies hatte zur Folge, dass die Silbe *qi* sich zu *ki* verschob. Während in der vorklassischen mongolischen Schriftsprache (also vor dem 17. Jh.) neben *ki* auch *qi* vorkam, hat das klassische Schriftmongolische nur *ki*, d.h. sowohl in vorder- als auch in hintervokalischen Stämmen. Die Silbe *ki* ist hinsichtlich der Lautharmonie sozusagen neutral geworden.

19.   *The same analysis was independently proposed in Jacobsen (1968). See also Zwicky (1970a).

20.   My analysis of Nez Perce vowel harmony as a kind of velar harmony is confirmed by the observation of Velten (cited from Aoki 1966: 759) that 'verbs with final suffixes containing a velar consonant (i.e. *g* or *x*) appear only with the vowels *a, o, i.*' In other words, velars act like the dominant vowels. This has obvious implications for distinctive feature theory.

21.   Cf. Panfilov (1962: 17-20). This language shows harmonic alternations between high and low vowels:

The process appears to be residual and unproductive in the present-day form of the language.

22.   I am grateful to Wayles Browne for calling my attention to the vowel harmony systems of these languages.

# Chapter 7

# Productivity in Phonology*

R. Skousen (1972) points out that 'by just looking at static data, there is no way at present for a linguist to determine what regularities speakers will capture'. He proposes that linguists (at least phonologists) should look at external evidence, such as language acquisition and language change, in order to determine what sorts of grammars are 'psychologically real'. In his paper, Skousen examines some putative rules of Finnish from this point of view, and concludes that they do not exist in the synchronic Finnish phonological system.

I completely agree with Skousen on the need for this line of research in phonology. However, I think that there is more to the Finnish data than Skousen brings out. The purpose of this chapter is to take a closer look at it, and to point out further facts, which reverse Skousen's conclusions. This re-examination has some general interest, since it illustrates pitfalls inherent in the use of historical evidence, and, more positively, since one of the specific examples turns out to bear unexpectedly on the question whether phonological rules are ordered, raised anew recently by several people.

Skousen is surely right when he says that a phonological rule is real if 'surface violations' of it (i.e. cases of opacity of type (i), cf. Kiparsky 1971) arising, e.g. by borrowing, or by the operation of other rules, tend to get eliminated. But the converse claim, also made by Skousen, that a rule is *not* real if surface violations of a rule do not tend to become eliminated, is too strong.

First, the failure of a specific change to occur in a specific language at a specific period means nothing, since no one has been able to show conditions under which a change, however natural, *must* take place.[1] Negative historical evidence must take the form of a *universal* statement to be of any value. A statement of the form: 'changes of type X never occur' needs a linguistic explanation, but a statement of the form: 'change X did not occur in language L at time T', in our present state of knowledge,

*    This paper was supported in part by a grant from the National Institutes of Mental Health (Grant number 2-PO1-MH13390-06).

does not. Hence, the failure of surface violations of a rule to be eliminated is no proof that the rule is a linguist's figment.

Second, all 'surface violations' of a rule need not be exceptions to it, and if they are not, there is no reason why they should become eliminated. One of Skousen's examples is the Finnish rule

(1)      $t \rightarrow s / \_i$

which accounts for, e.g. /vete/→*vesi* 'water', /halut+i/→*halusi* 'wanted'. It is quite true that words like *äiti* 'mother', *neiti* 'Miss', *tippa* 'drop' do not tend to turn into *\*äisi, \*neisi, \*sippa*. They are not felt as being phonologically deviant at all. But this does not justify Skousen's conclusion that rule (1) does not exist, and that speakers simply memorize several alternate forms for each stem, e.g. *vesi vete(+nä)*, as well as the lists of suffixes before which each stem form occurs. For rule (1) is a morphophonemic and not a phonetic rule, and there are indications that morphophonemic rules can apply only to *derived* forms (Kiparsky 1973a, section 2). Words like *äiti* are therefore not exceptions to this morphophonemic process, and there is no reason to expect their *t* to become *s*.

Aside from this, however, it seems that the Finnish rules in question *are* proved to be psychologically real by just the sort of historical evidence whose existence Skousen denies.

One rule discussed by Skousen is the rule of consonant gradation, which weakens single stops and geminate stops in the onset of closed syllables:

(2)      a.  p  →  v  
          t  →  d  
          k  →  ∅     } / _ VC  { C  
      b.  pp  →  p              #  
          tt  →  t  
          kk  →  k  }

Skousen denies the reality of rule (2) on the grounds that new words entering the language allegedly do not undergo it, and on the grounds that the rule does not adjust to new phonological changes which feed or bleed it. But examples of both kinds do exist, as far as degemination (part (b) of rule (2)) is concerned. For example, loanwords like *Kalkutta* 'Calcutta' are inflected in accordance with rule (2), e.g. gen. *Kalkutan*, iness. *Kalkutassa*, ess. *Kalkuttana*, etc. Even morpheme-internally there is a tendency to adjust violations of (2), which shows that it is close to being a phonetic rather than morphophonemic process.[2]

A phonological change which bleeds (2) is the change of the inessive suffix -*ssa* to -*sa* in some dialects, e.g. *kädessä→kädesä (käresä)*. The reduced inessive -*sa* continues to take stems in the gradated form, as if it still formed a closed syllable. This, according to Skousen, again shows that the gradation rule is not real. However, Kettunen (1960) cites some interesting facts from Votic, a closely related language in which the inessive -*ssa* also went to -*sa*. Here part (a) of the gradation rule continues to work as if -*sa* still closed the syllable, e.g. *rinta+sa→rinnaza*[3] 'in the breast', but part (b), the degemination rule, has 'caught up' with the new form of the suffix and fails to apply, e.g. /nokka+sa/→*nokkaza* 'in the beak' (not *\*nokaza*, which would be the historically expected form). It seems reasonable to assume that after the change of -*ssa* to -*sa* (e.g., /nokka+ssa/ →*\*nokassa→\*nokaza*), the degemination rule (2b) adjusted to the new inessive suffix (*\*nokaza→nokkaza*). This would be a case of opacity of type (ii) (Kiparsky 1971) being eliminated.

This kind of evidence does not exist, to my knowledge, for the other branch of consonant gradation. Undoubtedly the different behavior of the two parts of consonant gradation is related to the fact that degemination has hardly any exceptions, whereas loanwords, proper names, acronyms, etc. tend to be exceptions to plain weakening (Kiparsky 1971).

Historical evidence for the reality of the *t→s* rule is buried more deeply, but digging it up has proved to be well worth the effort. There is one form class where the rule does seem to have been extended to new cases meeting its structural analysis which arose after the rule entered the language: the past tense forms of vowel stem verbs. In these cases the vowel of the stem contracts, under certain conditions, with the past tense suffix -*i* into *i*, viz. *a+i→i, ä+i→i, e+i→i*. If this contracted *i* is preceded by *t*, it remains *t* in some words, and turns to *s* in others, with some verbs showing both forms. E.g.,

| | |
|---|---|
| /piirtä+i/→*\*piirti→piirsi* | 'drew' |
| /pitä+i/ → *piti* (↛*\*pisi*) | 'held' |
| /kiitä+i/→ *kiiti~kiisi* | 'sped' |

Historians of the Finnish language hold that the *s* forms are 'regular' and the *t* forms 'analogical'. That is, they view the historical chronology as being:

1. contraction
2. t→s

Forms like *piti*, according to this view, have secondarily reintroduced the *t*, replacing an earlier *\*pisi*. This is the view of Hakulinen (1961: 51) and Rapola (1966: 236-237), two standard reference works on the history of Finnish.

On looking at the facts, I can find nothing to substantiate this chronology. But I do find a certain amount of evidence for the opposite chronology:

1.    t→s
2.    contraction

On this chronology, it is rather forms like *piirsi* which are secondary, representing an extension of the *t→s* rule to the new *i*'s that came from contraction. Forms like *\*pisi*, therefore, never existed at all. In the following paragraphs I will give four arguments for this view.

(1) As Wiik (1967) has pointed out, the vacillation between *t* and *s* is *only* found before *contracted i* in the past tense. Before *uncontracted i* in the past, the *t→s* change takes place without exception, in Standard Finnish as well as in dialects and older Finnish. E.g.,

| /halut+i/ | →*halusi* | 'wanted' |
| /hakkat+i/ | →*hakkasi* | 'hewed' |
| /turpot+i/ | →*turposi* | 'swelled' |

These verbs are consonant stems, cf. pp. /halut+nut/→*halunnut*, 3p. imper. /halut +koon/→*halutkoon* contrasting with *piïrtänyt, piirtäköön*. Hence, their stem-final *t* precedes the *i* in the underlying representation, and no contraction is involved. Wiik notes that these verbs always undergo *t→s*, but carefully refrains from drawing any historical conclusions from this fact. However, it is fair to ask how this distribution could be explained. Under the usual historical assumptions I can see no explanation for the failure of *halusi* to become *\*haluti* in the same way that *\*pisi* (with *i<äi*) supposedly became *piti*. Whether the suffix vowel is contracted or not should make no difference if the analogy goes from *s* to *t*. If we start from (noncontracted) *halusi* but (contracted) *piti, kiiti, \*piirti*, i.e. if *t→s* came before contraction, then subsequent sporadic extension of *t→s* to the new contracted *i*'s gives us exactly the observed distribution in the imperfect.

(2) It is possible to gain some idea of the general direction of change by looking at earlier attested stages of Finnish, and by checking for productivity in the modern language. The forms cited from 16th and 17th century authors in Rapola (1933: 188) differ from the modern forms in having more cases of *t*: *pyysi, pysi ~ pyyti, pijijti, pyti* 'asked' (Standard Finnish *pyysi*), *hwsi ~ huuti, hwti, huudit, hwdhit, hwdit* 'shouted' (Standard Finnish *huusi, huusivat*), *löysi ~ löyti* 'found' (Standard Finnish *löysi*), *parandi* 'healed' (Standard Finnish *paransi*), *rakendi* 'built' (Standard Finnish *rakensi*), *wäänsin ~ wäännin* 'twisted' (Standard Finnish

*väänsin*), *wotij* 'leaked' (Standard Finnish *vuoti* ~ *vuosi*). The same is true for the language of the Kalevala. Penttilä (1963: 137) gives the following examples: *huuti* 'shouted' (Standard Finnish *huusi*), *kielti* 'denied' (Standard Finnish *kielsi*), *käänti* 'turned' (Standard Finnish *käänsi*), *lenti* 'flew' (Standard Finnish *lensi*), *kujerti* 'cooed' (Standard Finnish *kujersi*), *kumarti* 'bowed' (Standard Finnish *kumarsi*), *masenti* 'depressed' (Standard Finnish *masensi*), *murti* 'broke' (Standard Finnish *mursi*), *paranti* 'healed' (Standard Finnish *paransi*), *sivalti* 'chopped' (Standard Finnish *sivalsi*), *syventi* 'deepened' (Standard Finnish *syvensi*), *vuoti* 'leaked' (Standard Finnish *vuoti* ~ *vuosi*), *väänti* 'twisted' (Standard Finnish *väänsi)*.

In one type of case only does Standard Finnish have *-ti* as against older *-si*: when the stem ends in underlying /-kt/. Here *t* originally went to *s*, as in *läksi* 'went', current in older Finnish (Rapola 1933: 188) but now dialectal or obsolescent and replaced by *lähti* (where *k→h* before *t* by a general rule of Finnish phonology). There is a general curtailment of the rule in the case of this cluster, even before *i* from *e* in word-final position, where *t→s* is otherwise regular, as in nouns like *lahti* 'cove, bay' from older *\*laksi* (underlying /lakte/.). The rule remains in operation only in the numerals *yksi* 'one' and *kaksi* 'two'. The situation after *k* is special in that *t→s* does not take place after any other obstruents. The rule must be specifically blocked after *h*, *s* and *t* (*p* does not occur before *t*). Hence /kt/→*ks* is a really anomalous case, which is drifting out of the language.

The above lists of examples from older Finnish are not complete, but they are presumably representative. Throughout, the older language has *less* instances of *t→s*. Apart from the special case of *kt→ks*, I have not found any examples of the contrary case, i.e. past forms which have *-ti* in Standard Finnish but *-si* in the older language. Unless a more thorough investigation of older Finnish reverses these findings, we may conclude that *t* is on the way *out*, not in. This direction of drift is contrary to what the accepted chronology implies, and rather agrees with the opposite chronology which I have proposed.

In the synchronic system of contemporary Finnish, it is again *s* and not *t* which is the productive type. It is, first of all, far more frequent. Moreover, as has often been noted (e.g. Itkonen 1966: 202), many of the verbs retaining *t* do so 'because' *s* would result in ambiguity, e.g. *kynti* 'plowed' (inf. *kyntää*), cf. *kynsi* 'scratched (with nails)' (inf. *kynsiä*); *nouti* 'fetched' (inf. *noutaa*), cf. *nousi* 'rose' (inf. *nousta*); *kuti* 'spawned' (inf. *kutea*), cf. *kusi* 'pissed' (inf. *kusta*). The latter also belongs to a second predictable group of *t*-verbs: those with short initial syllables, e.g. *syti* 'throbbed', *päti* 'was valid', *iti* 'germinated', *veti* 'drew', *kyti* 'smoldered', *poti* 'was ill with'. In general, *-ti*-verbs are a closed set. All verbs with productive derivative suffixes in *-t* take *-si*, including recent neologisms like *valmentaa* 'train (in sports)', *täsmentää* 'make precise', *asentaa* 'install', coined in this century (Hakulinen 1961). These facts in themselves suffice to refute Skousen's challenge.

(3) Rapola (1966: 236) reports a remarkable fact about the regional dialects of Lower Satakunta. Here disallybic stems in -*ta* and -*tä* have optional -*t* in the third person only, elsewhere they have *s*. E.g. the singular paradigm of *huutaa* 'shout' is

1.    huusin
2.    huusit
3.    huusi ∼ huuti

Even in Standard Finnish, optional -*ti*- seems restricted to the third person in some verbs: 3.p. *mursi* ∼ *murti* 'broke', but 1.p. *mursin* sounds better than *murrin*. According to the generally accepted view, the *t*-forms are innovations. In the view I am defending here, they are on the contrary older forms. We have already seen that the historical facts from Finnish give some support to the latter view. The above dialectal paradigm allows us to confirm this conclusion by means of the following line of reasoning. As has been often pointed out, the third person is the 'basic' or 'unmarked' person in the indicative paradigm: it is more frequent than the other persons, it may be the only existing person in the paradigm (e.g. *quoth*), it is generally shorter, it is more often endingless than the other persons, and so on. First and second person forms are less well 'entrenched' in the system, and as a consequence, they are more subject to analogical change than third person forms.[4] An example will make this clear. The Sanskrit periphrastic future is historically derived from a syntactically participial agent nominalization in -*tar* with the copula (omitted as usual in the unmarked, third person). E.g. *dātāsmi* = *dātā asmi* 'I'm giving', *dātāsi* = *dātā asi* 'you're giving', *dātā* 'he's giving'.[5]

|     | sg.     | du.       | pl.       |
|-----|---------|-----------|-----------|
| 1.  | dātāsmi | dātāsvaḥ  | dātāsmaḥ  |
| 2.  | dātāsi  | dātāsthaḥ | dātāstha  |
| 3.  | dātā    | dātārau   | dātāraḥ   |

The third person retains the three-way number distinction in the nominal form (cf. nom. du. *dātārau*, nom. pl. *dātāraḥ*). But the first and second persons have eliminated it and generalized the singular form throughout (e.g. 1.pl. *\*dātāraḥ smaḥ > dātāsmaḥ*).

If, then, first and second person forms are more favored loci of innovation, this means that 1.sg. *huusin*, 2.sg. *huusit*, and the *s*-forms generally, are innovations replacing the *t*-forms.

(4) A fourth argument, which I think would alone suffice to establish the point, is the behavior of *t* before contracted *i* elsewhere than in the past tense. There are several such groups of forms: (a) the past impersonal, e.g. *mentiin* 'one went', from underlying /men+tä+i+hen/; (b) the conditional, e.g. *tuntisin* 'I would know', from /tunte+isi+n/; (c) derived verbs, e.g. *sotia* 'to wage war', from /sota+i+ta/; (d) derived adjectives, e.g. *vetinen* 'watery', from /vete+i+nen/; (e) derived nouns, e.g. *sontiainen* 'dung beetle', from /sonta+iai+nen/; (f) noun plurals, e.g. *sotina* (essive), *sotiin* (illative), *sodissa* (inessive) 'war', from /sota+i+na/, /sota+i+hen/, /sota+i+ssa/. Now, in all of these cases, not only is *t* the rule, but there are no traces of any kind, either in Standard Finnish, or in dialects, or in the older literary documents, of the *s* which the standard theory claims must once have existed in them. Rapola (1966: 237) remarks with reference to one of these cases ((a) above) that they are 'among the most thoroughly carried through cases of analogy in Proto-Finnic. There is not even a trace of *s*.' The same could be said for (b), (c), (d), (e), and (f). Why this discrepancy between contracted *i* in cases (a-e), which never triggers *t→s*, and the contracted *i* of the past tense, which normally triggers *s*?

The customary chronology allows no explanation. If instead we assume that *t→s* preceded contraction, the reason is clear. The difference between the past tense, where *t→s* was extended to the new *i*'s, and all other cases, where *t→s* was not extended, is that the change *t→s* before underlying /i/ happens to occur only in the past tense, viz. in consonant stems like /avat +i/→*avasi* 'opened', /halut+i/→*halusi* 'wanted'.[6] Prior to contraction, therefore, the process *t→s* was applicable in these forms in the past tense, but in no forms in the other categories (a-e). After contraction, the situation was, from a surface point of view, that *t* went to *s* always before *i* from final *e* (/vete/→*veti→vesi), sometimes before *i* in the past tense (/avat+i/→*avasi*, but /käänta+i/→*käänti*), and never before *i*'s in other categories (where all *i*'s came from contraction), e.g. /men+tä+i+hen/ →*mentiin*, /tunte+isi+n/→*tuntisin*. Hence, a 'model' for the extension of *t→s* to the new contracted *i*'s existed only in the past tense.

The formalization of this explanation is of extreme interest for the theory of generative phonology. Consider the stage of Finnish reached after contraction, as described in the preceding paragraph. The present theory would allow two ways of characterizing it. The first is to mark the categories (a-e) as not undergoing *t→s*, and to mark verbs individually as undergoing or not undergoing *t→s* in the past tense. The second is to order *t→s* before contraction. On grounds of simplicity, the second solution would be preferred. Yet the historical development from this stage to modern Finnish indicates rather that the first, 'marking' solution is right. Under this solution, the actual development is exactly what would be expected: the change of past *käänti* to *käänsi* is a simplification of the grammar, since it eliminates what in this theory is a lexical exception to the *t→s* rule; but a putative change of plural *sotiin* to *\*sosiin* would be a complication of the grammar, since the nonapplicability of *t→s* is a *general* property of noun plurals.

Under the rule ordering solution, however, the development which took place in Finnish is a complication of the grammar, and hence cannot be explained. In the rule ordering solution, one can only say that the grammar resulting immediately after contraction became *more* complex — either by reordering the rules and marking categories (a-e), as well as many verbs in the past tense, as exceptions to the *t→s* rule, or by adding a second *t→s* rule which applies only in the past tense (which is Wiik's synchronic solution for Finnish), *or* by splitting up contraction into two rules, one which applies to some past tense forms and is ordered before *t→s*, the other applying to remaining vowel sequences and ordered after *t→s*. None of these is a change of the kind one would expect to occur. Hence, the marking solution rather than the ordering solution gives the right analysis.

How must phonological theory be revised so as to make the marking solution more highly valued than the ordering solution at the stage immediately after contraction? One possible such revision is the recent idea of Kisseberth (1972) and Koutsoudas, Sanders, and Noll (1971) that marked ordering relations do not exist at all. The way in which the Finnish facts would have to be treated under this constraint is shown to be correct by the further history of the language.

This does not mean that the 'no ordering' theory is the *only* theory with the desired effect. There are less sweeping revisions of phonological theory which will also make the marking solution more highly valued than the ordering solution. For example, one might restrict the 'no ordering' proposal to a subclass of rules, perhaps the class of 'morphophonemic' rules (Kiparsky 1973a, section 2). At any rate, our example points to a way in which the issue can be resolved by means of historical evidence.

### Notes

1.    This is true of primary changes (e.g. sound change, analogy, etc.), not of restructuring, which is presumably obligatory.
2.    Skousen's example is *kettinki* 'chain', a loan from Swedish *ketting*. It is true that it has *tt* in the gradation context in Standard Finnish. But degeminated *ketinki* is a current substandard form. By chance I remember the phrase *ketingit päällä* 'with his chains on' used in reference to a mayor of Helsinki, then running for president of Finland, who was depicted in full regalia on his election poster.
3.    The voicing of *s* to *z* appears to be automatic after unstressed vowels (Kettunen 1960: 52-55).
4.    Often the change is in fact based on existing third person forms (Watkins 1962), though this is not the only possibility.
5.    Somewhat like the English progressive, too, it refers to a 'foreseeable' event

in the near future, e.g. *I'm giving him a book (tomorrow)* – *dātāsmi*, vs. *I will give him a book* – *dāsyāmi*.

6.    In cases (a), (c), (d), (e) the underlying sequence /t+i/ could never occur. In case (b), the underlying sequence occurs, but *t* is deleted by a rule which precedes *t→s*, e.g. /avat+isi/→*avaisi*.

# Chapter 8

# From Paleogrammarians to Neogrammarians*

Early nineteenth-century comparative linguistics is in some ways a predecessor of twentieth-century theoretical linguistics. This is not because it held any of the same views as modern linguistics, but because many of its basic concerns were the same, and because the radical changes it underwent contributed directly to the development of modern linguistics. The theoretical disputes among the nineteenth-century comparativists were rarely about the modern comparativist's problem of establishing reliable methods of linguistic reconstruction. More often they centered on topics which today would be considered questions to be settled outside of comparative linguistics. These included such issues of current relevance as the relation of form and meaning in language, the psychological reality and abstract nature of underlying representations, and the status of explanatory theories in linguistics.

That the field bore this character is mainly attributable to the influence of Franz Bopp. Ostensibly aimed simply at reconstructing Indo-European, Bopp's works also implicitly presented a specific and original linguistic theory. While this linguistic theory did not survive past the 1860's, Bopp's influential idea that the study of language change was the most worthwhile kind of linguistics managed to hold the field for a full century. Between the publication of Bopp's *Conjugationssystem* in 1816 and the publication of Saussure's *Cours* in 1915, the main empirical basis of linguistic theory was in diachrony. The purpose of this essay is to explore some controversies that arose in connection with Bopp's approach to comparative linguistics, and to relate them to the development of modern linguistics.

Bopp's basic assumption is often said to have been that the Indo-European endings are derived from pronouns and forms of the copula attached to the verbal root (the 'agglutination theory'). This is a true but

*This work was supported in part by the National Institute of Mental Health (Grant No. MH13390-04). A version of this paper was read at a symposium on the history of linguistics at the Newberry Library, Chicago, Ill., sponsored by the Wenner-Gren Foundation for Anthropological Research. I would like to express my gratitude to Dell Hymes for the great help he has given me in getting this essay into printable shape.

incomplete statement, which glosses over the sharp differences between
Bopp's views and those of later comparative grammar. It is merely the one
aspect of Bopp's hypothesis about the structure of the Indo-European
proto-language which later historians of linguistics, such as Delbrück,
emphasized and partly accepted. Bopp actually seems to have held that in
the proto-language the primitive semantic elements were by and large
expressed by separate morphemes. The morphology of a Proto-Indo-
European word, Bopp believed, was a representation of the elements of its
meaning. Obscured as this state of affairs was in the daughter languages,
because of phonetic decay, it was nevertheless reconstructible by the
comparative method (cf. Verburg 1950).

   Although Bopp in the *Conjugationssystem* was still strongly influenced
by the very different ideas of Fr. Schlegel, the germ of his notion of the
proto-language can already be found in this work. In a section on the
formation of the voices in Sanskrit (1816: 36-37), Bopp gives an interesting
semantic analysis of the active, middle, passive, and causative, by means of
two binary features referring to the functional relation of the grammatical
subject to the action denoted by the verb. In the active and the middle,
but not in the passive or causative, the grammatical subject is the agent of
the action, and in the middle and the passive, but not in the active or the
causative, the subject is the direct or indirect goal of the action.

|  |  |  | Subject = Agent | Subject = Goal |
|---|---|---|---|---|
| Active | karoti | 'makes' | + | − |
| Middle | kurute | 'makes (for) himself' | + | + |
| Passive | kriyate | 'is made' | − | + |
| Causative | kārayati | 'causes to make' | − | − |

He further notes that the middle and passive voices, and the passive and
causative, each have some morphology in common. The middle and passive
are characterized by a special set of endings (e.g., *-te* vs. *-ti* in the third
person singular), and the passive and causative are characterized by similar
suffixes *-ya* and *-aya*.

|  | -(a)ya | -te |
|---|---|---|
| Active | − | − |

| | | |
|---|---|---|
| Middle | − | + |
| Passive | + | + |
| Causative | + | − |

Bopp then takes the crucial step of linking the morphological and semantic analyses on the level of their primitive components. He associates with -*(a)ya* the meaning 'subject ≠ agent' and with the mediopassive endings the meaning 'subject = goal'.[1] Commenting on this analysis, he remarks:

> Es kann hierdurch gesehen werden, wie im Sanskrit ähnliche Modifikationen der Bedeutung durch ähnliche Modifikationen der Form angezeigt werden, und wie in gewissem Betrachte der Sinn der organischen Flexionen eben so bestimmt und unverändert bleibt, als jener der bedeutenden Stammsylben selbst. [This shows how in Sanskrit similar modifications of meaning are expressed by similar modifications of form, and how in a sense the meaning of the organic inflections remains as fixed and constant as that of the significant stem syllables.]

This was an important remark. No one had ever tried to penetrate Indo-European morphology in this way before. It subsequently became one of the main goals of Bopp and his school to show that such a one-to-one correspondence between morphological and semantic elements could be established more widely in the Indo-European proto-language by comparative reconstruction.

What Bopp brought to linguistics was, then, a *paradigm* of historical explanation, in the sense in which Kuhn (1962) has introduced this term. A historical explanation of an inflectional form was to him a demonstration that the form was derived from a proto-form in which each of the primitive concepts into which its meaning was analyzable was expressed by a separate morpheme. This paradigm was based on the belief that the methods of comparative reconstruction, applied to what Bopp considered the greatly decayed and disorganized morphological debris of the attested Indo-European languages, would yield a proto-morphology which reflects logical relations. As Curtius (1871: 213) succinctly put it:

> Ein Haupbestreben dieser Wissenschaft läuft darauf hinaus, aus den in mannichfaltiger Weise entstellten und verstümmelten Formen, wie sie in den einzelnen Sprachen vorliegen, die vollen, reinen Formen einer grundlegenden Periode zu reconstruieren. [A principal goal of this science (comparative linguistics) is to reconstruct the full, pure forms of an original state from the variously disfigured and mutilated forms which are attested in the individual languages.]

Especially significant is the remark: 'Erklärungen aber, welche die Hauptsache, nämlich die Bedeutung, dunkel lassen, sind nicht geeignet zu befriedigen' [But explanations which fail to elucidate what is of greatest importance, namely the meaning, cannot be satisfactory] (1871: 215).[2]

This paradigm of historical explanation can be represented by the following schema:

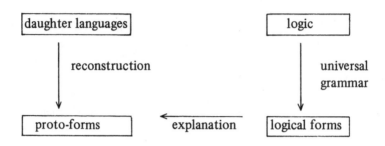

To say that Bopp and his followers operated according to this paradigm is not to say that such explanations were ever actually achieved. Needless to say, they were not. But linguists at the time thought that they had been achieved, and research in comparative grammar was for several decades oriented towards searching for them. It was the lack of any theory of reconstruction that made this whole schema of explanation quite empty in practice. Little thought was given to the rules whereby the actual forms of the daughter languages were derived from the reconstructed proto-forms, and hence these proto-forms could simply be set up ad hoc to fit the hypothesis that Proto-Indo-European had a morphology in which the salient elements of meaning corresponded to separate elements of form. A good illustration of this is the analysis of the personal endings of the verb which was developed by Bopp, Kuhn, and Schleicher, as summarized by Curtius, the last representative of this school of comparative linguistics (1877).

The basic assumption underlying this analysis was that the personal endings had originally been pronouns attached to the verb stem. This was at least given some phonological plausibility by an overall similarity between pronouns and the corresponding verb endings in the Indo-European languages. The first person singular was reconstructed as *-ma* and the second person singular as *-tva*. The derivation of the Greek second person singular endings from *-tva* was represented by Curtius (1877: 47) in the form of a tree as follows:

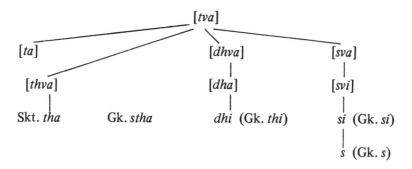

(Square brackets represent reconstructed forms.)

From here on the reconstruction proceeded on the basis of a purely semantic analysis. Plurals were analyzed as derived from conjunction, with 1.pl. *-ma-tva* and 2.pl. *-tva-tva*. The middle endings were also assumed to have had reduplicated pronouns, to reflect the double function of subject as actor and goal, e.g. sg.1.p. *-ma-ma* and 2.p. *-tva-tva*. But if the plural is formed by repeating singular endings, and the middle is formed by repeating the active endings, what of the plural middle endings? According to Curtius (who disarmingly remarks that this is one of the most difficult problems in IE morphology) they are to be reconstructed as 1.pl. *-ma-tva-tva* and 2.pl. *-tva-tva-tva*. Schleicher, more relentlessly logical, had set up *-ma-tva-ma-tva* and *-tva-tva-tva-tva*.

Characteristically, no one working in this framework of comparative grammar seems to have objected to all this on any phonological grounds. The argumentation was based on semantics (for example, an objection to 1.pl. *-ma-tva* was that this form should only have the meaning of an inclusive 'we', which Schleicher and Curtius countered by postulating the existence of a lost exclusive 'we' in the proto-language). No one was disturbed by the fact that the phonologically very different 2.p. active plural and middle singular endings were derived from exactly the same base form *-tva-tva*, or by the proposal that the 2.sg. present, past, perfect, and imperative endings all go back to *-tva*, as shown on the chart reproduced here from Curtius. Base forms as different as 2.sg. act. *-tva* and 2.pl.mid. *-tva-tva-tva* or *-tva-tva-tva-tva* were readily assumed to underlie forms as similar as Greek *-stha* and *-sthe*. Obviously it is not ignorance of phonetics but indifference to it that explains this. The actual shape of the forms in the daughter languages was not, in general, something that Bopp and his followers were interested in trying to explain. Attention was given to rules only insofar as they could serve to justify the choice of one base form over another. Otherwise they were satisfied with perfectly ad hoc statements. The idea did not occur to them that the anomalies of the daughter languages might have some interest in themselves.

What was the status of reconstructed forms thought to be? Usually, it seems to have been taken for granted that reconstruction results in the surface phonetic forms of the proto-language. But there was at least one important expression of dissent, which I should like to cite here to illustrate the fact that the same linguists who so neglected the formulation of sound changes were capable of highly sophisticated thinking on phonological theory. In a remarkable review of the first volume of Pott's *Etymologische Forschungen*,[3] Theodor Benfey in 1837 introduced the distinction between the phonetic value of a sound and its functional value, showing on the basis of a discussion of root and ablaut theory that they could differ greatly, and arguing that linguistic reconstruction yields functional as well as phonetic representations.

At the time, Indo-Europeanists accepted Pāṇinian root theory, in which roots are represented in the zero grade form in case they contain a sonant susceptible to vocalization (e.g., *kṛ, vid*), and in the full grade otherwise (e.g., *tap*). That is, base forms have the minimal vocalism, subject to the proviso that they must be pronounceable. This proviso was natural, indeed necessary, from the viewpoint of Indian linguistics, based as it was on an oral tradition.[4] Benfey pointed out that from a linguistic point of view it is indefensible, because it breaks the generality of the ablaut rules, and necessitates ad hoc statements like '*a* is its own guṇa'. In considering more consistent alternatives to the Indian system, Benfey asks the fundamental question: 'Denn wäre es nicht möglich, dass den unter sich zusammenhängenden *i, e, ya, ai; u, o, va, au; ṛ, ar, ra, ar* etwas im Sprachgeiste zu Grunde liege, was von ihnen allen verschieden wäre?' [For is it not possible that the related series *i, e, ya, ai*, etc., might have an underlying representation in the mind that differs from them all?] (1837: 15). Benfey's question is whether base forms of morphemes can be different from any of the phonetic forms in which they actually appear. He bases his affirmative answer on the very good point that whatever ablaut grade is chosen as the basic one, it can happen that some roots for irrelevant morphological reasons happen not to occur phonetically in that grade:

Wir haben bis jetzt Beispiele angeführt, wo sich neben den Formen mit *r* und anderm Vokal auch eine mit *ṛ* wirklich zeigte. Es versteht sich aber von selbst, dass es leicht geschehen konnte, dass eine solche Form gar nicht hervortrat oder wieder verschwand. Wir sind also berechtigt, auch solche Formen unter eine Wurzel zu bringen, welche begrifflich verwandt nur in Beziehung auf den das *r* begleitenden Vokal wechseln, selbst wenn eine sie äusserlich zusammenhaltende Form mit *ṛ* fehlt [Up to now we have cited examples where a form with *ṛ* actually appears alongside those with *r* + vowel. But it is self-evident that such a form might fail to appear in the first place, or might disappear again. We are therefore justified in deriving from a single root semantically related forms with alternations in the vowel accompanying *r*, even where there is no actual form with *ṛ* to superficially tie them together] (1837: 17).

Having thus justified abstract underlying representations, Benfey, after an analysis of the ablaut system, summarizes his conclusions as follows:

> Wir haben durch diese Untersuchung als Resultat erlangt, dass *r* im Sanskrit vom lautlichen Standpunkte aus ein wirklicher Vokal so gut wie *i, u* sei; dass alle drei functionell den Werth von Consonanten in Wurzeln haben; dass alle Wurzeln im Sprachgeiste nur consonantisch liegen, und *a* wo es in Wurzeln erscheint, Guna ist [In this investigation we have reached the result that *r* in Sanskrit is phonetically a true vowel just like *i, u* are; that functionally all three have the value of consonants in roots; that all roots are purely consonantal in the underlying representation in the mind, and that *a*, wherever it appears in roots, represents full grade] (1837: 23).

Of especial interest is the following comment on the status of reconstructed forms:

> Übrigens fürchten wir nicht, dass man uns eine so barock materielle Ansicht unterschieben möchte, als ob wir glaubten, dass die consonantischen Wurzeln, welche wir annehmen, je nackend oder ihrer Stufenfolge gemäss aufgetreten wären. In dieser Abstraction ruhten sie nur im Geiste, in der Erscheinung traten sie sogleich, je nach den Gesetzen, welchen die zwischen Laut und Begriff zu erstrebende Harmonie sie unterwarf, nach ihren verschiedenen Phasen auf [Incidentally we do not fear that anyone will impute to us the grotesquely physicalistic view that the consonantal roots which we set up ever appeared unmodified or in the order of their ablaut grades (?). In this abstract form they were represented only in the mind, their successive phonetic forms were from the outset determined by the rules to which they were subjected, which established the required harmony between sound and meaning] (1837: 24).

In the 1860's the reaction against Bopp began. It was on the arbitrariness of the analysis of Indo-European verb morphology described above that the critics first seized. In 1860 and 1870, Fr. Müller published articles in which he argued for something that is today accepted by all Indo-Europeanists, but which at the time was a startling and paradoxical idea: that the secondary endings (*-m -s -t*) were more original than the primary endings (*-mi -si -ti*), and that the augment was not an original part of past tense inflection. The primary endings, Müller suggested arose only through the addition of a deictic, pronominal element to the end of the verb to denote the 'here and now' of the present tense, just as the augment was added to the beginning as a sign of past tense. Müller criticized the baselessness of the standard derivation of verb endings and termed the basic assumptions of Boppian comparative linguistics 'unsupported dogma' (1870: 194). A number of linguists, such as Scherer (1868) and Westphal (1869), agreed with Müller in this. In a reply, Curtius reiterated his fundamental position (1871: 213): 'Dass das vollere das prius, das schwächere das posterius sei, das ist die gesammte vergleichende Grammatik umfassende

schwerlich anfechtbare Grundanschauung.' [That the full forms are prior
to the weaker forms is the basic, hardly disputable assumption underlying
all of comparative grammar.]

These critiques of Bopp reflect nothing less than a revolution, in the
sense of Kuhn (1962), which was taking place in comparative linguistics in
the 1860's. The Bopp paradigm of historical explanation, which had proved
unproductive, was abandoned, and a new one was adopted in its place. The
principal goal of comparative grammar now became the explanation of
phonological or morphological features of the individual daughter languages
on the basis of the reconstructed proto-language. The proto-language
ceased to be of semantic interest, and its new importance was that it
enabled the linguist to explain phenomena in the daughter languages which,
viewed in isolation, had no explanation. All the sensational new sound
laws discovered in the 1860's and 1870's were historical explanations
within this new paradigm. Verner's Law was the explanation of certain
anomalies in the Germanic consonantism on the basis of the Proto-Indo-
European accent as reconstructed from Sanskrit and Greek. The 'Palatal-
gesetz' was the discovery that the Sanskrit palatals could be explained if
the five-vowel system of the European languages was reconstructed for
Proto-Indo-European. Grassmann's Law showed that some Sanskrit and
Greek peculiarities could be explained on the basis of reconstructing the
double-aspirate roots indicated by Germanic and Latin. The new paradigm
illustrated by these discoveries, which might be called *formal explanation*,
can be represented by the following schema:

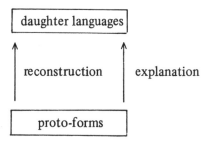

This new paradigm is so much a part of our thinking that it is hard to
think of it as ever having been an innovation in method. Nevertheless, it
was a very basic change. The results achieved in this new paradigm were
partly incomprehensible and partly uninteresting to the comparativists
operating in the older framework. Some of them even refused to accept
Grassmann's Law. Bopp ignored it in the 1870 (posthumous) edition of
his comparative grammar, and Pott attacked it in a long article, asking
essentially: 'how could monstrous roots like this have existed?' On the
other hand, proponents of the new paradigm of formal explanation saw

the new paradigm as a regeneration of the science of comparative linguistics. Writing in 1877, Ascoli criticized the older methods of reconstruction for their arbitrariness and contrasted with them the new explanatory paradigm as the properly scientific one, in a very modern-sounding passage:

> Ma chi vorrà per questo negare che la ricostruzione si debba dir solida, e nobilissimamente scientifica, quando ell'è, dall'un canto, la resultanza logicamente necessaria dei termini o de' fenomeni onde moviamo, e, dall'altro, riusce a rivelare, come per spontaneità sua propria, le ragioni istoriche d'altri termini o fenomeni, che non entravano nel calcolo pel quale siam riusciti a stabilirla? [But who would deny by this that the reconstruction must be termed solid, and eminently scientific, when it is, on the one hand, the logical consequence of the terms and phenomena on which it is based, and on the other hand, succeeds in revealing, spontaneously as it were, the historical reasons for other terms and phenomena, which did not enter into the calculations by which we succeeded in establishing this reconstruction?] (1877: 8).

The difference between the two paradigms can perhaps be clarified by an analogy from recent work in transformational grammar. The Bopp paradigm is roughly comparable to the line of investigation undertaken in Katz and Postal (1964). Bopp's program, ideally, was to show that reconstruction of Indo-European morphology, in principle a formal process, results in proto-forms with a one-to-one correspondence between morphemes and minimal semantic elements. Katz and Postal argue somewhat analogously that syntactic deep structures established on the basis of purely syntactic considerations will turn out to contain exactly the information needed for semantic interpretation. The difference is that Bopp's paradigm led to few results of any interest. The post-Boppian paradigm of formal explanation, on the other hand, is reminiscent of Chomsky's concept of explanatory adequacy as presented in *Current Issues in Linguistic Theory* (Chomsky 1964). As Ascoli put it very clearly, the application of the comparative method to a certain set of data enables the linguist, via the reconstructed proto-language, to explain other data found in these languages. Chomsky's point that a theory of phonology or syntax, applied to a set of data in a language, generalizes and makes predictions about data not in this initial set is formally comparable.

In linguistics textbooks the story of comparative linguistics usually gets told roughly as follows:

The early comparativists did badly because they knew no phonetics. ("One difficulty that limited Bopp, and especially Grimm, was an inferior understanding of articulatory phonetics" [Dinneen 1967: 182]). Increased attention to phonology, and a growing appreciation of articulatory phonetics, led gradually to greater rigor in the formulation of sound laws, and to a resulting refinement in the comparative method. ('From approximately 1820 through the 1870's scholars progressed from the notion of sound shifts between these language stages to sound laws that accounted for changes' [Dinneen 1967: 184]). This development culminated in the 'break-through' (Hockett 1965) of the Neogrammarian hypothesis that sound changes can have no exceptions.

I am inclined to question the alleged relevance of articulatory phonetics. I do not see that phonetics played much of a role in the sweeping revision of the comparative method between 1820 and the 1870's. There is nothing about the comparative method of Bopp or his followers which could be explained by their ignorance of some fact of phonetics. Arguments of many kinds were raised against Bopp by his critics in the 1860's, but no one at the time accused him of being a bad phonetician. As far as I know, *nothing* in the whole controversy about comparative linguistics ever turned either on any specific point of phonetics, or on any general considerations of phonetic theory. A much more plausible interpretation is that it was the new paradigm of historical explanation which made, for the first time, historical phonology a subject of interest. It was the realization that there were significant things to be said about the phonological detail of each language, and that explanation in this domain was possible, which caused comparative linguists to take an interest in articulatory phonetics.

Another facet of the story which needs rethinking is the role of the Neogrammarians. Since so many important advances in comparative grammar were made by the Neogrammarians, it is natural to think of them as the initiators of the revolution in the field. But the revolution was begun in the decade *before* the Neogrammarians made their appearance. Further-more, the new paradigm of historical explanation was in the 1870's accepted by linguists who stood on both sides of the controversy about the Neogrammarian theory of sound change. There exists a most regrettable myth that the belief in necessarily exceptionless sound change accounts for the discovery of the many new sound changes in the 1860's and 1870's. For example, Bloomfield (1933: 355) attributes Grassmann's discovery to this belief, and similarly Verner's discovery (1933: 359). But neither Grassmann nor Verner in fact believed that sound changes could not have exceptions. And why did linguists who specifically rejected the Neogram-marian theory of sound change once it had been formulated in the 1870's, such as Collitz, Ascoli, J. Schmidt, discover sound laws which were just as significant as those discovered by Neogrammarians, such as Brugmann, Osthoff, and Leskien? Neither side in the disagreement over the sound change issue seems to have had a bad effect on the linguists who embraced it. In fact, the two groups of linguists scarcely differed in the kind of actual historical linguistics they did. It is hard to see how a theory with so few actual consequences for comparative work should be considered a 'breakthrough'. A more important change in the field was surely the acceptance of the new paradigm of historical explanation. This far exceeds the sound change debate in productivity and concrete consequences, and is a far more likely historical source of the new discoveries in phonology. The disagreement between the Neogrammarians and their contemporary opponents seems utterly insignificant compared to the rejection by both groups of the Bopp-Schleicher-Curtius paradigm.

The switch in outlook had further consequences. First, it opened the way to the theory of proportional analogy. The connection is obvious. Bopp's followers were being quite consistent in rejecting the concept of analogical change when it first began to be offered by the new comparativists. As long as the morphologies of the attested Indo-European languages were seen as nothing more than pitiful, jumbled remnants of an earlier stage, there was no way of supposing that these morphologies could undergo any sort of systematic modification. Analogy as a form of language change presupposes some synchronic regularity which is being generalized beyond its proper confines. But linguists of Bopp's school were not in principle prepared to admit the existence of the kind of synchronic regularities in the historical Indo-European languages which could form the basis for analogical generalization. Analogy only became a conceivable form of change when it was admitted that the morphology of the daughter languages could be described as a system in its own terms. It is no accident that the linguists who first began to use proportional analogy as a principle of explanation were Scherer, Whitney, and the other linguists who headed the rejection of the Bopp paradigm in the 1860's.

It can also be argued that the concept of a synchronic system is ultimately connected with these changes in the prevailing views about language. At the very beginning of the reaction against Bopp, the objection was already being raised that his theory, which saw all change as decay, could make no sense out of the fact that the daughter languages had system and structure too. In Westphal (1869), a historical grammar of German in the framework of a K. F. Becker-like system of universal grammar, this is the most serious charge against Bopp:

> Erst dadurch, dass die ursprünglichen Auslaute zerschlagen und zertrümmert worden sind und nicht einer einzigen Form ihr ursprünglicher Bestand gelassen ist, erst durch diese zufällige Vernichtung des ursprünglichen Zustandes soll jener in sich so ganz und gar consequente Organismus der Endungen t ta, ti tai, tu tau u.s.w. der doch sicherlich ein festes und vernünftiges Prinzip zeigt, entstanden sien? Erst durch Depravation und Corruption soll es gekommen sein, dass die Endungen in ihrem Gegensatze zu einander als Träger logischer oder metaphysischer Kategorien dastahen und als solche mindestens dieselben Ansprüche auf Schönheit, ja auf unsere Bewunderung erheben, wie die bestimmten mathematischen Functionen folgenden Krystallformen der anorganischen Welt? [Is it only by the destruction and wreckage of the old terminations, which has not left a single form untouched, only by this random annihilation of the original state, that the internally quite coherent system of endings t ta, ti tai, tu tau etc., which surely shows

a solid and rational principle, is supposed to have originated? Is it only by decay and corruption that the endings have come to stand in opposition to each other as carriers of logical or metaphysical categories, and as such deserve to be considered, indeed admired, as being beautiful, to at least the extent that inorganic crystals which follow certain mathematical functions deserve it?] (1869: 179).

Westphal seems to have had virtually no influence. But the paradoxical relationship between synchrony and diachrony which he was perhaps the first to point out continued to disturb linguists like Kruszewski (1881; cf. Jakobson 1965), and became the key problem of Saussure's *Cours*.

## POSTSCRIPT (1973)

The great handbooks of the Neogrammarians form a kind of massive wall behind which the working Indo-Europeanist today rarely finds it necessary to go for either facts or theories. Consequently, our prevailing views of the earlier nineteenth-century Indo-Europeanists have been shaped mainly at second hand, through the historiography of men like Delbrück, Streitberg, and Pedersen, who take a very partisan view and understandably misrepresent the aims of their predecessors in terms of their own concerns. In discussing Bopp, for example, they play up issues which were of little concern to Bopp (such as the regularity of sound change, and what later came to be called the 'comparative method'), and virtually ignore the issues that Bopp was mainly interested in (such as the relationship of form and meaning in language). The main purpose of my essay is to qualify their account of the nineteenth century (which may be caricatured as 'Bopp + Ausnahmslosigkeit = Brugmann') and to emphasize the fact that the program that guided Bopp's work was very different from that which led to the *Grundriss*.

I think that my essay, which appears here substantially as written over five years ago, is right in its major points. However, I would now say that I depicted the contrast between the two approaches rather too luridly. Contrary to what I say in the essay, the development of a theory of phonetic features was rather important in the development of the new comparative grammar. A deeper analysis of the period would also have to take into account the long development of Bopp's own ideas, and (as Y. Malkiel rightly remarked during the conference) the role of men like Rask, Grimm, and Diez.

Perhaps the conflict between Bopp and the later Indo-Europeanists ultimately is a reflection of the two basic reasons why man has always found the study of language so fascinating: on the one hand the elusive relationship between form and meaning, and on the other hand the intricate but perhaps slightly less elusive intrinsic patterning of linguistic forms.

Sometimes one must be bought at the price of the other, for reasons which we are still a long way from understanding. The nineteenth-century Indo-Europeanists were by no means the only linguists to feel this conflict. In the essay I compare the difference between Katz and Postal's and Chomsky's 1964 ideas of linguistic explanation. These have since been polarized into two major schools of generative grammar, which in practice at least have been distinguished by the fact that one has focused its search on the semantic basis of linguistic form, and the other on its intrinsic patterning. In a work in preparation, S. D. Joshi and I hope to show that over two thousand years ago the same conflict arose in India, between Pāṇini and a school (probably antedating Pāṇini himself) represented by his greatest critic Kātyāyana. A major underlying theme of Kātyāyana's *vārttikās*, or critical remarks on Pāṇini's rules, is to tie syntax to semantics more closely, by attempting to show that *kārakas* (deep syntactic relations) are semantically based, and by arguing for highly 'abstract' underlying representations quite similar to those which would be required by generative semantics today.

In the past, the study of intrinsic form came out with more lasting results than the search for semantic explanations: Pāṇini achieved more than Kātyāyana, and the Neogrammarians achieved more than the Bopp school. The reason was the cavalier treatment of meaning which was possible and tempting in the absence of a well-motivated framework for representing meaning. That gap has still hardly begun to be filled. Semantics is as observable as phonetics, and yet we know much less about the nature of semantic representations than about phonetic representations. Quite possibly, the semantic representations appearing in present-day works on generative grammar will seem as amusing 100 years from now as Grimm's phonetic representation of German *Schrift* with the eight sounds [skhripht] seems to us today.

## Notes

1. Bopp later proposed different solutions to these problems.
2. As Keith Percival has pointed out to me, Bopp did not require that base forms be uniquely interpretable. Ambiguities could be introduced, for example, by what today would be called the scope of negation. Bopp's (in fact erroneous) derivation of the tense-marking augment from the negative prefix had called forth a scathing attack by Lassen on the absurdity of assuming 'I saw' to have been expressed as 'I do not see'. Today the issue would not even arise because of the phonological impossibility of the derivation. In Bopp's days, it provoked an interesting semantic discussion – probably one of the first treatments of scope phenomena in the Western linguistic tradition. In his comparative grammar (1870 edition, Vol. 2, pp. 417-20) Bopp tried to defend his position by pointing out that one could view the present tense only, and not the verb, as negated, i.e., 'I do not see *now* (but I saw earlier)'. As a parallel he mentions that *not one* could mean either 'no-one' (cf. English) or 'several' (cf.

Sanskrit *an-eka*). He then makes explicit that the ideal one-to-one correspondence between meaning and form is never reached. Reconstructions, he says, result not in full semantic representations, but only in representations of the most salient semantic properties: 'Die Sprache drückt niemals etwas vollständig aus, sondern hebt überall nur das am meisten hervorstechende, oder ihr so erscheinende Merkmal hervor. Dieses Merkmal herauszufinden ist die Aufgabe der Etymologie. Ein Zahn-habender ist noch kein Elephant, ein Haarhabender noch kein Löwe, und dennoch nennt das Sanskrit den Elephanten *dantin*, den Löwen *kesin* . . . somit dreht sich die Sprache in einem Kreise der Unvollständigkeiten herum, bezeichnet die Gegenstände unvollständig durch irgend eine Eigenschaft, die selber unvollständig angedeutet ist. Gewiss aber ist, dass die Nicht-Gegenwart die hervorstechendste Eigenschaft der Vergangenheit ist, und diese mit grösserem Rechte bezeichnet, als *Zahn-habender* den Elephanten.' [Language never expresses anything completely, but everywhere brings out only the most salient feature, or what seems to her to be the most salient feature. It is the task of etymology to discover this feature. Just having teeth (tusks) doesn't make you an elephant, just having hair (a mane) doesn't make you a lion, and yet Sanskrit calls the elephant *dantin*, the lion *kesin* . . . thus language turns in a circle of imperfections, denoting objects incompletely through some property which is itself incompletely expressed. But certainly non-presentness is the most conspicuous property of the past, and denotes it with greater justice than 'tusk-carrier' denotes the elephant.] It is interesting to note that the Sanskrit animal names are also used by Humboldt in his discussion of sense and reference. The whole passage of Bopp is a nice illustration of the pitfalls of homemade semantics.

3.     Benfey (1837), quoted from the reprint in Benfey (1890).

4.     This restriction on pronounceable roots perhaps accounts for other peculiarities of Pāṇini's phonology, such as his relatively inelegant treatment of the Grassmann's Law phenomena.

# Chapter 9

# On the Evaluation Measure*

The evaluation measure can be construed as an explication of the concept 'learnability of the abstract system of a language' (Koefoed 1974). It interacts with the long-established factors of ease of perception and ease of production in setting the direction of linguistic change. It is evident that the three factors can impose mutually conflicting requirements on the grammar. For example, phonological processes, as well as syntactic trans-formations, serve to facilitate speech production and perception, but both generally do so at the cost of making the structure of the linguistic system harder to discover. Moreover, the functions of production and perception can themselves partially conflict with each other.

Natural languages appear to stay close to an optimum beyond which ease of production, perception, and acquisition can not be jointly increased, and improvements in any one respect entail sacrifices in the others. There is, however, no fixed point of balance between the three factors. In the first place, variation in the relative weight of the factors, depending on the demands imposed by the speech situation, creates a stratification of speech into functionally determined styles. Rapid speech forces maximization of speakability, and familiar speech also allows it by virtue of decreasing the conflicting perceptibility requirement. Formal speech, and speech over a noisy channel (e.g. a bad phone connection) require maximal perceptibility. There is also considerable variation in structural complexity, cf. the maxi-mally simplified styles of speech used with children and foreigners (Ferguson 1971b).

Secondly, alongside this kind of functionally governed stylistic variation there is fluctuation over time. The teleology of change is 'local' in the sense that changes can be motivated by any single factor, and they are not, as far as has been shown, blocked if they have bad effects with respect to some other factor. For example, Martinet's contrary claim that the likeli-hood of a sound change depends (other things being equal) on the amount of homonymy it would create has never to my knowledge received more

*This paper was read at the Natural Phonology Parasession, organized by the Chicago Linguistic Society, 18 April, 1974.

than anecdotal support, and has failed attempts at statistical verification
(King 1967). The changes seem to take place anyway, and are then followed
by further change which corrects the damage done by the first. That is,
language practises 'therapy' (Gilliéron) rather than prophylaxis. Discussing
the effects of vowel syncope in Odawa, Kaye (1974) comments: 'Why a
rule should enter the language which simultaneously opacates a stress rule,
destroys a surface alternating stress pattern and causes wholesale allomorphy, seems a question worth pondering.' More generally, we could ask:
why are changes locally rather than globally motivated? It is likely that the
answer lies at least in part in the conventionalizing and spread of originally
functionally restricted styles of speech.

The distinct functional targets of change are not necessarily reached in
formally distinct ways (as suggested in Vennemann 1972). Any of the
three modes of optimalization could in principle be implemented by any
possible kind of change. Thus, reordering into feeding order can reduce
phonetic complexity, as in nearly all the cases noted in Bailey (1973), e.g.
*jus' yet* becoming *juš' yet* in faster speech by ordering the deletion of final *t*
in clusters to precede palatalization of *s*. It can also reduce cognitive
(structural) complexity. This will be the case when the fed rule is morphologically conditioned. This happens, for example, in German dialects which
apply umlauting to derived back vowels. There are dialects of Swiss
German where *æi* turns into *ā* before consonants and word-finally (Jutz
1931: 116), e.g. *ā* 'egg' ~ *æiər* 'eggs', *tswā* ~ *tswæiər* 'two-deciliter bottle',
*šrā* 'a scream' ~*šræiə* 'to scream'. Originally, and still in the dialects of part
of the Kanton of Schaffhausen (Wanner 1941), the *æi* → *ā* rule precedes
umlauting, so that the secondary back vowels it produces are not fronted
in the umlaut contexts, as in the diminutive form *āli* 'little egg', or in the
plural *šrā* 'screams'. In most dialects, however, the rules are placed in
feeding order, with *ā* from *æi* undergoing fronting to *æ* in umlauting
contexts, giving forms like *æli* in place of original *āli* (e.g. Enderlin 1913,
for the dialect of Kesswil in Oberthurgau). As umlauting is a purely morphological process, its extension to derived back vowels can have no
phonetic motivation, but rather reduces the opacity of the umlaut rule.
Presumably only the first kind of reordering is favored in fast or careless
speech, and only the second can be regarded as an instance of analogical
change in the usual sense.

In rule generalization there is again a phonetically and a systemically
motivated variety. For example, fast speech brings about a more general
application of many rules in English, such as syncope. On the other hand,
the generalization of the consonant assimilation rule $l+n → l+l$ in Finnish
(e.g. *tul+nut* → *tul+lut*)  to the form $C_i+n → C_i+C_i$ (e.g. *pur+nut* → *pur+
rut, pes+nyt* → *pes+syt*) can hardly be phonetically motivated. The reason
is that it does not eliminate *Cn* clusters from the language, as these are

retained morpheme-internally (for further discussion, see Kiparsky 1973a: 71).

The analogous observation can be made also for sound change. Cf. especially Stampe (1972) on polarization and assimilation as, respectively, perceptually and articulatorily motivated phonological processes. One might say that the only limitations on what functions a given formal change can serve are purely logical ones. Thus, rule generalization or reordering into feeding order can scarcely decrease perceptual difficulty, as their effect is generally to suppress contrasts that would otherwise appear on the surface. And it is hard to think of cases in which it would be possible for the addition of a new rule to make the abstract system more learnable.

Taken together, these considerations imply that there could be no single function of a grammar which would predict the directions of possible change. There are rather several independent factors, whose effect moreover seems to take the form of a loose interplay of local optima.
optima.

Although we can generally recognize what sorts of things each of the factors is to account for, a precise explication of any of them is still lacking. Relatively much effort has been devoted to finding out what is involved in learnability (e.g. Brink 1974, Miller 1973, Kaye 1974, Schindler 1974). All recent writings on the subject that I have seen hold that simplicity combined with the current form of grammars does not suffice. More adequate solutions have been sought in two directions: one, taking learnability itself to be determined by several independent subfactors, and the other, seeking to justify reanalyses of grammars and revisions of linguistic theory which have the effect of making simplicity work.

A proposal made in Kiparsky (1971, 1972) was that learnability depends on three things: in addition to (1) formal simplicity, also (2) paradigm coherence, or degree of allomorphy, and (3) transparency of rules. It immediately brings up a problem parallel to the one concerning the mutual relationship of the three functional factors: how are the supposed subfactors that determine learnability in turn related to each other? On the face of it, there are clear cases where they conflict, as would be expected if the factors are indeed truly independent. What are the domains of conflict, and how is it resolved? The answer could be that there is some ranking or partial ranking of factors such that if A ranks over B, then (i) there are changes where A is optimized at the cost of B, and (ii) there are no changes where B is optimized at the cost of A (cf. King 1972 for some discussion). It might also be the case that the resolution is indeterminate, or determined by the grammar or by the language learning situation in some way.

A priori, this whole approach does not seem very satisfactory. Especially the distinction of simplicity and allomorphy is suspect, as Koefoed (1974) has noted: 'It sounds like a paradox that a reduction of allomorphy could ever complicate a rule system that has as its main task precisely to account for allomorphy'. Some kind of reduction in the components of the evaluation measure would therefore be welcome, especially if it could reduce the questions of the preceding paragraph to pseudo-problems.

Consider, from this point of view, first the principle of minimization of allomorphy. One possible way of getting rid of it would be to claim that given the right theory of grammatical form, minimization of allomorphy is always correctly represented as formal simplification of the system. One could in effect deny the independence of the notion of allomorphy, if it were the case that simply by virtue of the way grammars work, a reduction in allomorphy (in whatever sense that term appears to be linguistically relevant) must formally simplify the grammar, and any increase in allomorphy must correspondingly complicate it. (The converse would not necessarily have to be true). Koefoed notes that a large step can be taken towards this situation by redefining 'degree of allomorphy' in terms of alternation types rather than alternation tokens. Then, the degree of allomorphy is given by the number of alternating pairs of segment types rather than by the number of pairs of allomorphs exhibiting such alternations. A consequence of this is to make allomorphy dependent in most cases just on the presence of a rule, not on its generality. Given this definition of degree of allomorphy, Koefoed claims, simplification in the rule system never leads to new alternation types. He excepts only cases where this simplification is motivated 'by phonetic factors rather than by the abstract tendency to formally simpler rules'. That is, new alternation types can have phonetic but not systematic causes. But even with this proviso, the claim is not strictly true. The Swiss German and Finnish examples mentioned earlier are typical counterexamples. Koefoed could of course respond to this objection by defining 'alternation type' at a still higher level of abstraction, in terms of classes of segments, or features. On this definition, the cited reordering of the umlaut rule does not produce a new alternation type, but merely extends an old one, viz. the alternation between front and back in the vowels. Some further redefinition would be required for rules involving deletion, total assimilation (as in the Finnish example), and so on.

But this would still be insufficient, for it leaves allomorphy frequently failing to correspond to formal complexity. This happens, on the one hand, where a rule accounts for more than one surface 'alternation', and on the other, where more than one rule accounts for a single paradigmatic target.

A single rule can account for more than one alternation when its output is differentiated by rules that apply after it. Because of this possibility, rule generalization can increase allomorphy in the sense of creating new alternations, if these are defined as types of differences between related surface forms. An example is Kuryłowicz's (1968: 298) derivation of IE lengthened grade by the proportion $RT:eRT = eT:\bar{e}T$. This corresponds to a generalization of an inherited ablaut rule $(\phi \rightarrow e)$ from $CRC$ stems ($RT \rightarrow eRT \rightarrow eRT$) to CVC stems ($eT \rightarrow eeT \rightarrow \bar{e}T$), creating a new type of alternation in length by analogy to an existing one that involves the presence or absence of a short vowel. Since allomorphy is by definition a relation involving surface representations, such cases show that allomorphy cannot possibly translate point by point into complexity, as required by the proposal we are considering.

The opposite type of case, where more than one rule converges on a single allomorphic target, likewise falsifies the strict reducability thesis. A uniform paradigm could, given the present theory of grammar, easily be due to several rules which separately would not produce this result. In such cases, the uniform paradigm could formally arise through the addition of a rule (a complication of the system), and correspondingly, an elimination of one of the rules (a simplification) could introduce new allomorphic variation into surface structure. Not only is this a logical possibility, but analyses have been proposed in which just the described situation holds. Apparent systemic complications resulting in paradigm leveling under such conditions were indeed the original motivation for the proposal that a principle of minimization of allomorphy be introduced as part of the evaluation measure in addition to simplicity. The standard examples include phenomena like columnar stress in inflectional paradigms, which in generative analyses of several languages, e.g. Spanish (Harris 1973) and Sanskrit (Kiparsky 1973c) mysteriously arises from an elaborate set of conditions of a morphological sort on the stress rule, or even from the interaction of several stress rules, and the leveling of the original *s/r* alternation in the Latin nouns of the type *honor*, where the change from *honōs:honōris* to *honor:honōris* seemed to require a new branch of rhotacism in the nominative singular. Since these are at least *possible* analyses, the claim that allomorphy is *necessarily* equivalent to formal complexity evidently breaks down here.

The remaining possibility of eliminating a separate principle of minimization of allomorphy is more promising. This is to find a theory of grammar in which it will be true that actually *occurring* types of leveling will always constitute formal simplifications. It involves conceding the formal point that leveling could involve a complication of the grammar, and replacing it with the empirical claim that it in fact never does. It also involves withdrawing the claim that simplification could never result in an increase of allomorphy, which, as we have seen, is dubious anyway. Leveling would then simply be a reflex of some types of simplification, rather than a factor in its own right.

What is interesting about this version of the proposal to eliminate a principle of elimination of allomorphy from the evaluation measure is that it restricts leveling to cases where it is associated with a formal simplification of the system. Other, theoretically imaginable types of leveling accordingly should not be attested in actual change.

The crucial test cases are precisely those in which leveling has been analyzed as resulting from a formal complication in the grammar. If the proposal is to go through, reanalyses must be motivated for these examples, in which the relative formal simplicity of the stages before and after the changes is reversed. It is significant, then, that a more detailed analysis by Harris (1975) of the development of columnar stress in Spanish has indicated that the steps in this development constitute progressive simplifications of the stress rule that arose when the quantity distinction of Latin was first lost. In the Latin example, it seems reasonable to suppose that the change of *honōs* to *honor* involves not a new environment for the rhotacism rule, but simply a reanalysis of *-ōs* stems to *-ōr* stems. This hypothesis would at once explain the restriction of the leveling to masculine and feminine polysyllables, for it is precisely in these categories that stems in *-ōr* existed at all (Schindler 1974, who further refers to Szemerényi). Recently Redenbarger (1976) has argued that in the context of the Latin morphophonemic system the change reduces to a reordering of two rules.

The evidence for an independent principle of minimization of allomorphy that has so far been presented is thus rather poor. However, the decision to abandon it should not be made lightly, as it has some surprising consequences. Vennemann (1974) has pointed out, in connection with motivating his theory of Natural Generative Grammar, that the reduction of leveling to formal simplification is often possible only if phonological representations are assumed to be more superficial than those countenanced in standard generative phonology. A particularly clear instance is the change in Canadian English from the [rəyt] : [raydṛ] type of dialect to the [rəyt] : [rəydṛ] type, thoroughly discussed by J. K. Chambers (1973). The effect of this change is to eliminate the *a:ə* alternation arising in diphthongs through the well-known interaction of voicing with the 'Canadian Raising' rule. As far as I can see, this must be considered a case of analogical leveling, and there is no other reasonable motivation for the change. Yet it can be represented as a formal simplification only if we assume that the raised dipthongs prior to the change are lexicalized before underlying voiceless stops, as in *write* /rəyt/, with a lowering rule then applying before voiced consonants to give forms like *writer* [raydṛ]. The change from the type [raydṛ] to the type [rəydṛ] would then be the loss of the lowering rule. Current generative phonology would however require the redundant difference between [ay] and [əy] to be taken out of underlying representations and introduced by a phonological rule instead.

Turning now to the question whether opacity might be similarly eliminable as a separate factor in the evaluation measure, we face the same two possible strategies as in the case of allomorphy, except that the difficulties this time turn out to be overwhelming. One possibility, again, is that under the right formulation of grammar opacity might turn out to be dispensable because it always translates into complexity. Any increase in opacity would then have to formally complicate the grammar, and any decrease in opacity would have to simplify it. But this is hardly ever so. For one thing, every case of rule reordering is a counterexample, as it causes a decrease in opacity with no corresponding change in formal complexity of the grammar. True, disallowing extrinsic ordering (Koutsoudas, Sanders, and Noll 1974) generally has the effect of forcing a reformulation of nonfeeding ordering by some device which complicates the system (e.g. an extra restriction on the fed rule). What the standard theory would represent as reordering into feeding order (necessarily a gain in input transparency) would then constitute a formal simplification. This would eliminate the need for an independent factor of opacity in certain cases. Aside from the problems that the exclusion of extrinsic ordering meets with (e.g. Campbell 1973) it remains true that outside of this class of disputed cases, opacity does not (even under the no-ordering theory) correspond to complexity as far as we can now tell. This is true for reordering into bleeding order, which brings a gain in environment transparency. The Koutsoudas-Sanders-Noll theory of rule ordering does not guarantee the correct directionality in such cases. Until a principled basis is given for translating environment opacity into complexity, the elimination of extrinsic ordering does not do away with the need for opacity.

Indeed, to find cases where opacity does not correspond to formal complexity we need not turn to rule ordering at all. The Finnish case cited above, where a rule is generalized and becomes opaque in the process, illustrates the basic independence of the two concepts.

Still less acceptable is the second alternative possibility of eliminating opacity, whose counterpart turned out to be rather promising in the case of allomorphy. This would be to give up the equivalence of opacity with complexity, which fails in such obvious ways, and to rather claim that opacity can be reduced to simplicity in those cases where it is apparently relevant to linguistic change. A review of the cases we have just mentioned quickly refutes this try too. In precisely those cases where opacity is completely independent of complexity its historical effect is most clearly apparent, as for example in reordering of rules. Moreover, opacity seems to play a role in the theory of loan phonology and in the theory of exceptions (Kiparsky 1971). The postulation of a separate principle of opacity in the evaluation measure seems unavoidable.

As to the relative weight of simplicity and opacity where the two principles conflict, the only thing that can be said with certainty so far is that simplification can take place in such a way as to create opacity. We have mentioned an example from Finnish which shows this possibility. The question whether a hierarchical relationship holds, with simplicity dominating transparency, therefore depends on whether opacity is ever eliminated at the price of complicating the grammar.

Our conclusions can be summed up as follows:

(1) Minimization of allomorphy, of opacity, and of complexity are formally independent, in the sense that none of them can be defined in terms of any of the others.

(2) No unequivocal evidence exists for considering minimization of allomorphy as a separate motivating factor in linguistic change. Actually attested cases of leveling can usually with some plausibility be represented as formal simplifications, though this in some cases involves nontrivial and perhaps false assumptions about the form of grammars.

(3) Minimization of opacity must, however, be considered to function as a separate motivating factor in linguistic change, and hence (by our assumption about the source of such change) also as a separate component of the evaluation measure.

The idea that the 'learnability' of a system depends on at least two separate factors, complexity and opacity, which we have reached on strictly language-internal evidence, might be generalized naively as follows. Learning an abstract system from a corpus of examples involves two distinct tasks: discovering what the system is like, and fixing it in one's memory. A source of difficulty for the latter task is the sheer amount of information which must be processed and stored. Thus, a long list of random digits is hard to learn simply because it takes up a lot of memory space. A linguistic counterpart would be suppletive morphology. There is another source of difficulty, of the sort which is for example maximized in cryptography, to make it hard to 'learn' codes. A formally very simple set of rules can produce a hard-to-figure-out relation between input and output, though it might be easy to remember the rules once they have been discovered. As Koefoed (1974: fn. 4) notes, the transparency of a rule might be considered to depend in addition to the factors so far proposed also on the phonetic similarity of its input and output. Even a single, formally simple rule can be hard to discover and might therefore be considered transparent, as for example the rule for turning English into Pig Latin (it is just this fact which is the whole point of using Pig Latin). The difficulty would of course be compounded by several such rules applying sequentially. It is natural to identify these dimensions of learning difficulty with what we have identified linguistically as complexity and opacity. Complexity could be thought of as a measure of the amount of information which must be processed and stored. Opacity would then be a measure of one factor determining the ease with which the structure of the system may be discovered (which is not to deny that complexity would not also have an effect on it). Perhaps this speculation can take us to a point where linguists' hypotheses about language acquisition can finally begin to make contact with findings of experimental psychology.

# Chapter 10

# Remarks on Analogical Change*

One of the things we ought to require of a theory of language change is that it tell us, for a given language, what possible changes it may undergo. If we represent the history of a language as a succession of stages, then we can construe this part of the theory of change as specifying the possible pairs $(S_i, S_{i+1})$ of successive historical stages of languages. We would also like the theory to rank the changes in an order of plausibility or 'naturalness' on some principled basis. It is only to be expected, of course, that the distinction between implausible and impossible changes will necessarily be left vague in many respects.

I do not mean to imply in any way that delimiting possible changes and ranking them according to plausibility is the only goal of historical linguistic theory. Much would remain to be done even if we had already reached this goal, and much can be done before we ever do. In particular, it is necessary to find out correctly *how* changes are implemented in a speech community. But the specification of 'possible linguistic changes' is important, as it gives us the first-order theoretical basis both for linguistic reconstruction and for bringing historical facts to bear on linguistic theory. It gives a basis for reconstruction because the basic notions such as 'proto-language', 'related language', 'daughter language', 'internal reconstruction', 'comparative reconstruction' are all definable in terms of the successor relationship as a primitive, in fairly obvious ways. E.g. two languages M and N are genetically related if and only if they have the history

$$(M_o, M_1, \ldots M_{p-1}, M_p) \quad (N_o, N_1, \ldots N_{q-1}, N_q), \text{ where } M_o = N_o$$

And it gives a basis for relating history to synchronic issues because the typical argument there takes the form of deducing the correctness of a

\* This work was supported in part by Grants from the National Institute of Mental Health (Grant #MH13380) and from the National Institutes of Health (Grant #HD14378) to The Massachusetts Institute of Technology. A version of this paper was read at the First International Conference on Historical Linguistics, University of Edinburgh, 2-7 September, 1973.

particular grammar, and thereby of a particular linguistic theory, by showing that it is required by an attested historical change in terms of some prior notion of 'possible change'. For example, we might have two versions of linguistic theory, LT and LT', which in a certain language lead to the respective grammars $G_i$ and $G_i'$. We observe that the directly following stage has the grammar $G_{i+1}$, let us say under both LT and LT'. If now either $(G_i, G_{i+1})$ or $(G_i', G_{i+1}')$ is not a possible pair of successive stages, then we can argue that $G_i$ or $G_i'$, as the case may be, is the wrong grammar, and correspondingly LT or LT' is a wrong linguistic theory. The more sharply we can delimit possible changes, the more compelling we can make this form of argumentation.

The succession of historical stages is both a succession of *language states* $L_p$, $L_{p+1}$, .... and a corresponding succession of *grammars* $G_p$, $G_{p+1}$, . . . , where $G_i$ generates $L_i$.[1] Consequently, there are three possible approaches to the task of delimiting the class of possible changes:

(1)    In terms of language states, viz. $L_p > L_{p+1}$.

(2)    In terms of grammars, viz. $G_p > G_{p+1}$.

(3)    In terms of both language states and grammars, viz.
       $(L_p, G_p) > (L_{p+1}, G_{p+1})$.

The first approach is to look for functions mapping language states into their possible successor states, without reference to the grammar. This is the approach of Hermann Paul and the other Neogrammarians, and of de Saussure in the *Cours de linguistique générale*. In the domain of sound change, it takes the form of the claim that phonetic factors only, and no grammatical ones, may condition sound change. In the domain of analogy, it takes the form of the claim that the proportional schema, applied to the utterances of a language, generates the possible analogical changes which the language can undergo. The Neogrammarians were committed to such a theory of change by their view of language, which did not countenance any abstract morphophonemic and syntactic structure. It was assumed that the mind stores language in the form of sample utterances in phonetic representation, with associative bonds between morphological segments, and that speech production itself is really the solving of analogical proportions. But in the twentieth century, the same view of change tended to be retained even as structuralist linguistics was developing increasingly abstract theories of grammar. There emerged a dual view of change: extra-grammatical (and in the case of sound change even quasi-physical) processes of primary change secondarily causing restructuring of the grammar itself. Sound change or analogy could for example lead to rephonemicization or loss of grammatical categories, though the changes per se were independent of these repercussions. The mechanisms of change were not either conditioned or motivated by the structure on which they ultimately impinged. This gap between change and structure was explicitly maintained by de Saussure and Bloomfield, who believed that they had found reasons why it should exist, and attempted to deduce inportant consequences from it. Jakobson, on the other hand, perceived it as a latent contradiction, which he tried to resolve by demonstrating that sound change must be viewed as a psychological and grammatical process, and not as a purely physical one. Studies of the functionally based grammatical conditioning of sound change (e.g. Kiparsky 1972) and socio-linguistic studies of sound change in progress (e.g. Labov 1972a) have now converged to establish Jakobson's point beyond any doubt. A somewhat parallel effort in the domain of anological change was made by J. Kuryłowicz (1949), who argued that grammatical structure is essential in this type of change too. However, the 'annotated' proportions suggested by Kuryłowicz suffer from some of the same defects as the plain proportions of the Neogrammarians. These defects are related in interesting ways to the defects of taxonomic grammar in general. In addition, Kuryłowicz's theory of analogy has various problems of its own, some of which we will encounter below.

The problem with any proportional theory of analogy is that it is both too weak and too strong. On the one hand, it allows many kinds of analogical change which we do not find in the actual history of languages. As long as we merely require that *some* relationship hold between the terms in a proportion (and more we cannot legitimately require without introducing the very system of grammatical rules which the proportional theory of analogy is supposed to do without) we cannot distinguish absurd proportions from those which a historical linguist would consider as defining truly potential analogical changes. For example, we do not expect a new lexical item *heye* meaning 'to see' to arise from the proportion *ear*: *hear* = *eye* : x, though this proportion cannot without the grammar be distinguished from that which generated an actual analogical form such as *brothers*, e.g. *sister*: *sisters* = *brother* : x. Or in syntax, we do not expect to hear *Mary, who John knows Bill and*, though this is the solution to the proportion *John knows Mary: Mary, who John knows = John knows Bill and Mary* : x. In general, the relationship between the terms of a proportion is one which corresponds to a *grammatical* operation which functions or could function in the language at hand. Therefore it must for one thing correspond to a possible or actual rule, and the rule must furthermore be applied in a way which conforms to valid conditions on rule application. In our first example, *heye* is excluded because the relationship *ear* : *hear* evidently does not correspond to a rule in English grammar. In the second example, the proportion does correspond to a rule, but is applied in such a way as to violate the Coordinate Structure Constraint.

Conversely, it is well known and admitted even by proponents of proportional analogy that cases of *bona fide* analogical change exist for which no proportional representation can be given. In morphology, analogical 'double' plurals of the type *mices, feets, mens* which are common in American dialects as well as in child language, simply do not fit the proportional schema in any way. A similar case from the earlier history of English is *kine*, replacing *kye* as the plural of *cows*. Another large class of counterexamples are changes affecting isolated, nonderived words, where a proportional schema cannot in principle be set up. For example, loanwords in English in time tend to become adapted to the native vocabulary in stress and other phonological characteristics, e.g. *garáge* > *gárage*. In so far as such words do not participate in any derivational morphology, it is impossible to represent their adaptation as the resolution of any kind of proportion between surface forms.

Finally, the proportional model, if we interpret the terms of a proportion as concrete words or utterances, carries with it the implication that analogical change should be an essentially sporadic, lexical-item-by-lexical-item process. This is indeed how analogical change is traditionally described. But in reality it is only morphological analogy which is typically sporadic; in the case of syntactic phenomena on the one hand, and purely phonological phenomena on the other, analogical changes proceed typically (though not always) across-the-board. That is, they do not depend on this or that lexical item but simply on some configuration of syntactic or phonological elements. We could try to represent this type of analogy by allowing the terms of proportions to be syntactic or phonological categories rather than concrete utterances. Besides the fact that we have then ended up reintroducing grammar by the back door, we would still not thereby have explained why it is that morphological analogy is typically sporadic, whereas syntactic and phonological analogy is typically across-the-board.

The second approach to specifying possible changes is to look for functions mapping grammars directly into their possible successor grammars. These have been discussed occasionally in the framework of generative grammar under the term 'metarules' or 'epirules' (e.g. George Grace, R. Lass); a recent treatment with specific reference to analogical change is Thomason (1973). This is the exact opposite of the first approach in that it implies that change can be defined on grammars alone, without any reference to the surface structures they generate. The difficulty with this is that many analogical changes are made possible only by ambiguities or near-ambiguities of analysis. Small differences in output can correspond to large differences in grammar. To the extent that this is the case analogical restructuring can lead to substantial structural change. For example, morphological recutting, as when the boundary between stem and suffix is redrawn, characteristically has multiple consequences for the system. In the Maori case described in Hale (1973), there is a *simultaneous* change in

(1) The underlying forms of suffixes (e.g. /ia/ > /tia/, /ria/, /kia/ etc.);
(2) The underlying forms of stems (e.g. /afit/ > /afi/, /maur/ > /mau/, /hopuk/ > /hopu/ etc.);
(3) The system of phonological rules (e.g. the rule that deletes word-final consonants ceases to become necessary in the grammar);
(4) The morpheme structure conditions (e.g. the canonical form of stems changes in that all stems must now end in vowels).

The consequences of this drastic reanalysis are quite small in the output, however. It follows that metarules that map grammars into grammars must allow for multiple changes of this magnitude. But it is obvious that not any random assortment of such changes in the grammar is a possible analogical innovation. For example, if some other change in the form of suffixes was substituted for (1) in the above complex of changes, the result taken as a whole would clearly no longer be a possible analogical development. Indeed, (1) or (2) alone would hardly be possible changes. Advocates of the metarules approach to analogy must therefore show how they propose to allow for the sorts of substantial grammatical restructurings that do occur, without at the same time letting through an enormous mass of formally similar putative restructurings which we can assume could not occur. If we ask why (1) in the Maori example could not be replaced by some other similar change, or omitted altogether, the answer is obvious: the resulting complex of changes would involve a radical and unmotivated modification of the language. The change that actually took place, however, was a plausible reinterpretation of the system which involved (initially at least) very few changes in the surface forms of the language. The metarules approach would seem to preclude this kind of answer. From the viewpoint of the grammar *per se* the change that actually took place is formally indistinguishable from the change which we agree is impossible.

Therefore, the class of possible analogical changes that a language can undergo cannot be characterized on the basis of grammar alone, any more than it can be characterized on the basis of surface structure alone. The failure of the first two approaches brings us by default to the third, in which reference is made to *both* grammar and surface structure. Of course, this overall approach could be given many different concrete interpretations. As a starting point I would like to take my earlier formulation in Kiparsky (1965). This could be summarized by saying that the *direction*

of analogical change is optimalization in terms of the evaluation measure
provided by the theory of generative grammar, and the *range* of analogical
change is constrained by the requirement that the change in surface
structure be small (where it is of course necessary to elaborate on what
is meant by 'small').

Such a characterization of analogical change must meet the test of
fitting the historical data. It can also be supported by the fact that it itself
follows from a natural model of the actual process of change that is
involved. We can view this process as one of *imperfect learning*, in which
residues of the intermediate grammars created by children during the
acquisition of language are carried over into the adult system. There is
abundant evidence from studies of child language that the successive
grammars constructed in the process of language acquisition are normally
both increasingly adequate analyses of the language and increasingly
complex systems. If, then, aspects of these grammars survive correction,
and are adopted by other speakers in the community, a linguistic change
will have taken place which will normally have produced a more highly
valued grammatical system. And it follows also that analogical change can
only result in such differences as could reasonably survive in a speech
community. That is, the change cannot have overly radical effects on the
surface forms of the language. Thus, the overall contributions of grammar
and surface structure to circumscribing the direction and range of analogical change are neatly accounted for if we ascribe analogical change
to imperfect language learning, while understanding language learning in
the way suggested by the theory of generative grammar.

This basic idea must of course be elaborated in several ways before it
can approach anything like empirical adequacy. Let us note, though, that
even in this simplest possible form it readily solves the difficulties which
we earlier found in both alternative approaches to analogical change. For
example, the asymmetry of analogical change is built into this theory
by virtue of the asymmetry inherent in the linguistic evaluation measure.
The difference between sporadic and across-the-board analogy seems to
reduce simply to the difference between the effect of simplifying a general
(phonological or syntactic) rule, or a morphological or lexical rule applying only to designated lexical items. Cases like *mices* fit in as *partial
regularizations*, where the regular suffix -*s* is adopted but the irregular
vowel change in the stem is retained. And the overly radical changes permitted by a purely grammatical characterization are ruled out when we
require that the surface structures of the old and new grammars be sufficiently similar that the change can persist in the speech community.

Consequently, the evaluation measure assumes a different role in the
theory than was originally meant for it. Rather than just functioning as a
procedure for selecting the 'right' grammar among a number of grammars

that generate the same language, it now is required to define a hierarchy of complexity even among grammars that generate different languages. We can, in fact, think of the evaluation measure as a theory of the order in which alternative hypotheses are entertained in the process of language acquisition.

Of course, this approach to analogical change is not committed to any specific version of the evaluation measure. It merely says that *whatever* the right evaluation measure of grammars ultimately proves to be will also describe the direction of analogical change in language. But to be tenable, it should be consistent with the historical facts in so far as the evaluation measure is firmly established on empirical grounds. Originally it was assumed that the evaluation measure could be reduced to simplicity, measured in phonology by the number of feature specifications within some descriptive format specified by the theory of grammar. Difficulties with this particular view of the evaluation measure became apparent very soon. It was found that the ordering of rules is asymmetrical, in that for certain pairs of rules one order is more highly valued than its opposite. Such an asymmetry, like many of the less obvious aspects of grammatical theory, could hardly be discovered from strictly descriptive considerations, but requires evidence from historical linguistics, developmental psycholinguistics, or other external sources. More serious blows were dealt to any monolithic version of the evaluation measure by the finding that the complexity or 'learnability' of a grammar cannot be determined just from its form, but involves also the relationship between the rules of the grammar and the surface forms (degree of opacity) and the distance between paradigmatically related surface forms. In addition, requirements of perception and production dictate other aspects of linguistic structure and evolution, and we can conjecture that they play a role in the acquisition of language as well (Kiparsky 1972). For an illuminating discussion of these questions see Koefoed (1974).

Some people have expressed uneasiness about the dissolution of the unified simplicity measure into a set of distinct specific principles. This move is necessary because the facts require it, but in any case it should not be thought of as somehow undesirable on a priori grounds. It would seem that both in the social sciences and in fields like biology it is normal to find an interplay of separate factors which may in particular cases conflict with each other, in others reinforce each other, and in still others be independent of each other. In our case, these factors are the acquisition, perception, and production of language. The structure and development of language is guided by the requirements of 'learnability', 'perceptibility' and 'producibility', each of these factors themselves being complex and operating at several levels of structure.

All this is only one of the ways in which one could try to account for the way analogical change is constrained by grammar and surface structure. There is especially one other plausible alternative which has often been mentioned in this connection. We could assume that the source of analogical change lies not in language acquisition by children, but in the slips of the tongue that occur naturally in speech, especially when a speaker is tired or nervous. Such slips of the tongue could become adopted as normal parts of the language by the speech community. It is undeniable that 'slips of the tongue' often look like analogical forms, and that many of them can only be understood in grammatical terms, and not in terms of the peripheral speech apparatus alone. I do not see any reason to assume that some analogical changes might not in fact originate in this way. However, there are compelling reasons why *all* analogical change cannot be understood so. Any change involving substantial reanalysis of the rules and/or the underlying representations, such as the sort of recutting illustrated by the Maori example cited above, could obviously not be brought about by a simple slip of the tongue. We know on other grounds (such as the phenomenon of hypercorrection) that radical restructuring does not easily take place in mature speakers. Therefore, any case of analogy involving such restructuring must be attributed to fresh analyses imposed by learners on the language they hear.

A question which the theory of analogical change must face is how residues of child language could ever be carried uncorrected all the way into the adult system, and how they could ever be adopted by the speech community as a whole. Some empirical research will no doubt be more useful here than any speculation we can offer now. However, it seems inescapable that we must assume some positive reception of new forms by mature speakers. Some analogical forms 'sound good' and are picked up, perhaps as a joke within the family at first. The potential analogical changes are thus 'in the air', and one might think of child language (and perhaps slips of the tongue) as merely releasing tendencies which are already latent in the language.

I would now like to turn to some aspects in which the above discussion has been oversimplified. Analogical changes in morphology normally do not extend to all applicable cases, but are typcially sporadic. A curious corollary of this is that a change which constitutes a regularization within the domain where it takes place can nevertheless end up creating irregularity in the grammar as a whole. One class of such cases is *lexical split*, in which words are regularized in certain meanings or uses, while remaining irregular in others. A standard example is the split of the plural of *brother* into *brothers* and *brethren*. Clearly this split has been caused by the tendency to regularize the plural, but since the regularization affected only some uses of the word and not others, the net effect has strictly speaking been a de-regularization of the grammar. The rule for the plural of *brother* is now more complicated than before the analogical innovation took place. Another important class of analogical changes is *morphologization*, that is, analogical regularization in specific morphological categories. New light on this traditional topic has recently been shed by the studies of Robinson (1972) on German dialects and Harris (1974) on the Spanish of the Southwestern United States (Chicano). Robinson shows that analogical changes affecting the Umlaut rule, by the rule either becoming inapplicable or reordered with respect to another rule, usually proceed by suffix or by morphological category. Harris, basing himself on an analysis by Rogelio Reyes of Chicano Spanish, describes the levelling out of the rule that diphthongizes stressed mid vowels (as in *calíento* ~ *calentámos* 'heat', *cuézo* ~ *cocémos* 'cook'). In Mexican Spanish, this rule applies independently of morphological categorization, though it is restricted to certain lexically marked mid vowels only. In Chicano, the alternation is leveled out in verbs of the first (*a*-) conjugation only, e.g. *vuelo – volamos – vuelo – vuelamos*. For some speakers, both front and back diphthongs are leveled, for others (including Reyes himself) the leveling touches only the *back* diphthongs:

|    |       |       |          |
|----|-------|-------|----------|
| 2. | conj. | tiéne | tenémos  |
| 2. | conj. | puéde | podémos  |
| 1. | conj. | piénsa | pensámos |
| 1. | conj. | vuélo | vuelámos |

Although this plainly constitutes a regularization of a certain subclass of verbs, it equally plainly constitutes a complication of the grammar as a whole, for from its point of view the alternation has simply become more messy than ever. To deal with such facts, it is not enough to speak simply about regularization or optimalization; we have to come to grips with the way the effects of analogical regularization can be counteracted by an opposing tendency to resist change, resulting sometimes in lexical split or morphologization with a net loss in regularity for the system as a whole.

Consider in more detail what happens in cases of lexical split. According to Kuryłowicz's widely accepted Fourth Law of Analogy, the new (analogical form) will in such cases assume the primary function while the old form is retained in the secondary function:

Quand à la suite d'une transformation morphologique une forme subit la différenciation, la forme nouvelle correspond à sa fonction primaire (de fondation), la forme ancienne est réservée pour la fonction sécondaire (fondée). (Kuryłowicz 1949).

Recent textbooks of historical linguistics cite this principle with appro-
bation and give an example or two in support of it, e.g. *brothers/brethren*,
*older/elder*, or lexicalized past participles of the type *wrought* (vs. *worked*),
*straight* (vs. *stretched*). Only Lehmann (1962) adds an apparent contrary
example. But it is not pointed out that Kuryłowicz's principle is contradicted by numerous changes of a quite everyday sort, in which a form is
regularized in some special function but remains irregular in its 'primary
function'. These behave exactly in the opposite way from what
Kuryłowicz's principle predicts. I list the major categories of relevant
cases below, with representative examples of each.[2]

The most common case is perhaps regularization in metaphorical usage:

| | | |
|---|---|---|
| *wolfs* | 'aggressive men' | vs. *wolves* |
| *sweet tooths* | | vs. *teeth* |
| *mouses* | 'black eyes' | vs. *mice* (Mark Liberman) |
| *weaved* | (through traffic) | vs. *wove* |
| *crowed* | obligatorily in the sense 'exulted', | |
| | | otherwise *crew* is possible (British) |
| *badder* | 'tougher', *baddest* | vs. *worse, worst* |

Nouns regularize when used as disparaging epithets:

*Those louses!*
*Silly gooses!*
*Oxes!*

Other types of derived meaning:

| | | |
|---|---|---|
| *selfs* | 'egos' | vs. *selves* |
| *halfs* (of a game or term) | | vs. *halves* |
| *lifes* optional for 'biographies' | | vs. *lives* |

Names tend to regularize:

*Mickey Mouses*
*Mother Gooses*
*Maple Leafs*

A fortiori, the same is true of names used metaphorically, e.g. *mickey
mouses* 'police cars' (Robert Jeffers) or 'trivial ones (e.g. easy courses)'
(Susan Giuliana).

There is a tendency for compounds to get regularized. This tendency is
particularly strong for exocentric (bahuvrihi) compounds:

| | | |
|---|---|---|
| *flatfoots* | 'policemen' | vs. *forefeet* |
| *still-lifes* | | vs. *afterlives* |
| *silverleafs* | 'white poplars' | vs. *tealeaves, cloverleaves* |
| *cloverleafs* | 'intersections' | 'leaves of clover' |
| *sabertooths* | 'tigers' | vs. *buckteeth* |
| *loudmouths* [θ] | | vs. *rivermouths* |
| *jackknifes* | 'dives' | vs. *jackknives* |
| *powerhouses* [s] | 'powerful or active people', | |
| *tollhouses₁* [s] | 'tollhouse cookies' (Don Churma) | |
| | | vs. *powerhouses, tollhouses* |

But not all exocentric compounds regularize, cf. *Blackfeet*. And even some endocentric compounds have a tendency to regular inflection:

| | |
|---|---|
| *backslided* ~ *backslid* | vs. *slid* (\**slided*) |
| *gainsaid* [-seyd] | vs. *said* |
| *guineafowls* | vs. *fowl* (George Stalker) |
| *barrelcactuses* | vs. *cacti* (Lynn Heaton) |
| *steak-, pocketknifes* | along with *-knives* (Susan Giuliana) |

None of these tendencies are specific to English. Each could be illustrated with examples from other languages. Thus, we have regularization of compound verbs in

| | | |
|---|---|---|
| French | *prédisez, contredisez* | vs. *dites* |
| German | *Staub, gesaugt* 'vacuum cleaned' | vs. *gesogen* 'sucked' |
| Latin | *dēmpsī* | vs. *ēmī* 'bought' |
| Swedish | *frambesvärjde* or *frambesvor* 'conjured up', but only *besvor* 'adjured'. | |

We seem to be faced with two diametrically opposed sets of examples, one supporting Kuryłowicz's Fourth Law of Analogy, the other contradicting it.

| | | |
|---|---|---|
| Old form: | *elder* ('secondary function') | *worse* ('primary function') |
| New form: | *older* ('primary function') | *badder* ('secondary function') |

Is there a resolution to this conflict? Must we conclude that there is no regularity to lexical split, or is there a deeper generalization underlying these types of change?

A simple formalism will help to give a clearer picture here. I will use a rightward wedge $>$ to denote historical change and a downward arrow $\downarrow$ to denote a synchronic derivation. A lexicalized derivation, i.e. one which is no longer synchronically operative, so that the derived form has been reanalyzed as an independent lexical item, can be symbolized by a slashed downward arrow $\not\downarrow$. I indicate regular forms or paradigms by $(\quad)^R$, and irregular or exceptional forms or paradigms by $(\quad)^X$. Of course, the regularity or irregularity is always to be understood in regard to a particular morphological rule. In this fashion the morphology of *ox* can be represented as follows:

$$(\text{ox, oxen})^X$$
$$\downarrow$$
$$(\text{ox, oxen})^X > (\text{ox, oxes})^R$$

where the downward arrow stands for the metaphorical derivation that gives the meaning 'stupid person', in which the word's plural has been regularized.

Similarly,

$$(\text{bad, worse})^X$$
$$\downarrow$$
$$(\text{bad, worse})^X > (\text{bad, badder})^R$$

where of course it is also possible that the word was never irregular in the particular derived meaning at issue,

$$(\text{bad, worse})^X$$
$$\downarrow$$
$$(\text{bad, badder})^R$$

More generally, regularization begins at the end of a derivational chain. Where there are several stages of derivation, as in

$$(\text{leaf, leaves})^X$$
$$\downarrow$$
$$(\text{maple leaf, -ves})^X$$
$$\downarrow$$
$$(\text{Maple Leaf, -ves})^X \qquad \text{'emblem of Canada'}$$
$$\downarrow$$
$$(\text{Maple Leafs})^R \qquad \text{'Toronto hockey team'}$$

the regularization of any link in the chain implies the regularization of the links below it.

Consider now what happens when the derivational chain is broken and a historically derived form is lexicalized. For example, the original past participle of *stretch* is *straight*. Like such participles as *closed* in current English, *straight* developed an adjectival function in addition to its function as a participle. In general, all past participles of change-of-state verbs appear to have an adjectival twin. When the participle was regularized by acquiring the normal *-ed* suffix, the lexicalized adjective could not be affected. Since it was an independent lexical entry, it was regular already.

$$(\text{stretch, straight}_{\text{pp.}})^X \quad \rightarrow \quad (\text{stretch, stretched})^R$$
$$\downarrow$$
$$(\text{straight}_{\text{Adj.}})^R$$

Our principle that regularization starts at the end of a derivational chain remains valid for such cases too. But now note that *straight* is a typical example of the sort used to justify Kuryłowicz's Fourth Law of Analogy. There is of course the difficulty for Kuryłowicz that there is no independently justified sense in which the adjectival function of *straight* could be called secondary relative to its participal function. But this is not the point which I wish to make here. More essential is the fact that as we have just seen, no such principle is needed at all to explain why adjectival *straight* fails to change. It follows from the uncontroversial assumption that *straight* was lexicalized as an adjective before the analogy took effect. Since it was in that function no longer derived from *stretch*, it was thereby regular and could not be further 'regularized'.

My contention is that *whenever* there is regularization in a 'primary meaning', in apparent violation with my principle and in apparent agreement with Kuryłowicz's Fourth Law, special conditions of this type hold, by virtue of which the irregularity in a secondary usage is fixed in the lexicon. The most common type of case, in fact, is of exactly the type of *straight*, where a derived form is lexicalized. There are, of course, large numbers of adjectives of similar origin, e.g. *drunken, clean-shaven, sodden, horror-stricken, fraught.*

An irregular form might also survive analogical change by being preserved in fixed expressions. For example, *molten* and *burnt* are surely still synchronically related to *melt* and *burn*. The regularized participles *melted, burned* are also used adjectivally (*melted cheese, burned toast*). But relatively fixed phrases like *molten lava, burnt offerings* (note \*completely burnt offerings) preserve the older form.

Sometimes verbs shed lexicalized forms at several points in their history.

Two examples illustrating the variety of possible situations are *cleave* and *gild*, whose morphology is represented in our formalism as follows:

$$\text{(cleave, cloven)}^{X1} > \text{(cleave, cleft)}^{X} > \text{(cleave, -ed)}^{R}$$

(cloven) e.g. *hoof*      (cleft) e.g. *palate*

$$\text{(gild, gilt)}^{X} > \text{(gild, -ed)}^{R}$$

(gilt) e.g. *edges* (gild, -ed)$^{R}$

(gilded) e.g. *youth*

A third way in which an irregular form can be preserved is by being fixed in a special style or usage. For example, *brethren* is retained in reference to members of religious or fraternal groups.

Of course it is possible for several of these conditions to hold simultaneously in the same word. For example, the old comparative of *old* survives on the one hand in the lexicalized noun *elder* (as in the *elders of a church*), and on the other hand (along with *eldest*) in fixed phrases like *elder brother, elder statesman*. In support of this view we may note that *elder brother* is not the same as *older brother*. *Elder* implies seniority, not just an earlier time of birth. For example, of two twin brothers the one who was born first would hardly be the *elder brother* (in our culture at least), though he would be the *older brother*. Similarly, *wrought* persists as an adjective in *wrought iron, overwrought*, and as a verb form in religious usage (*what hath God wrought*) and in a few fixed verb phrases such as *wrought wonders*.

My claim, then, is that *all* cases that apparently support Kuryłowicz's Fourth Law of Analogy are really due to one of the above special factors causing retention of the irregular form in a restricted function. Therefore, Kuryłowicz's Fourth Law is not needed as an independent principle at all. In the general case, where these special factors do not operate, we in fact require a principle with exactly the opposite effect, which governs the class of examples of the type analyzed earlier.

The format $A > B$ is a macroscopic representation of change. The wedge actually stands for two distinct historical processes: the introduction of the new form and the loss of the old one. As has been often pointed out, these processes must be distinguished, because they do not necessarily take place at the same time. Most commonly, the new form competes for a time with the old one before finally ousting it (e.g. *dreamt/ dreamed, lit/lighted, knelt/kneeled, dwarves/dwarfs*). Less frequent is the complementary case, which makes the point even more dramatically. Here the old form is lost but the new one is not yet usable. The result is a *copout* — a gap in the paradigm at points of choice in the rule system. For example, *stride* lacks a past participle in most people's speech — neither *stridden* nor *strided* seems quite acceptable. In Russian, certain verbs lack first person singular forms in an otherwise complete paradigm. These turn out to be stems in *-d* in a conjugation where a choice must be made in 1.sg. forms whether to palatalize *d* into *-žd-*, the old (Church Slavic) form, or *ž*, the new form. For example, neither *\*pobežu* nor *\*pobeždu* 'I shall win' is acceptable (V. Kiparsky 1967: 217). A well-known case in Spanish is the gap in the paradigm of certain verbs like *abolir* 'abolish' in those forms where a decision must be made whether or not to apply a vowel change rule (*o~ue*), e.g. 1.sg. *\*abuelo/\*abolo*. In Finnish, certain verbs of the type *erkanee* 'is separated out' are not used in environments in which the consonant gradation rule would be applicable (e.g. 1.sg.pres. *erkanen*, pres. part. *erkaneva*, but not inf. *\*erata*, past part. *\*erannut*). The analogical history of these paradigms is not clear to me, however.

Another place where copouts can be found is in the process of back-formation from compound nouns, which is a major source of new verbs in English. A kind of path to verbhood is apparent, where the principal stations are: Noun or Adjective (Agent *-er*, gerund and Participial *-ing*) — Tenseless Verb (Infinitive, Progressive) — Tensed Verb. An example of the most nominal type is *bloodsucker, a bloodsucking parasite*. No verbal forms are possible, whether tenseless (*\*he wants to bloodsuck, \*he is bloodsucking tonight*) or tensed (*\*he bloodsucked with the Count every month*). The type *sightseer, sightseeing* allows tenseless verbal forms (*I like to sightsee, they're sightseeing*) but not tensed ones (*\*sightsees, \*sightsaw*). The third type, *ghostwriter*, allows all verb forms (*to ghostwrite, ghostwrites, ghostwrote*).

Note now that certain back-formations with strong verb bases allow a present but not a past: *skywrites* but not *\*skywrote, \*skywrited, freethrows* but not *\*freethrew, \*freethrowed, joyrides* but not *\*joyrode, \*joyrided, skydives* but not *\*skydove, \*skydived*. Weak verbs, even those whose past tense involves vowel shortening, seem to have no copouts, but make a (possibly regularized) past tense if they make a present tense, e.g. *daydreamed, (daydreamt), shotputted, inputted, outputted, broadcast (-ed), forecast (-ed), backslid (-ed)*.

It remains to discover the concrete mechanisms of change by which lexical split and morphologization of this type can take place. On the assumption that analogical change is related to language acquisition as suggested above, we may make the following tentative conclusions.

We know from empirical studies of child language that a morphological rule is learned in a characteristic progression of steps (Ervin 1964, Zwicky 1970b). In the first stage, the most frequent forms, whether regular or irregular, are learned by the child as unanalyzable wholes. When a rule is then learned, it is often overgeneralized even to irregular lexical items which are not subject to it in the adult language, though the right forms may have been produced in the first stage. Finally, the irregularities are acquired or reacquired, lexical item by lexical item, as these are marked as not undergoing the rule.

We have a sequence of grammars

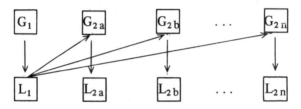

where $G_{2a}$, $G_{2b}$, ... are approximations to $G_1$, usually of increasing adequacy and decreasing value (i.e. increasing linguistic 'complexity').[3] The child's progress consists in modifying his grammar so as to accommodate the counter-evidence in $L_1$. Any individual piece of data can always be accounted for by several different modifications of the grammar. Morphological structure is in part so idiosyncratic that a projection from a small amount of data is likely to be either an overgeneralization or an undergeneralization which will require modification later on. Suppose, for example, that a child has learned the regular past tense suffix, and produces both correct forms like *walked* and incorrect forms like *goed, singed, bringed*. If he now hears *sank* and *sang*, one possible response would be to set up an $i \rightarrow a$ rule, and another would be to enter them in the lexicon (as *went* must be dealt with). The former is an overgeneralization; the fact that children at least sometimes do it is shown by the fact that they produce forms like *brang*, where the new rule is extended to a verb it properly does not apply to. The latter is an undergeneralization, which we may infer whenever forms subject to a rule are introduced singly (e.g. *sang* but *sinked*).

The examples of lexical split and morphologization we have discussed are due to undergeneralization. They imply that at least in the case of lexically conditioned rules the optimal generalization may be missed in language acquisition. While they are compatible with the claim that $G_{2a}$, $G_{2b}$, ... are increasingly adequate and of decreasing value, they show that these stages may in some respects be less highly valued than $G_1$.

## Notes

1.      Variation enters this picture at two points: each $G_i$ presumably contains a number of 'optional' rules, and each speech community has coexisting in it several stages of the language.

2.      Where I do not credit a specific informant or source, the example is either found in *Webster's Collegiate Dictionary* or has been attested to me by more than one speaker.

3.      Of course this is in many respects an idealization which for certain purposes will represent an oversimplification. But at least it does not represent language acquisition as instantaneous, which (whatever its convenience when discussing e.g. the question of innate ideas) is misleading and useless as far as historical linguistics is concerned.

# Chapter 11

# Analogical Change as a Problem for Linguistic Theory*

## 1. Simplification vs. proportions

Recent linguistics has moved from the structuralist segregation of synchronic and diachronic study of language towards a reintegration of the two, based on the idea that structure can determine change, with the corollary that change can therefore be diagnostic of structure. This program has had consequences on both sides of the equation. On the synchronic side, it is mainly through evidence from change that phonologists have argued for such factors as opacity and recoverability in the evaluation measure, and for the imposition of restrictions on the abstractness of underlying phonological representations. On the historical side, the new conception of linguistic structure evolved through efforts to construct explicit formal generative grammars has provoked some rethinking of the nature of both sound change and analogy.

As an example of the relevance of synchronic work for historical linguistics we may take the classic issue of whether sound change admits nonphonetic conditioning. Formal grammar as well as sociolinguistic research on linguistic variation has shown that phonology is intimately connected to higher linguistic levels. This undermines the structuralist concept of autonomous phonology, and thereby in turn casts doubt on the companion concept of 'blind' sound change. Morphological and other nonphonetic conditioning of sound change was previously ascribed to grammatical analogy secondarily acting upon the results of a quasiphysiological process of sound change. It is now more simply taken to be part and parcel of the phonological process itself, as a reflection of the inherent contextually determined and functionally governed variability characteristic

*This essay was read at the Forum Lecture Series presented at the 1978 Linguistic Institute of the Linguistic Society of America, hosted by the University of Illinois, 12 June – 5 August, 1978. It is extracted from a monograph on analogy to be published separately. It presents the main line of argument in a condensed form, omitting most of the critical discussion of alternative views and nearly all supporting data. This work was supported in part by the National Institutes of Mental Health Grant No. 5 PO1 MH13390-12.

of all new rules. This permits a more restricted and therefore more predictive theory of analogy.

In general, the theory of grammar has opened up the possibility of structural explanations as alternatives to be considered in many cases where so far only a historical explanation was available. Noting a change $(A > A', B > B')$ in two classes of items, the traditional historical linguist would tend to seek its origin in one class and postulate its analogical spread to the other:

(1)    A , B
　　　　↓
　　　A' , B
　　　　↓ ——— analogy
　　　A' , B'

In many cases, however, there turns out to be a structural explanation in the form of a shared property of A and B which allows us to assume a common origin for the phenomenon in both classes:

(2)    A , B
　　　　↓
　　　A' , B'

Thus the investigation of clusters of co-occurring changes becomes an important method of probing into the organization of linguistic phenomena.

The issue to which I should like to address myself here is analogical change.[1] Traditionally visualized as the extension of surface patterns (in terms of proportional schemata) it has more recently been given another interpretation as the elimination of arbitrary complexity in the linguistic system (in terms of the evaluation measure developed in the theory of grammar). At the back of this lies a new view about the nature of the concrete process of analogical change and how it relates to the acquisition and use of language. A proportional view of analogy fits naturally into a theory of language acquisition based on substitution-in-frames techniques and equivalent 'taxonomic' devices. The idea that analogy is simplification of grammar jibes better with the idea that language acquisition is based on a general rule schematism in conjunction with an evaluation measure which selects the simplest grammar from the set of alternatives compatible with the data encountered by the learner, and assumes that learners progress to the adult grammar through a series of intermediate stages of increasing adequacy and complexity. Analogical changes are then interpretable as retentions of features of these intermediate stages into the adult system.

The difference between the views is not so radical in practice as it seems from the above formulation. Both approaches, to be at all plausible, require some elaboration, which may take and in fact has taken different terms. Other factors than simplification have been introduced by proponents of grammar-based theories. An example is transparency (Kiparsky 1971, 1973b), which determines the directionality of rule reordering, indifferent as far as simplicity is concerned. Proposals have been made to bring in paradigmatic factors independently of simplicity considerations (Harris 1973; Kiparsky 1972). The general effect of these modifications is to bring the theory into closer agreement with proportional theories. Under the radically 'concrete' analyses of Natural Generative Phonology and Upside-Down Phonology the treatment of analogy as simplification yields predictions which resemble those of proportional theories.

On the other hand, diverse proposals exist to replace bare proportions by interpreted ones. Typical is this passage from von Wartburg (1969: 59): '... analogy does not operate blindly. The Neogrammarians, and Saussure also, made the mistake of regarding analogy as a purely proportional process. Paul (p. 116) simply asserts that, for a new form to arise, there must be three elements present in the equation. He cites as an example *animus : animi = senatus : x; x = senati* (instead of Class. Lat. *senatus*). This conception accounts for only a limited number of instances of the working of analogy. In most cases, analogy does not arise merely as the result of a formal resemblance; the two words so linked are also closely linked by their semantic environment.' Similar ideas are found earlier in Hermann (1931). Another kind of 'annotated proportion' was developed by Kuryłowicz (1956, 1964, and many other works). Kuryłowicz argued that both the terms of the proportions and the relation between the terms have to be interpreted in terms of certain abstract structural notions. For example, the relation between *a* and *b* and between *c* and *x* in the proportional schema could not be just any relation, but only that between a 'forme de fondation' and a 'forme fondée'. And the terms themselves may have to be different from what is actually pronounced in the language, as in the following proportions:

(3)  a.  $\underset{o}{R} : eR = e : X \, (X = ee = \bar{e})$

b.  $ReT : RuT = RewT : X \, (X = RuwT = R\bar{u}T)$

(3a) was proposed to account for the rise of *vṛddhi* (long grade) in nouns (Kuryłowicz 1968: 298). (3b) was proposed as the explanation of the Germanic verbs of the type *lūkan* (Kuryłowicz 1969). These proportions critically depend on the equivalence within the early Indo-European phonological systems of syllabic and nonsyllabic resonants $(R = \underset{o}{R})$ and long vowels and geminate vowels $(\bar{e} = ee)$.

In this way, analogical proportions come look in some ways rather like the rules of a generative grammar. The relation between forme de fondation and forme fondée is something like the relation between input and output of a rule, and proportions where terms are 'virtual' in that they abstract away from certain overtly present surface features are comparable to rules which apply to abstract representations at nonterminal stages in derivations. For example, (3a) and (3b) can be construed as representing the generalization of ablaut rules at a point in the synchronic derivation of Indo-Iranian and Germanic which precedes the application of vowel contraction and of the rules which determine the distribution of syllabic and nonsyllabic sonorants. Indeed, Kuryłowicz (1964) has explicitly justified the abstract character of analogical change by the principle that *redundant* features or elements are to be disregarded in setting up proportions. In our terms that translates into the claim that rules can generalize even when followed by other rules which add those redundant features or elements. Thus, Kuryłowicz (followed by Watkins 1969) considers the proportion (4) a valid account of the replacement of Indo-Iranian mid.3. pl. *ra* by *nta*:

(4)    act. 3.sg. $t$ : 3.pl. $nt$ = mid. 3.sg. $a$ : X (X = $nta$)

Here the suffix $-t$ of the unmarked finite verb form (act. 3.sg.) is to be stripped away, as it were, in order for the terms to match properly.

Still, even in their modified forms, both theories retain many inadequacies. Either side can easily adduce examples of indubitable analogical changes which do *not* agree with the claims of the other. In fact, much of the debate around analogy over the last ten years or so has consisted of generative linguists showing up various problems for the proportional theory (such as analogical changes that depend in various ways on abstract properties of grammatical structure — significantly more abstract than even the work of Kuryłowicz assumed) and the opposition countering with cases of analogical processes which complicate grammars rather than simplify them. A detailed assessment of some of this evidence is presented in the fuller version of the present work. It fully confirms Hock's (1975) conclusion that analogy can involve different levels of abstraction: there are some changes 'which can be plausibly explained or motivated only in terms of (the generalization of) sometimes fairly abstract rules, and not (or only with great conceptual difficulties) in terms of classical surface-oriented analogy', and other changes which show a sovereign disregard of those abstract rules and are 'explainable only in terms of surface analogy'.

Because of space limitations I shall omit entirely any discussion of the first type of case, which contradicts recent proposals to revive surface proportions and reaffirms the fundamentally grammar-based, simplificatory character of analogical change. What follows is a brief outline of the problems posed by cases of the second type, cases which appear to show just the opposite. I shall argue that they too can be analyzed as simplifications provided we take into account certain kinds of interaction between the language learner and his linguistic environment and certain kinds of inertia inherent in the process of language acquisition. That is, the difficulties turn out to be artifacts due to the simplifying idealizations of the ideal speaker-hearer and instantaneous language acquisition, which are appropriate in the study of formal grammar but should not be imported into historical linguistics.

Cases where analogy produces complication in the grammar can be grouped into two main types, not necessarily mutually exclusive or in all cases clearly separable, but still broadly distinct in their symptoms and causes: *partial analogy* and *false analogy*.

## 2. Partial analogy

The characteristic feature of partial analogy is that an analogical process which *would* be a simplification if it took place across the board ends up actually complicating the grammar because it is not fully carried through. Each type of simplification can be partial in this sense. As a counterpart to the *loss* of a rule (and in fact usually as the first step in that process) we find its curtailment, i.e. *partial loss*. For example, Sadock (1973) finds that the loss of the word-final devoicing rule in Yiddish went via an intermediate stage at which it applied in a phonologically restricted context. 'First, it was lost everywhere except in the final cluster *-nd*, and then after the loss of final schwas, the rule was dropped entirely.' Thus 'the Yiddish word-final devoicing rule in all likelihood was made considerably more complex (i.e. it became more restricted in its application) before it was lost' (p. 793). Other cases have been presented in Andersen (1969), Dressler (1972), Ralph (1975: 161 ff.). As a counterpart to the generalization of a rule, we find its *partial generalization* in some subenvironment only (Thomason 1976, Ralph 1975 : 172 ff.). As a counterpart to *reordering*, we find a new order of application introduced for only *some* of the cases (Kiparsky 1973a: 93-101, Robinson 1976, Bley-Vroman 1975).

In such cases, the old form of the rule, or (in case of reordering) the old order remains in the grammar and continues to be applicable to a subset of forms, which must be identified by a contextual restriction added to the rule, or by an arbitrary rule feature marked on some lexical entries — and at worst, by a combination of both. The regularization may, for example, go through only:
- in inflection as opposed to derivation
- in some morphological category (e.g. plurals but not singulars)
- in some inflectional subclass (e.g. the most productive declension or conjugation)

- — in some subset of the vocabulary (often the less common words)
- — in some phonologically definable circumstances (often in cases which are in various ways relatively less salient)
- — in just one sense of a word (often e.g. in metaphorical use)

In all such cases, the result is a more complex grammar.

Can even such changes be due somehow to the mechanism of simplification? The obvious possibility to consider is to reassess the form of grammars or the evaluation measure (or both) in the hope of discovering that the grammars which are actually learned by speakers are such that even in the apparently 'bad' cases the new grammar turns out to be more highly valued after all. Methodological considerations would recommend this approach because it would give both the simplest and the most restrictive theory of analogy — provided of course that the required kinds of synchronic grammars could be justified in their own right independently of the historical changes which we wish to explain.

Several such attempts have in fact been made. One is to maintain the evaluation measure unchanged while assuming grammars of a much 'shallower' type than generally envisaged. The best-known solution of this type is embodied in the theory of Natural Generative Grammar (Vennemann 1974b, Hooper 1976; cf. the related ideas of Skousen 1975). As Hooper notes, the gradual spread of certain kinds of leveling (rule loss) through the lexicon could be characterized as simplification if phonological rules and representations were made very 'concrete'. If, for example, a morpheme was entered in the lexion as the set of its allomorphs, then any analogical change which reduces the number of allomorphs — all cases of rule loss, for example, are of this type — would entail a simplification in the phonological representation of any item subject to the analogical change. If marked ordering of phonological rules did not exist, then for example what now are treated as counterfeeding orderings would really be lexical exceptions to the counterfed rule, and a 'reordering' into feeding order would really be the elimination of this exception feature, which one would expect to take place word by word, as does any idiosyncratic lexical marking. If we could assume that subrules are not collapsed as is claimed in the theory of generative grammar, but are to be kept separate, then obviously the independent generalization of those subrules would not be a problem. In short, the fragmentation observed in the problematic cases of *change* could be ascribed to the synchronic *system* in which the change takes place.

This line of thinking, however, destroys the basis for understanding the normal situation where a rule is generalized in the *same* way in different subenvironments. The splits effected by partial analogy are so varied that in order to turn them all into simplifications we end up with no synchronic generality at all, so that each individual case of alternation is governed by a 'rule' of its own. The result is a synchronically wrong description and a treatment of analogy which suffers from the same kinds of defects as the proportional model.

A more promising-looking attempt to motivate partial analogy in synchronic theory is sketched out in Andersen (1969). Though he too proposes fairly shallow underlying forms, he explicitly assumes single (nondisjunctive) representations related to the phonetics by extrinsically ordered rules, among which he distinguishes morphophonemic and phonological rules. The key to his solution is not so much the 'concreteness' of grammars as the idea that at the stage of the language which immediately precedes the appearance of the analogical forms, speakers learn as it were the 'wrong' grammar, which is such that the subsequent spread of the analogy in fact constitutes a simplification. The scenario for word-by-word extension of a rule would then be as follows: at some point language learners acquire the rule in *overgeneralized* form. 'When this is the case, lexical items which for historical reasons are not subject to the rule (i.e. do not constitute an environment for its application) have to be specified as exceptions to the rule. The extension of the domain of the rule consists in gradual elimination of such exceptions.' ... 'The first phase can be understood as motivated by the need to formulate grammatical rules in as simple (general) terms as possible. The second phase follows as the traditional forms are imperfectly passed on to succeeding generations of learners. It entails a simplification of the lexical component of the grammar. The first phase is necessarily abrupt – but it is covert and goes unnoticed by the speakers. The second phase is gradual and may be more or less apparent to the speakers as older and newer forms are utilized as indices of style' (p. 822).

In order to account for word-by-word curtailment, Andersen then supposes that speakers can also *undergeneralize*: 'If we suppose that this rule in its original formulation applied only to morphemes specifically marked as subject to the rule, then we can understand its curtailment – and eventual elimination – as the result of a simplification of the lexicon, exactly analogous to the one we defined for the extension changes. Here then, as in the extension changes, we have two phases: first a morphophonemic rule is formulated in such a way that individual lexical items have to be marked with respect to that rule; then the marking of these items is gradually omitted. The difference is that where the marked items are exempt from the rule, the simplification of the lexicon results in an extension of the domain of the rule; but where the marked items are the ones that are subject to the rule, the result of a simplification is a curtailment of the domain of the rule' (p. 823). The idea is, simply put, that language learners failed to discover the context of the rule and consequently had to mark the forms subject to it with an ad hoc rule feature, whose elimination case by case curtails and eventually liquidates the rule.

The interesting feature of this theory is that it claims to predict the direction in which a rule will change. Whether a rule is extended (eliminating the exceptions to the rule) or curtailed (eliminating the rule) is determined by its status (as major or minor, motivated or unmotivated, etc.). As things stand, this apparent explanatory power is dubious because there is no theory that tells us *independently* of the change itself what the relevant character of the rule in fact is. It is well enough recognized that the productivity of a rule is not at any rate a simple function of the frequency with which it is applicable (whether counted by types or tokens). Rules which are originally restricted to a handful of forms may spread, and conversely, dominant rules may lose out. Andersen also appeals to the naturalness of a rule: phonetically motivated rules are extended but phonetically unmotivated rules are curtailed. This is beset with the same circularity because the status of a rule as motivated or unmotivated may depend on the choice of distinctive features, which in turn is made by looking at the subsequent changes that depend on it.

It would appear that this solution does not remove the indeterminacy but simply shifts it: instead of determinate synchronic systems but unpredictable alternative possibilities of eliminating points of linguistic complexity, we have indeterminate synchronic systems of which each alternative sets a fixed path for future analogical change. In effect, this is an attempt to reduce partial analogy to false analogy.

There are difficulties with extending Andersen's theory to partial analogy in general. It does not work where the subset of cases affected is structurally (phonologically or morphologically) rather than lexically defined. At the intermediate stage of the loss of final devoicing in Yiddish, if Sadock is right, the domain of the devoicing rule was cut back from all obstruents to just *-nd*. The rule at this stage has added on a phonological context which unarguably makes it more complex than before. Even if we suppose that the rule had, before its curtailment, somehow become a minor rule (which in itself does not seem a justifiable assumption), it surely cannot be maintained that adding contextual restrictions even to minor rules makes them simpler! Only the kind of curtailment that comes from eliminating features on lexical items that mark them as subject to minor rules can be plausibly regarded as simplification. It is also impossible to suppose that the devoicing rule itself remained in its original general form and the curtailment was effected by marking lexical items as exceptions to it. Apart from the difficulty that the prior status of devoicing as a minor rule again cannot be justified, this would amount to saying that it is only accidentally true of the words which maintain devoicing at the intermediate stage that they all end in *-nd*. How could such a regularity have arisen if it was not apprehended as a rule by language learners at some point? The possibility of a purely item-by-item specification is excluded still more clearly in Thomason's Slavic example. The class of lexical items to which the rule applies at the two stages must be specified in a general way in the rule itself since the class of Animate nouns is an open one. It then follows that the generalization of the Accusative = Genitive rule results in a more complex rule.

A second general type of approach is keeping more or less orthodox assumptions about the form of grammars and instead looking for some other version of the *evaluation measure* which would reduce instances of partial analogy to legitimate optimalization.

A plausible scheme for revising the evaluation measure might be to keep simplicity in it but to have it interact with other parameters in some way. One such proposal, due to Ralph (1975: 179), is to adopt Chen's (1973, 1974) device of 'metarules' as a regulator of partial analogy. These are akin to the 'marking conventions' introduced by Chomsky and Halle (1968: Ch. 9) to account for the 'intrinsic content' of the features, and still more to the scales of environments utilized by Foley (1977 and many earlier writings), but they implement the idea in a rather different way. Suppose we assign a higher 'index' to the fronting of long and rounded vowels than to the fronting of the corresponding short and unrounded (or lower) vowels, e.g. for the special case that is relevant to Old Swedish palatal umlaut as discussed by Ralph:

$$(5) \quad \begin{array}{c|c c} & 2 & \mathfrak{d} & \bar{\mathfrak{d}} \\ & 1 & a & \bar{a} \\ \hline & & 1 & 2 \end{array}$$

Then multiplying (or adding) the indices for each feature will give a ranking of multifeature contexts which corresponds to their historical order of appearance:

(6)  a            1      palatalized first
     ā,ɔ          2      palatalized next
     ɔ̄           4      palatalized last

Given a general theory of 'metarules', the order of generalization would be predicted by the principle that rules are generalized in the order of increasing indices.

In one respect this approach represents a major advance over the others we have considered so far: it implies, correctly, that the pattern of partial generalization is not random. It makes the interesting and, I suspect, correct prediction that no language will be found in which such a fronting process has unfolded in the reverse order, although from the viewpoint of the classical simplicity measure that order would be exactly equivalent to what actually happened in Old Swedish.

226 Explanation in phonology

No doubt the metarules as conceived by Chen and adopted by Ralph are lacking in generality. To assume that a table like (5) needs to be specially set up to index the possible contexts of every phonological process is to assume that there are no general principles behind the ordering of contexts, which is scarcely credible. Many cases fall under the rather simple overarching principle that assimilation proceeds in the order of increasing phonetic 'distance' between focus and environment, as measured by the number of relevantly shared feature specifications between them. The more alike two segments are, the more prone they are to assimilate, other things being equal. For example, velars will be assimilated (palatalized) by an adjacent [-back] segment in the following order: palatalized consonants, $y$, $i$, $e$, $æ$. By the same principle, $i$ fronts $a$ before it fronts $ɔ$. I do not wish to claim that this is the only principle at work: I would suppose, for example, that there are other reasons why the short vowels are fronted before the long vowels. Perhaps the explanation for the ordering of contexts will turn out to be exceedingly complex. This would still be better than a list of 'metarules', which can at best claim to be a summary of the observed facts but not an explanation.

Moreover, neither metarules nor even a more general set of principles which would predict the order of contexts would yet address the entire problem of partial analogy. It is hard to see how these ideas could be extended to cases of partial analogy in *morphological* subcontexts, and the lexical cases are evidently quite impossible to handle that way.

For the morphological and lexical cases there does exist another proposal which is entirely different from metarules in content but resembles it formally in that it involves enriching the evaluation measure. This is the idea of Harris (1973), Kiparsky (1972) and others that paradigmatic uniformity has to be recognized as an independent factor in change, not *instead* of but *alongside* simplicity (cf. Schindler 1974 for discussion). In effect, it says that the evaluation measure is to somehow check the outputs of grammars (it is impossible to tell just from the rules) and assign a 'cost' to allomorphic variation in paradigms. That is, it claims that the language learner preferentially selects grammars whose outputs have certain 'transderivational' properties. This is a retreat to a much weaker theory, since the evaluation measure otherwise is defined purely on the grammar. It is also distressingly vague because crucial aspects of the proposal were left in the air: is allomorphy to be quantified by types or tokens? What are paradigms? How are the relative contributions of allomorphy and complexity in terms of the number of feature specifications (not to speak of opacity) to be weighted relative to each other (King 1972, Kiparsky 1974)? In itself, that does not mean that the idea of a complex evaluation measure relying on allomorphy or some equivalent concept as one of its several components is necessarily wrong. The vagueness could be eliminated by exact definitions of 'allomorphy', 'paradigm', and other key notions of the theory, and some of it may indeed have to be retained as an inescapable correlate of the indeterminacy of analogical change itself. A priori there is no reason why there should not be independent criteria of evaluation in as functionally complex a system as language is, and why their relative weight should not be in certain respects indeterminate — all the more so if it can be shown that the weighting varies with linguistic function, so as to create styles adapted to the special requirements of speaker, hearer, and learner (Kiparsky 1975).

There is another general consideration which ought to give one pause. The status of 'paradigm uniformity' and other such criteria in the theory of generative grammar would be quite different from the role of the corresponding notions of analogy in the Neogrammarian theory. In the latter, proportional analogy is assumed to underlie language acquisition and speech production, and its role as a mechanism of change is simply a reflection of its more basic function. In the theory of generative grammar, simplicity has a corresponding role in language acquisition, and its relevance to analogical change would therefore be expected. Proportions, paradigmatic uniformity etc. do not figure in the theory of generative grammar and it would therefore be surprising to find them directing change. It would mean that there would be no essential relation between the way language changes and anything else about it.

Although some authors (e.g. Lass 1976) have welcomed the proposal to introduce paradigmatic notions into the evaluation measure, I believe Bever and Langendoen (1971) were closer to the mark in criticizing it, or rather the program of which it formed a part, for treating function as structure: that is, for attempting to explain *within* the linguistic system a phenomenon which originates in the interaction of that system with other systems. The commonsense explanation for the uneven progress of analogy is that speakers resist some kinds of innovations and readily adopt others. To make something of this idea we surely have to go beyond the formal theory of grammar to the theory of language *use*, specifically to that part of it which concerns the way speakers deploy the variation deposited in their grammars by ongoing linguistic change (Labov 1972a). I shall consider here one way in which such a program might be worked out.

One could picture partial analogy arising through the interplay of language acquisition and synchronic variation by a process somewhat analogous to that by which the conditioning of sound changes is crystallized out of their initially variable application. A three-part scenario for it would be:

(1) Language learners can acquire different grammars even when exposed to the same language, because of random differences in the speech data they are exposed to, in the order in which they are exposed to it, in

the way they analyze indeterminate cases, and possibly because of other reasons. Such 'imperfect learning' (along with language contact and other sources of linguistic innovation) constantly replenishes the language with a fresh supply of coexisting variants.

(2)    Some of the variants arising this way will tend to be avoided in speech because they are dysfunctional or because they become stigmatized. Others will be favored in speech because they can be used to make things easier to say or to understand. These effects will show up in varying degrees depending on the circumstances.

(3)    Some of the bias in the deployment of variants will in turn be grammaticalized, with favored variants being acquired as obligatory and disfavored variants being lost.

The assumption is, in short, that the variation due to 'imperfect learning' which we postulate as the source of analogical change is channeled jointly by the conservative influence of the established norm and by the functional needs of the system. Their combined effect should, if the assumption is right, predict whatever is predictable in the patterns of partial analogy. Let us consider the two factors in turn.

The first way an analogical innovation might end up incompletely effected would be, then, that it gives way in particular subenvironments and/or in particular lexical items to the older standard, whether through self-monitoring by language learners, through explicit correction by other speakers, or both. Would any general type of pattern be likely to emerge from such a process? Presumably there could be no completely predictable pattern, if only because the linguistic data which bring about the partial adoption of the older system will come to the attention of different individuals in different orders and at different stages in their evolving grammars. Still, one would expect some innovations to stick out against the norm more than others, and thereby to have a diminished life expectancy. The innovations most likely to succeed would be the least 'blatant' or 'salient' ones, for they have the best chance of surviving the language learners' own efforts to accommodate their speech to the community norm, and are also least likely to provoke outright correction or ridicule by other speakers.

Intuitions on what exactly defines the crucial dimension of relative saliency are bound to be vague. Fortunately we have some slight empirical foothold on it, for dialectologists have long operated with the notion of relative saliency in studies of interdialectal adaptation.

The relevance of certain kinds of saliency in syntactic change has recently been demonstrated in an important article by Naro and Lemle (1977). They investigate the loss of subject-verb agreement in Brazilian Portuguese and conclude that the process spreads through the language in order of increasing saliency. They take the relative saliency of an innovation against the background of the old form to be a composite function of distinct factors, of which they name two:

(1)    An innovation which is more differentiated from the old form is more salient than one which is more similar to it.

(2)    An innovation is more salient in monitored (formal) speech than in unmonitored speech.

It is plausible to add to this the following factors:

(3)    An innovation in a frequent form is more salient than an innovation in a rare form.

(4)    An innovation which alters surface structure or phonotactics is more salient than one which does not.

This permits us to interpret many types of partial analogy: the tendency for 'small' alternations to be eliminated before 'big' ones (1), stylistic differentiation (2), frequency (3), and various 'structure-preserving' effects (4).

In addition to an overall normative pressure which pushes back particularly the most salient innovations, we are also supposing as another selective process, in line with traditional functionalist thinking, that innovations which serve the needs of speakers well or ill will be resisted or favored accordingly. Here is where the familiar functional factors find a natural interpretation.

Obviously the factors that control the use of variants in speech, whatever they turn out to be, can have nothing to do with analogy per se, for variation from *any* source must be patterned in the same way once it is in the language (Samuels 1972: 87). This is borne out by the resemblances in the characteristic profiles of partial analogy and variable rules (Kiparsky 1972). We have in effect ended up dividing the explanation of analogical change between two different theories, one dealing with the *source* of the innovations (imperfect learning) and the other with their *selection* in speech and eventually in grammar. (A vague parallel might be the theory of evolution as a function of genetic variation and natural selection.) The constraints on analogical change are, then, jointly determined by the properties of imperfect learning and of variation.

This part of my proposal is close in general spirit to Samuels (1972), who also distinguishes between the components of 'variation' and 'systemic regulation' in change (see especially p. 135 ff.). He remarks that 'neither sound-change nor analogy can be regarded as providing any more than the raw material of change; the *process* of change, from its initiation to its acceptance in a system, is considerably more complex than this . . .' (p. 136). Samuels devotes his attention mainly to 'systemic regulation' and rather underestimates the structural conditions of change. I cannot agree with him, though, that new variants always reduce information-content and that subsequent selection is a 'compensatory mechanism' which 'consists of the restoration of the distances lost in [variation]' (p. 178).

A certain amount of discussion has centered on the question whether change originates in competence or performance (see Dressler 1976 for recent discussion). From the present point of view, the question is rather misleadingly posed, since change involves *both* competence and performance. This is also the conclusion reached through a different line of reasoning by Vincent (1974: 436): '. . . analogy is neither a competence nor a performance phenomenon, but rather a sort of line linking these two aspects of language.'

## 3. False analogy

There is a second fallacy in assuming that the retention of forms from intermediate stages of language acquisition must simplify the grammar: they might be residual projections from an analysis which, even though optimal for the restricted linguistic data available to the learner at some stage, is not part of the optimal grammar of the whole language. If they are retained anyway, the result is analogy which creates a complication of the grammar. Everyone knows how the crucial data that may decide between competing analyses can lurk in obscure corners and elude the linguist working from a limited corpus. It would not be surprising to find the language learner occasionally in the same predicament. Accordingly, the assumption that analogy must represent simplification with respect to the *adult* grammar is entirely unwarranted. The most that we can legitimately claim is that analogical innovations represent analyses which are optimal at the particular stage of language acquisition at which these analyses arise and for the particular set of primary linguistic data which is under consideration by the language learner at that stage. Even a partial retention of these innovations may force a complication on the grammar when it is reanalyzed on the basis of a fuller set of data.

It is obvious that the sort of *paradigmatic leveling* which fails to simplify and possibly complicates the adult grammar is often ascribable to a simplification at an earlier stage in language development. For a learner of Latin whose relevant data includes only the oblique case forms *honōrem, honōris* etc., *honor* is the simplest projection for the nominative singular. Never mind that having later learned *honestus* and acquired an intervocalic $s \to r$ rule anyway for cases like *flōs*~*flōris* he might be better off with the older *honōs* after all: the horses are already out of the barn. For a learner of Canadian English who has not acquired the $ay$~$əy$ and vowel shift rules, *write* would simply be underlying /rəyt/, and the simplest projection for the suffixed forms *write + er, write + ing* would be [rəydər], [rəydIŋ] – though once the dependence of $ay$ vs. $əy$ on the voicing of the following consonant is learned, the transparent ordering which yields the older forms [raydər], [raydIŋ] might be preferable.

Similarly, cyclic ordering can be a structural accommodation of analogy which imposes on derived words the surface features of stems they contain. It is not necessary, if this is so, to suppose that cyclic ordering is to be assigned preferred status by the evaluation measure, for the tendency of rules to shift into the cycle can be explained without it.

This inertia of the language learner's own mistakes is perhaps the minimal assumption which can be made to account for 'false' analogy. It should be distinguished from McCawley's (1977) more radical, by no means implausible idea (cf. Fodor 1978: 62) of an inertial effect in the language learner's own *grammars*. One version would be that language learners resort to restructuring only 'under duress', perhaps if the grammars they have formulated cannot be patched up to incorporate new data in a way which satisfies some criteria — which remain to be specified by a theory of language acquisition. Alternatively, one could imagine the degree of resistance to restructuring depending how great the restructuring would be, perhaps as weighed against the amount of simplification it would afford. These hypotheses would entail that the evolving grammar is not necessarily at any particular stage, including the finished grammar, optimal for the data it covers, though it of course *might* be. Even more severe would be the assumption that *all* language acquisition is, in effect, a patchup job, with new data always being absorbed by means of the smallest possible grammatical adjustments, without restructuring (cf. also Haber 1975 for some related observations). That would mean that the child's first hypotheses always fix the future course for the evolving grammar. The optimal grammar would on this view be an ideal construct which was perhaps never realized by any actual language learner.

Similar in spirit is Andersen's (1973) idea of 'adaptive rules'. It amounts to assuming that the learner may be stuck with a nonoptimal analysis which in itself generates the wrong output and is mapped into the right one by 'adaptive' rules. Andersen illustrates his concept with an interpretation of a sound change which takes palatalized labials to dentals. He assumes that at some point language learners began to *interpret* palatalized labials as being dentals ([p'] as /t/ etc.). To account for their actual pronunciation as [p'] rather than [t] they therefore required an *adaptive* rule which turned dentals to palatalized labials (/t/ → [p'] etc.). Having thus become 'virtual' dentals by reanalysis, the palatalized labials changed to dentals phonetically by the loss of the adaptive rule. I admit to finding this unconvincing as a proposal about sound change. The thought that language learners would somehow come to analyze palatalized labials as being really dentals, without any phonological motivation for doing so, and later start to pronounce them in accordance with this reanalysis is too idealist for my taste. For analogical change Andersen's notion of adaptive rules might make more sense. Even there, however, they seem to me to underestimate the flexibility of the language learner.

These hypotheses make different but largely overlapping predictions about analogy. They share the essential property of allowing for the real-time course of language acquisition to determine aspects of the system that eventually emerges. The precise causes of the inertia, and the degree to which it is mediated by the structure itself, could well be some combination of those mentioned here. The essential empirical difference between my assumption that the language learner freely restructures his grammar when encountering new data that motivates it, and McCawley's and Andersen's assumption of more limited adaptive measures for coping with new data, would seem to be the following. On the assumption of continuous restructuring, a certain amount of selection and organization would be expected to be imposed on the innovations by the adaptive system, due to the efforts of the learner to integrate the new data into his grammar in the optimal way. If on the other hand the new data is accommodated by tacking on 'patchup' rules or 'adaptive' rules, to the already formulated grammar, no such structural effects should presumably show up. Herein lies the relevance of cases where the result of analogical leveling is systematically adopted into the language precisely where it can be accommodated in a simple way into the system, and suppressed elsewhere. This would be incomprehensible if we did not assume grammatical reintegration rather than makeshift 'adaptive' rules.

'Adaptive' rules do appear to be the right mechanism for certain sorts of cases, hypercorrect forms, for example. They show precisely the distinction between the ordinary result of language acquisition, where reanalysis takes place, and the special situations caused by limited access to the relevant linguistic data, which lead to hypercorrection.

If this view of paradigmatic leveling is right, then it follows that efforts to combine paradigmatic leveling and 'distinctness' effects in terms of a unified set of 'paradigm conditions' (Kiparsky 1972) or 'Humboldt's Universal' (Vennemann 1974b) were fundamentally misguided. Paradigmatic leveling is a direct reflex of language learners' tendency to simplify grammar, whereas avoidance of homonymy, distinctions of grammatical categories etc. are imposed on the system by the purposive selection of speech variants from whatever source, including ordinary sound change. As a result of their different etiology, they are also implemented in the grammar in different ways. It is striking that 'distinctness' may be effected by the most varied structural means. Even for one category within one grammar it is possible to demonstrate the characteristic 'conspiracy' situation where the distinction between morphological markers is maintained by numerous rules and restrictions on rules acting in concert (cf. Kiparsky 1972: 214). Hogg (1975) has pointed out that such cases do not seem to occur with paradigmatic leveling. This is predicted from our assumption that the selection of variants favors category distinctness but is neutral as to paradigmatic leveling.

We have argued that 'paradigm' conditions can be eliminated from the evaluation measure. It is tempting to try a similar reduction for opacity. Can we interpret shift into transparent rule order as the result of incorporating into the language the projections of the simplest grammar for some set of core data, as we did for paradigmatic leveling? That would let us pare down the evaluation measure even further by taking even opacity out of it, essentially restoring it to its original form of a pure simplicity measure.

Let $R_1$, $R_2$ be two opaquely ordered rules which are reordered into the transparent order $R_2$, $R_1$. Consider now how the reordering can be analyzed as the grammatical reintegration of the projection from $R_1$ at a stage when $R_2$ has not been acquired. Taking first reordering into feeding order, suppose we have the rules

(7)  i. $a \rightarrow b$  $/ - c$
     ii. $d \rightarrow c$  $/ - e$

where (ii) counterfeeds (i), e.g. /ade/ $\rightarrow$ *ace*, not *\*bce*. Suppose that the primary linguistic data under consideration by the language learner at stage $S_n$ is enough to motivate (i) but not (ii). Such instances of the output *ce* from (ii) as are encountered are therefore incorrectly analyzed as derived from /ce/ rather than /de/ at $S_n$. From *a+ce* the grammar therefore projects the 'wrong' output *bce* by (i). Suppose that at stage $S_n+1$, rule (ii) has been learned. The wrong output *bce* of $S_n$ can be reintegrated into $S_n+1$ simply by ordering the rules in the transparent order (ii,i). If the analogical *bce* wins out, reordering has taken place. If correction to *ace* prevails, normal language transmission has taken its course. So it is possible to account for reordering into feeding order by the process of grammar simplification (imperfect learning) *without* supposing that feeding order, or transparency, is in itself more highly valued, if the entirely natural additional assumption of learners' output inertia is made and we further postulate an order of acquisition. Note that our scenario *predicts* the asymmetry of reordering. A switch from feeding to nonfeeding order would be inexplicable by the process we have outlined.

The above proposal is extreme in that it reduces assumptions about the factors governing language learners' structuring of data to the SPE minimum (simplicity) and puts the whole burden of explaining transparency effects, as was done with leveling, on the postulated inertia of learner's own earlier speech forms and on assumptions about the order of acquisition of rules. There is also a more moderate version of the same general idea, where the role we have so far assigned to the order of acquisition of rules is given to a minimal additional assumption about the language learners' structuring of data:

(8)   For any set of data D, learners select the shallowest underlying
      representations compatible with the simplest grammar of D.

All that this says is that speakers do not indulge in gratuitous abstraction
over and above what is required for linguistic generalizations. (8) is of
course quite distinct from such constraints as the Alternation Condition,
which limit the abstractness of underlying representations *regardless* of
any resulting grammatical complications. It has, I think, been generally
accepted even by those who reject these severer constraints, and would
seem to be independently necessary even if these are accepted, in order to
predict the restructuring on nonalternating outputs of neutralization rules
(for example, word-final obstruents restructured as unvoiced in isolated
forms in languages like German, Yiddish, etc., with final devoicing rules,
where the Alternation Condition does not predict the choice of the
devoiced obstruents as basic because the devoicing rule applies in a derived
environment).

   Most of the predictions about transparent ordering can be had this way
too. Instead of assuming a stage where only (i) has been learned, suppose
that (ii) has been learned but that those outputs of it (*ce*) for which the
learner is not (yet) in a position to motivate an underlying source /de/ are
systematically represented by him as /ce/, even though the more abstract
/de/ would be equally simple. (So far we have done without this assumption.) Then the grammar projects in such cases from *a+ce* the output *bce*
rather than *ace*. If retained, it must be structured in terms of feeding order
in all cases where *ce* is reanalyzed by the learner as /de/ on the basis of
data encountered later.

   Another likely victim of our reductionist rampage is the revised
Alternation Condition (Kiparsky, 1973b), which stipulates that obligatory
neutralization rules (or, in a milder formulation, obligatory nonautomatic
neutralization rules) apply only to derived inputs.

## 4. Conclusions

To summarize, we have discussed two recalcitrant types of analogy, *partial*
and *false* analogy, and concluded that they too yield to the interpretation
of analogical change as simplification under a more realistic interpretation
of change which allows for inertia in the acquisition process and for inter-
ference between the learner's system and the target norm of the speech
community. This is partly good news and partly bad news. The bad news is
that linguistic change can no longer be used as a probe into linguistic
structure in the direct and naive sense that many of us used to think. Before
we can exploit historical evidence for synchronic purposes we need a firm
theory of the intervening factors — the effect which the concrete process

of acquisition itself and differential saliency can have on what is acquired. It follows for example that the arguments concerning abstractness will have to be rethought in so far as they are based on historical evidence. The good news is that we can restore the integrity of the evaluation measure by eliminating from it the accretions which it had acquired. These accretions have two suspicious properties in common. First, they require reference not to the *form* of the grammar (as simplicity does) but to the relationship of the *output* of the grammar to something else — either to other output forms (paradigm conditions), to rules (opacity), or to underlying forms (recoverability, Hale's (1973) deep/surface disparity avoidance). Second, they were motivated practically exclusively from *historical* evidence. Arguments that they are required to select the synchronically correct grammar have not been forthcoming. The elimination of these considerations from the evaluation measure would therefore be a gain rather than a loss.

We wind up with a surprising conclusion. There are two assumptions of the theory of generative grammar that have been subjected to strong criticism: the simplicity metric, and the idealizations of instantaneous language acquisition and the ideal speaker-hearer. What we have seen is that by eliminating the second from historical linguistics we overcome the objections to the first. We seem to have found a way of retaining the simplicity measure without giving up what is right about traditional functionalist thinking. Structural and functional considerations both play an essential role but as part of separate systems. This relieves the evaluation measure of the burdens which purely structural theories unjustly placed on it and eliminates the unfortunate 'teleological' element of traditional functionalism, as well as its inability to account for structural patterning in analogical change. The 'teleological' effect can now be seen to follow from the functionally and structurally determined 'filtering' of the variation generated by the process of imperfect learning, while the structural patterning follows from the source mechanism of imperfect learning as well as from the grammaticalization of the functionally patterned variation.

## Notes

1. There is a terminological confusion to be cleared up. The term *analogy* has become established in reference to both a particular type of *phenomenon* in linguistic change, whose existence is not in dispute, though there may be disagreement about where its exact boundaries lie, and a particular theoretical *interpretation* of this phenomenon, namely the proportional schema or its equivalent, whose correctness has certainly been cast into doubt. My own practice earlier was to simply avoid the term, and to replace it, in both senses mentioned above (the phenomenon and the process I was proposing to account for it) by *simplification*. The term is also avoided by Andersen (who likewise objects the traditional interpretation and speaks of simplification (1969: 824), though from a somewhat different point of view): 'The changes with

which we will be concerned would be called analogical by some. We will not use this term, for terms like "grammatical analogy" as traditionally used are highly ambiguous, and we need to be specific' (p. 807). Others have continued to use the term *analogy* to refer to the mechanism as traditionally understood, that is, to the extension of surface patterns by the proportional schema or its equivalent (e.g. Chomsky and Halle 1968: 156, fn. 12; Isačenko 1970). Finally, King (1969) and others maintain the term in ambiguous use both 'as a cover designation for . . . *instances of change*' (p. 128) and as a term for the proportional mechanism (e.g. p. 182). The ambiguity would seem to be easily resolved by context but has nevertheless spawned a fatuous line of argument where generative criticisms of the surface proportional theory of analogy are called 'attacks on analogy', and their authors are then, absurdly, denounced for failing to distinguish between analogy and sound change!

None of these ways is satisfactory. It is best to have a separate, neutral term, for the type of historical change whose interpretation is at issue, and distinct terms for the various processes which have been proposed to account for it. I will here use *analogical change* (or sometimes just *analogy*) for the historical phenomenon and *proportional analogy* for the general class of processes by which it is traditionally explained (suitably qualified when necessary to devote specific versions of it), and *simplification* for the general class of processes which has been more recently suggested in its stead (again suitably qualified when necessary).

# Bibliography

Adams, D. et al. (eds.) 1971. *Papers from the seventh Regional Meeting of the Chicago Linguistic Society,* Chicago. Ill.

Andersen, H. 1969. A study in diachronic morphophonemics: the Ukrainian prefixes. *Language* 45: 807–30.

Andersen, H. 1973. Abductive and deductive change. *Language* 49: 765–93. Reprinted in Baldi and Werth (eds.), 313–47.

Anderson, J.M., and Ch. Jones (eds.) 1974. *Historical Linguistics II, theory and description in phonology.* North-Holland, Amsterdam.

Anderson, S.R. 1969. *West Scandinavian Vowel Systems and the Ordering of Phonological Rules.* Ph.D. diss., MIT, Cambridge, Mass. Reproduced by Indiana University Linguistics Club, Bloomington, Ind., 1971.

Anderson, S.R., and P. Kiparski (eds.) 1973. *A Festschrift for Morris Halle.* Holt, Rinehart, and Winston, New York.

Aoki, H. 1966. Nez Perce vowel harmony and Proto-Sahaptian vowels. *Language* 42: 759–67.

Ascoli, G.I. 1877. Squarci d'une lettera concernente le ricostruzioni paleontologiche della parola. Studi Critici II: 1–29. Roma.

Bach, E. 1968. Two proposals concerning the simplicity metric in phonology. *Glossa* 2: 128–49.

Bach, E., and R.T. Harms (eds.) 1968. *Universals in Linguistic Theory.* Holt, Rinehart and Winston, New York.

Bailey, Ch.-J.N. 1970. Building rate into a dynamic theory of linguistic description. *Hawaii Working Papers in Linguistics* 2/9: 161–233.

Bailey, Ch.-J.N. 1973. Variation resulting from different rule orderings in English phonology. In Bailey and Shuy (eds.), 211–52.

Bailey, Ch.-J.N., and R.W. Shuy (eds.) 1973. *New Ways of Analyzing Variation in English.* Georgetown University Press, Washington, D.C.

Baldi, P., and R.N. Werth (eds.) 1978. *Readings in Historical Phonology, Chapters in the Theory of Sound Change.* The Pennsylvania State University Press, University Park and London.

Bechert, J. 1971. Ad-hoc Merkmale in der generativen Phonologie. In Von Stechow (ed.), 29–37.

Benfey, Th. 1837. Review of Pott (1833). *Ergänzungsblätter zur (Halleschen) allgemeinen Literatur-Zeitung,* Dec. 1837, no. 114–7, Col. 905. Reprinted in Benfey (1890).

Benfey, Th. 1890. *Kleinere Sprachwissenschaftliche Schriften.* Ed. by A. Bezzenberger, Berlin.

Bever, T.G. 1970. The cognitive basis for linguistic structures. In Hayes (ed.), 279–352.

Bever, T.G., and D.T. Langendoen. 1971. A dynamic model of the evolution of language. *Linguistic Inquiry* 2: 433–64. Reprinted in Bever et al. (eds.), 115–48.

Bever, T.G., and D.T. Langendoen. 1972. The interaction of speech perception and grammatical structure in the evolution of language. In Stockwell and Macaulay (eds.), 32–95.

238

Bever, T.G., J.J. Katz, and D.T. Langedoen (eds.) 1976. *An Integrated Theory of Linguistic Ability*. Crowell, New York.

Bhat, D.N.S. 1969. A new hypothesis on language change. Linguistic Survey Bulletin 13.

Binnick, R., A. Davison, G.M. Green and J.L. Morgan (eds.) 1969. *Papers from the fifth Regional Meeting of the Chicago Linguistic Society*, Chicago, Ill.

Bley-Vroman, R. 1975. Opacity and interrupted rule schemata. In Grossman et al. (eds.), 73–80.

Bloomfield, L. 1933. *Language*. Holt, New York.

Bloomfield, L. 1934. Review of Havers (1931). *Language* 10: 32–9.

Boas, F. (ed.) 1911, 1922, 1938. *Handbook of American Indian Languages*, vols. I, II, III. Government Printing Office, Washington, D.C.

Boas, F. 1963. Introduction to the reprint of Boas (1911–38), ed. by C.I.J.M. Stuart. Institute of Languages and Linguistics, Georgetown, University Press, Washington, D.C.

Bogoras, W. 1922. Chukchee. In Boas (ed.), vol. 2: 631–903.

Bolodin, A.P., and A.N. Zhukova. 1968. Itel'menskij jazyk. *Jazyki narodov SSSR* 5: 334–52.

Bopp, F. 1816. *Ueber das Conjugationssystem der Sanskritsprache in Vergleichung mit jenem der griechischen, lateinischen, persischen und germanischen Sprache*, in der Andreäischen Buchhandlung, Frankfurt-am-Main. Portions reprinted in Lehmann (ed.), 38–45.

Brame, M.K. 1972a. On the abstractness of phonology: Maltese G̣. In Brame (ed.), 22–61.

Brame, M.K. 1972b. The Segmental Cycle. In Brame (ed.), 62–72.

Brame, M.K. (ed.) 1972c. *Contributions to Generative Phonology*. University of Texas Press, Austin, Texas.

Bresnan, J. 1971. On sentence stress and syntactic transformations. *Language* 47: 257–81. Reprinted with some revisions in Brame (ed.), 73–107; and in Hintikka et al. (eds.), 3–47.

Brink, D.T. 1974. Characterizing the natural order of application of phonological rules. *Lingua* 34: 47–72.

Bruck, A., R.A. Fox, and M.W. LaGaly (eds.) 1974. *Papers from the Parasession on Natural Phonology*, Chicago Linguistic Society, Chicago, Ill.

Campbell, L. 1973. Extrinsic ordering lives. Technical Report no. 80, Center for Research in Social Behavior, University of Missouri, Columbia. Reproduced by Indiana University Club, Bloomington, Ind., 1973.

Campbell, L. 1974. Phonological features: problems and proposals. *Language* 50: 52–65.

Campbell, M.A. et al. (eds.) 1970. *Papers from the sixth Regional Meeting of the Chicago Linguistic Society*, Chicago, Ill.

Campbell, R.S., M.G. Goldin, and M.C. Wang (eds.) 1974. *Linguistic Studies in Romance Languages*. Georgetown University Press, Washington, D.C.

Carstairs, A. 1970. A transderivational constraint in Greek phonology. Ditto.

Chambers, J.K. 1973. Canadian Raising. *Canadian Journal of Linguistics* 18: 113–35.

Chen, M. 1973. On the formal expression of natural rules in phonology. *Journal of Linguistics* 9: 223–49.

Chen, M. 1974. Natural phonology from a diachronic vantagepoint. In Bruck et al. (eds.), 43–80.

Chen, M., and H.-I. Hsieh. 1971. The time variable in phonological change. *Journal of Linguistics* 7: 1–13.

Chinebuah, I.K. 1963. The category of number in Nzema. *Journal of African Languages* 2: 244–59.

Chomsky, N. 1964. *Current Issues in Linguistic Theory*. Janua Linguarum 38, Mouton, The Hague. Reprinted in Fodor and Katz (eds.), 50–118.

Chomsky, N., and M. Halle. 1968. *The Sound Pattern of English*. Harper and Row, New York.

Christie, W. (ed.) 1976. *Current Progress in Historical Linguistics*. North Holland, Amsterdam.

Coats, H.S. 1970. Rule environment features in phonology. *Papers in Linguistics* 2: 110–40.

Crothers, J. 1971. On the abstractness controversy. *POLA* 12, second series, CR1-29, University of California, Berkeley. Reprinted by Indiana University Linguistics Club, 1971.

Curtius, G. 1871. Zur Erklärung der Personalendungen. *Studien zur griechischen und lateinischen Grammatik* 4: 211–33.

Curtius, G. 1877. Das verbum der griechische Sprache. Seinem Baue nach dargestellt. Leipzig, 2nd. ed.

Darden, B. 1970. The fronting of vowels after palatals in Slavic. In M.A. Campbell et al. (eds.), 459–70.

Davison, A. 1971. A problem concerning the relative naturalness of phonological rules and phonological representations. In Adams et al. (eds.), 332–9.

Demers, R. 1971. Rule insertion in Alemanic. Paper presented at the First Meeting of the New England Linguistic Society, Cambridge, Mass.

Dingwall, W.O. (ed.) 1971. *A Survey of Linguistic Science*. Linguistics Program, University of Maryland, College Park, Md. (first ed.). Second ed.: Greylock Publ., Stamford, Conn., 1978.

Dinneen, F.P. 1967. *An Introduction to General Linguistics*. Holt, Rinehart, and Winston, New York.

Dressler, W. 1972. On the phonology of language death. In Peranteau et al. (eds.), 448–57.

Dressler, W. 1976. How much does performance contribute to phonological change? *Wiener Linguistische Gazette* 13: 3–18.

Enderlin, F. 1913. *Die Mundart von Kesswil im Oberthurgau*. Beiträge zur schweizer-deutschen Grammatik 5. A. Bachmann, ed., Huber, Frauenfeld.

Erteschik, N. 1971. The BeGeD-KeFeT or BeKeF Mystery. Unpubl. ms., MIT, Cambridge, Mass.

Ervin, S.M. 1966. Imitation and structural change in children's language. In Lenneberg (ed.), 163–90.

Fasold, R., and R. Shuy (eds.) 1977. *Studies in Language Variation*. Georgetown University Press, Washington D.C.

Ferguson, Ch.A. 1971a. 'Short A' in Philadelphia English. *Stanford Occasional Papers in Linguistics* 1: 2–27.

Ferguson, Ch.A. 1971b. Absence of copula and the notion of simplicity: a study of normal speech, baby talk, foreigner talk, and pidgins. In Hymes (ed.), 141–50.

Fodor, J.D. 1978. What kind of exception is *have got*? *Linguistic Inquiry* 9: 45–65.

Fodor, J.D., and M. Garrett. 1966. Some reflections on competence and performance. In Lyons and Wales (eds.), 135–54.

Fodor, J.D., and J.J. Katz (eds.) 1964. *The Structure of Language*. Prentice-Hall, Englewood Cliffs, N.J.

Foley, J. 1965. *Spanish Morphology*. Ph.D. diss., MIT, Cambridge, Mass.

Foley, J. 1977. *Foundations of Theoretical Phonology*. Cambridge University Press.

Fromkin, V. 1965. On system-structure phonology. *Language* 41: 601–9. Reprinted in Makkai (ed.), 283–9.

Fudge, E.C. 1967. The nature of phonological primes. *Journal of Linguistics* 3: 1–36. Reprinted in Makkai (ed.), 500–21.

Fudge, E.C. (ed.) 1973. *Phonology*. Penguin Education, Harmondsworth.

Fujimura, O. (ed.) 1973. *Three Dimensions of Linguistic Theory*. TEC Co., Tokyo.

Garde, P. 1965. Review of *American Contributions to the Fifth International Congress of Slavists, Word* 21: 141–7.

Goyvaerts, D.L., and G.K. Pullum (eds.) 1975. *Essays on the Sound Pattern of English*. E. Story – Scientia, Ghent.

Grossman, R.E., L.J. San, and T.J. Vance (eds.) 1975. *Papers from the eleventh Regional Meeting of the Chicago Linguistic Society*, Chicago, Ill.

Gumperz, J.J., and D. Hymes (eds.) 1972. *Directions in Sociolinguistics*. Holt, Rine-hart, and Winston, New York.

Haber, L.R. 1975. The muzzy theory. In Grossman et al. (eds.), 240–56.

Hakulinen, L. 1961. *Suomen kielen rakenne ja kehitys*. Otava, Helsinki.

Hála, B., M. Romportl, and P. Janota (eds.) 1970. *Proceedings of the sixth International Congress of Phonetic Sciences*. Academia, Prague.

Hale, K. 1970. The passive and ergative in language change: the Australian case. In Wurm and Laycock (eds.), 757–81.

Hale, K. 1973. Deep-surface canonical disparities in relation to analysis and change: an Australian example. In Sebeok (ed.), 401–58.

Halle, M. 1961. On the role of simplicity in linguistic description. In Jakobson (ed.), 89–94.

Halle, M. 1962. Phonology in generative grammar. *Word* 18: 54–72. Reprinted in Fodor and Katz (eds.), 324–33, and in Makkai (ed.), 380–92.

Halle, M. 1970. Markedness. In Hála et al. (eds.), 61–72.

Halle, M., and T. Lightner. ms. Relative chronology and the synchronic order of rules.

Harada, S.I., and K. Imai. 1970. Where do English vowels come from? *Energeia* 2: 54–72.

Harris, J.W. 1967. *Spanish Phonology*. Ph.D. diss., MIT, Cambridge, Mass. Publ. as Harris (1969a).

Harris, J.W. 1969a. *Spanish Phonology*. MIT Press, Cambridge, Mass.

Harris, J.W. 1969b. Rule exception features versus [± Foreign] : evidence from Spanish. MIT RLE *Quarterly Progress Report* 94: 223–6.

Harris, J.W. 1973. On the order of certain phonological rules in Spanish. In Anderson and Kiparsky (eds.), 59–76.

Harris, J.W. 1974. Morphologization of phonological rules: an example from Chicano Spanish. In R.S. Campbell et al. (eds.), 8–27.

Harris, J.W. 1975. Stress assignment rules in Spanish. In Milan et al. (eds.), 56–83.

Havers, W. 1931. *Handbuch der erklärenden Syntax*. Winter, Heidelberg.

Hayes, J.R. (ed.) 1970. *Cognition and the Development of Language*. Wiley, New York.

Heeschen, C. 1967. Lithuanian Morphophonemics. MIT RLE *Quarterly Progress Report* 85:284–96.

Hermann, E. 1931. *Lautgesetz und Analogie*. Abhandlungen der Geselschaft der Wissenschaften zu Göttingen. Phil.-Hist. Klasse, Neue Folge 23/3, Weidmannsche Buchhandlung, Berlin.

Hintikka, K.J.J., J.M.E. Moravcsik, and P. Suppes (eds.) 1973. *Approaches to Natural Language*. Reidel, Dordrecht.

Hjelmslev, L. 1953. *Prolegomena to a Theory of Language*. Transl. by F.J. Whitfield, University of Wisconsin Press, Madison, Wis. Originally publ. as *Omkring Sprogteoriens Grundlaeggelse*, Copenhagen, 1943.

Hoard, J.E. 1972. Naturalness conditions in phonology, with particular reference to English vowels. In Brame (ed.), 123–54.

Hock, H.H. 1975. Current trends in historical linguistics. Read at the first meeting of the Kentucky Interdisciplinary Conference on Linguistics.

Hockett, Ch. 1958. *A Course in Modern Linguistics*. Macmillan, New York.

Hockett, Ch. 1965. Sound Change. *Language* 41: 185–204.

Hockett, Ch. 1968. *The State of the Art*. Mouton, The Hague.

Hoenigswald, H.M. 1960. *Language Change and Linguistic Reconstruction*. University of Chicago Press, Chicago, Ill.

Hogg, R.M. 1975. The place of analogy. *Neophilologus* 59: 109–13.

Hooper, J. Bybee. 1976. *An Introduction to Natural Generative Phonology*. Academic Press, New York.

Hotzenköcherle, R. 1934. *Die Mundart von Muten*. Beiträge zur schweizerdeutschen Grammatik 19. Albert Bachmann (ed.), Frauenfeld.

Householder, F.W. 1965. On some recent claims in phonological theory. *Journal of Linguistics* 1: 13–34. Reprinted in Makkai (ed.), 442–56.

Hurford, J. 1971. Review of Bach and Harms (eds.), *Journal of Linguistics* 7: 132-48.

Hyman, L.M. 1970a. How concrete is phonology? *Language* 46: 58–76.

Hyman, L.M. 1970b. The role of borrowing in the justification of phonological grammars. *Studies in African Linguistics* 1: 1–48.

Hymes, D. (ed.) 1971. *Pidginization and Creolization of Languages*. Cambridge University Press.

Isačenko, A.V. 1970. East Slavic morphophonemics and the treatment of jers in Russian: a revision of Havlik's Law. *International Journal of Slavic Linguistics and Poetics* 13: 73–124.

Itkonen, E. 1945. Onko kantasuomessa ollut keskivokaaleja? *Virittäjä*, 158–82.

Itkonen, E. 1966. *Kieli ja sen tutkimus*. Werner Söderström, Helsinki.

Ivić, P. 1958. *Die serbokroatischen Dialekte (ihre Struktur und Entwicklung)*, Mouton, The Hague.

Jacobsen, W.H. 1968. On the prehistory of Nez Perce vowel harmony. *Language* 44, 819–29.

Jakobson, R. 1929. Remarques sur l'évolution phonologique de russe comparée a celle des autres langues slaves. *Travaux du Cercle Linguistique de Prague II*. Reprinted in Jakobson (1962), 7–116.

Jakobson, R. 1931. Ueber die phonologischen Sprachbunde. *Travaux du Cercle Linguistique de Prague IV*: 234–9. Reprinted in Jakobson (1962), 137–43; and as 'On the theory of phonological associations among languages' in Keiler (ed.), 241–52.

Jakobson, R. 1942. Kindersprache, Aphasie, und allgemeine Lautgesetze, *Sprakvetenskapliga Sällskapets i Uppsala förhandlingar* 1940–2 (= *Uppsala Universitets Årsskrift* vol. 9), 1–83. Reprinted in Jakobson (1962), 328–401. English translation as Jakobson (1968).

Jakobson, R. 1948. Russian Conjugation. *Word* 4: 155–67. Reprinted in Jakobson (1971), 119–20.

Jakobson, R. (ed.) 1961. *Structure of Languages and its Mathemetical Aspects*, Proceedings of the Twelfth Symposium in Applied Mathematics, American Mathematical Society, Providence, R.I.

Jakobson, R. 1962. *Selected Writings I: Phonological Studies*. Mouton, The Hague.

Jakobson, R. 1965. L'importanza di Kruszewski per lo sviluppo della linguistica generale. *Ricerche Slavistiche* 13: 3–23.

Jakobson, R. 1968. *Child Language., Aphasia, and Phonological Universals*. Mouton, The Hague. Translated by A. Keiler.

Jakobson, R. 1971. *Selected Writings II: Word and Language*. Mouton, The Hague.

Jespersen, O. 1949. *Efficiency in Linguistic Change*. Historisk-filologiske Meddelelser 27:4. Munksgaard, København, 2nd ed.

Joos, M. (ed.) 1957. *Readings in Linguistics I*. American Council of Learned Societies. New York.

Jutz, L. 1931. *Die allemannischen Mundarten*. Saale, Halle.

Kachru, B.B., R.B. Lees, Y. Malkiel, A. Pietrangeli, and S. Saporta (eds.) 1973. *Issues in Linguistics, Papers in honor of Henry and Renée Kahane*, University of Illinois Press, Urbana, Ill.

Karttunen, F. 1970. *Problems in Finnish Phonology*. Unpubl. Ph.D. diss., University of Indiana, Bloomington, Ind.

Katz, J.J., and P.M. Postal. 1964. *An Integrated Theory of Linguistic Description*. MIT Press, Cambridge, Mass.

Kavanagh, J.F., and J.E. Cutting (eds.) 1975. *The Role of Speech in Language*. MIT Press, Cambridge, Mass.

Kaye, J.D. 1971. A case for local ordering in Ojibwa. In Kaye et al. (eds.), 3–10.

Kaye, J.D. 1974. Opacity and recoverability in phonology. *Canadian Journal of Linguistics* 19: 134–49.

Kaye, J.D., G.L. Piggott, and K. Tokaichi (eds.) 1971. *Odawa Language Project*, First Report, Anthropology Series no. 9, Department of Anthropology, University of Toronto.

Kazazis, K. 1969. Possible evidence for (near-) underlying forms in the speech of a child. In Binnick et al. (eds.), 372–9.

Keiler, A.R. (ed.) 1972. *A Reader in Historical and Comparative Linguistics*. Holt, Rinehart, and Winston, New York.

Kenstowicz, M., and Ch. Kisseberth. 1970. Rule ordering and the asymmetry hypothesis. In M.A. Campbell et al. (eds.), 504–20.

Kenstowicz, M., and Ch. Kisseberth. 1973a. Unmarked bleeding orders. In Kisseberth (ed.). 1–13. Also available in *Studies in the Linguistic Sciences* 1:1, Dept. of Linguistics, University of Illinois, Urbana, Ill., 1971, 8–28.

Kenstowicz, M., and Ch.W. Kisseberth (eds.) 1973b. *Issues in Phonological Theory*. Mouton, The Hague.

Kenstowicz, M., and Ch. Kisseberth. 1977. *Topics in Phonological Theory*. Academic Press, New York.

Kettunen, L. 1960. *Suomen lähisukukielten luonteenomaiset piirteet.* Mémoires de la société finno-ougrienne 119, = Suomalais ugrilaisen seuran toimituksia 119, Helsinki.

Kettunen, L. 1962. *Eestin kielen äännehistoria*. Suomalaisen Kirjallisuuden Seurn Toimituksia 156, Helsinki, 3rd ed.

Kim, C.-W. 1972. Two phonological notes: A-sharp and B-flat. In Brame (ed.), 155–70.

King, H. 1970. On blocking the rules for contraction in English. *Linguistic Inquiry* 1:134–6.

King, R.D. 1967. Functional load and sound change. *Language* 43: 831–52. Reprinted in Baldi and Werth (eds.), 190–217.

King, R.D. 1969. *Historical Linguistics and Generative Grammar*. Prentice-Hall, Englewood Cliffs, N.J.

King, R.D. 1972. A note on opacity and paradigm regularity. *Linguistic Inquiry* 3: 535–9.

King, R.D. 1974. Can rules be added in the middle of grammars? Reproduced by Indiana University Linguistics Club, Bloomington, Ind.

Kiparsky, P. 1965. *Phonological Change*. Ph.D. diss., MIT, Cambridge, Mass. Reproduced by Indiana University Linguistics Club, Bloomington, Ind., 1971.

Kiparsky, P. 1966. Ueber den deutschen Akzent. *Studia grammatica* 7: 69–98. Akademie-Verlag, Berlin.

Kiparsky, P. 1967. A propos de l'histoire de l'accenturation grecque. *Languages* 8: 73–93.

Kiparsky, P. 1968a. Linguistic universals and linguistic change. In Bach and Harms (eds.), 171–202. Reprinted in this volume.

Kiparsky, P. 1968b. How abstract is phonology? Reproduced by Indiana University Linguistics Club, Bloomington, Ind. Published with some revisions as part 1 of Kiparsky (1973a), 5–56. Reprinted in this volume.

Kiparsky, P. 1971. Historical Linguistics. In Dingwall (ed.), 576–649 (first 1971 ed.); and 33–62 (second 1978 ed.). Reprinted in this volume.

Kiparsky, P. 1972. Explanation in phonology. In Peters (ed.), 189–227. Reprinted in this volume.

Kiparsky, P. 1973a. Phonological representations. In Fujimura (ed.), 1–136.

Kiparsky, P. 1973b. Abstractness, opacity and global rules. Part 2 of Kiparsky (1973a), 57–86. Also available in Koutsoudas (ed.), 160–86.

Kiparsky, P. 1973c. The inflectional accent in Indo-European. *Language* 49: 794–849.

Kiparsky, P. 1974. On the evaluation measure. In Bruck et al. (eds.), 328–37. Reprinted in this volume.

Kiparsky, P. 1975. Comments on the role of phonology in language. In Kavanagh and Cutting (eds.), 271–80.

Kiparsky, V. 1967. *Russische historische Grammatik II. Die Entwicklung des Formensystems*, Winter, Heidelberg.

Kisseberth, Ch. 1969. On the abstractness of phonology: the evidence from Yawelmani, *Papers in Linguistics* 1:248–82.

Kisseberth, Ch. 1970a. On the functional unity of phonological rules. *Linguistic Inquiry* 1: 291–306. Reprinted in Fudge (ed.), 257–74.

Kisseberth, Ch. 1970b. The Tunica stress conspiracy. Mimeographed.

Kisseberth, Ch. 1970c. Vowel elision in Tonkawa and derivational constraints. In Sadock and Vanek (eds.), 109–39.

Kisseberth, Ch. 1970d. The treatment of exceptions. *Papers in Linguistics* 2: 44–58.

Kisseberth, Ch. 1973a. On the alternation of vowel length in Klamath: a global rule. In Kenstowicz and Kisseberth (eds.), 9–27.

Kisseberth, Ch. 1973b. Is rule ordering necessary in phonology? In Kachru et al. (eds.), 418–41.

Kisseberth, Ch. (ed.) 1973c. *Studies in Generative Phonology*. Linguistic Research, Edmonton.

Klima, E. 1964a. Relatedness between grammatical systems. *Language* 40: 1–20. Reprinted in Reibel and Schane (eds.), 227–46.

Klima, E. 1964b. Negation in English. In Fodor and Katz (eds.), 246–323.

Koefoed, G. 1974. On formal and functional explanation: some notes on Kiparsky's 'Explanation in phonology'. In Anderson and Jones (eds.), 277–96.

Koutsoudas, A. (ed.) 1973. *The Application and Ordering of Grammatical Rules*. Mouton, The Hague.

Koutsoudas, A., G. Sanders, and C. Noll. 1971. On the application of phonological rules. Reproduced by Indiana University Linguistics Club, Bloomington, Ind. Revised as Koutsoudas et al. (1974).

Koutsoudas, A., G. Sanders, and C. Noll. 1974. The application of phonological rules. *Language* 50: 1–28. Revised version of Koutsoudas et al. (1971).

Kreidler, Ch.W. (ed.) 1965. *Report of the Sixteenth Annual Round Table Meeting on Linguistics and Language Studies*, Georgetown University Monograph Series on Languages and Linguistics 18, Washington, D.C.

Kruszewski, M. 1881. Ueber die Lautabwechslung. Universitätsbuchdruckerei, Kazan. Reprinted in Baldi and Werth (eds.), 64–91 as 'On Sound Alternation'; transl. by R. Austerlitz.

Kuhn, T. 1962. *The Structure of Scientific Revolutions*. University of Chicago Press.

Kuryłowicz, J. 1956. *L'apophonie en indo-européen*. Prace Jezykoznawce 9, Polska Akademia Nauk, Wrocław.

Kuryłowicz, J. 1964. *The Inflectional Categories of Indo-European*. Winter, Heidelberg.

Kuryłowicz, J. 1968. *Indogermanische Grammatik*, Band II: *Akzent-Ablaut*. Winter, Heidelberg.

Kuryłowicz, J. 1969. Les verbes germaniques du type *lūkan*. *Melanges Fourquet*, Paris/München, 157–62. Reprinted in *Esquisses Linguistiques II*. Fink, München, 382–7.

Labov, W. 1963. The social motivation of a sound change. *Word* 19: 273–309.

Labov, W. 1965. On the mechanism of linguistic change. In Kreidler (ed.), 91–114. Reprinted in Gumperz and Hymes (eds.), 512–38; and in Keiler (ed.), 267–88.

Labov, W. 1969. Contraction, deletion, and inherent variability of the English copula. *Language* 45: 715–62.

Labov, W. 1972a. *Sociolinguistic Patterns*. University of Pennsylvania Press, Philadelphia.

Labov, W. 1972b. The internal evolution of linguistic rules. In Stockwell and Macaulay (eds.), 101–71.

Labov, W., P. Cohen, C. Robins, and J. Lewis. 1968. A study of the nonstandard English of the Negro and Puerto Rican Speakers of New York City. Cooperative Research Report no. 3288, vol. I. Columbia University, New York.

Ladefoged, P. 1964. Igbirra notes and word-list. *Journal of West African Languages* 1: 27–37.

Lakoff, G. 1965. On the nature of syntactic irregularity. Harvard Computation Laboratory, Report no. 16; published as *Irregularity in Syntax*, Holt, Rinehart, and Winston, New York, 1970.

244

Lamb, S. 1966. Prolegomena to a theory of phonology. *Language* 42: 536–73. Reprinted in Makkai (ed.), 606–33.

Langacker, R.W. 1969. Mirror image rules II: lexicon and phonology. *Language* 45: 844–62.

Lass, R. 1976. *English Phonology and Phonological Theory. Synchronic and Diachronic Studies.* Cambridge University Press.

Laver, J. 1967. A preliminary phonology of the Ayele dialect of Esako. *Journal of West African Languages* 4: 53–60.

Lehmann, W.P. 1962. *Historical Linguistics: an Introduction.* Holt, New York.

Lehmann, W.P. 1967. *A Reader in Nineteenth-Century Historical Indo-European Linguistics,* Indiana University Press, Bloomington, Ind.

Lenneberg, E. (ed.) 1966. *New Directions in the Study of Language.* MIT Press, Cambridge, Mass.

Levomäki, M. 1973. Vierasperäisten sanojen suffiksaali vokaalisointu, *Virittäjä* 254–61.

Lightner, T. 1965. On the description of vowel and consonant harmony. *Word* 21: 224–50.

Lindgren, K.B. 1953. *Die apokope des mhd. -e in seinen verschiedenen Funktionen,* Ann. Ac. Sc. Fenn. B78/2, Helsinki.

Luick, K. 1964. *Historische Grammatik der englischen Sprache,* vol. i. Blackwell and Tauchnitz, Oxford and stuttgart. Reprinted from the first 1921 ed.

Luján, M., and F. Hensey (eds.) 1976. *Current Studies in Romance Linguistics,* Georgetown University Press, Washington, D.C.

Macdonell, A.A. 1910. *Vedic Grammar.* Strassbourg.

Mackel, E. 1905–7. Die Mundart der Prignitz. *Niederdeutsches Jahrbuch* 31: 65–164; 32: 1–54; 33: 73–105. Norden and Leipzig.

Makkai, V.B. (ed.) 1972. *Phonological Theory. Evolution and Current Practice.* Holt, Rinehart, and Winston, New York.

Mandelbaum, D.G. (ed.) 1969. *Selected Writings of Edward Sapir.* University of California Press, Berkeley/Los Angeles.

Mascaro, J. 1976. *Catalan Phonology and the Phonological Cycle.* Ph.D.diss., MIT, Cambridge, Mass. Reproduced by Indiana University Linguistics Club, Bloomington, Ind.

Mattews. G.H. 1970. Some notes on the Proto-Siouan continuants. *IJAL* 36: 98–109.

McCawley, J.D. ms. Finnish Phonology.

McCawley, J.D. 1967. Sapir's phonological representations. *IJAL* 33: 106–11. Reprinted in McCawley (1979), 3–9.

McCawley, J.D. 1968. *The Phonological Component of a Grammar of Japanese.* Mouton, The Hague.

McCawley, J.D. 1974. Review of Chomsky and Halle (1968). *IJAL* 40: 50–88. Reprinted in Goyvaerts and Pullum (eds.), 145–97.

McCawley, J.D. 1977. Acquisition models as models of acquisition. In Fasold and Shuy (eds.), 51–64.

McCawley, J.D. 1979. *Adverbs, Vowels, and other Objects of Wonder.* The University of Chicago Press, Chicago, Ill.

McNeill, D. 1966. Developmental psycholinguistics. In Smith and Miller (eds.), 15–84.

Milan, W.G., J.J. Staczek, and J.C. Zamora (eds.) 1975. *1974 Colloquium on Spanish and Portuguese Linguistics.* Georgetown University Press, Washington, D.C.

Miller, D.G. 1970. The Pāli two-mora conspiracy: historical origin. Mimeo, University of Illinois, Urbana, Ill.

Miller, D.G. 1973. On the motivation of phonological change. In Kachru et al. (eds.), 686–718.

Mirčuk, N.J. 1964. Formy l-oji-osoby odyny dijesliv teperišnjogo času v ukrajinskyx govorax, *Ukrajinska dialektologija i onomastyka* (zbirnyk statej) 1: 80–94, Kiev.

Moore, S. 1927. Loss of final -n in inflectional syllables of Middle English. *Language* 3: 232–59.

Moulton, W. 1960. The short vowel systems of Northern Switzerland. A study in structural dialectology. *Word* 16:155–82.

Moulton, W. 1961. Lautwandel durch innere Kausalität: die ostschweizerische Vokalspaltung. *Zeitschrift für Mundartforschung* 28: 227–51.

Müller, F. 1860/70. Zur Suffixlehre des indogermanischen Verbums. *Sitzungsberichte der kaiserlichen Akademie der Wissenschaften.* Philosophisch-historische Classe 34: 8–16; 66: 193–212.

Naro, A., and M. Lemle. 1977. Syntactic diffusion. *Ciencia e Cultura* 29: 259–68.

Narten, J. 1964. *Die sigmatischen Aoriste im Veda.* Harrassowitz, Wiesbaden.

Nerger, K. 1869. *Grammatik des meklenburgischen Dialektes; älterer und neuerer Zeit. Laut- und Flexionslehre.* Brockhaus, Leipzig.

Newman, P. 1968. The reality of morphophonemics. *Language* 44: 507–15.

Nishihara, S. 1970. *Phonological Change and Verb Morphology of Japanese.* Unpubl. Ph.D.diss., University of Michigan, Ann Arbor.

Pandit, P.B. 1961. Historical Phonology of Gujarati vowels. *Language* 37: 54–66.

Panfilow, V.Z. 1962. *Grammatika nivxskogo jazyka,* vol. I. Izdatel,stvo Akademii Nauk, Moscow-Leningrad.

Pāṇini, 1962. *The Ashṭādhyāyi of Pāṇini,* vols. I and II. English translation by S. Vasu; Motilal Banarsidass, Delhi.

Paul, H. 1886², 1920⁵. *Prinzipien der Sprachgeschichte.* Niemeyer, Tübingen.

Penttilä, A. 1963. *Suomen kieloppi.* WSOY, Helsinki.

Penttilä, A. 1966. *Suomen kielen ääunehistorian luennot,* Suomalaisen Kirjallisuuden Seura, Helsinki.

Penzl, H. 1949. Umlaut and secondary umlaut in Old High German, *Language* 25: 223–40.

Peranteau, P.M., J.N. Levi, and G.C. Phares (eds.) 1972. *Papers from the eighth Regional Meeting of the Chicago Linguistic Society,* Chicago, Ill.

Peters, S. (ed.) 1972. *Goals of Linguistic Theory.* Prentice-Hall, Englewood Cliffs, N.J.

Piggott, G. 1971. Some implications of Algonquian palatalization. In Kaye et al. (eds.), 11–38.

Poppe, N. 1960. *Vergleichende Grammatik der altäischen Sprachen.* Harassowitz, Wiesbaden.

Postal, P. 1968. *Aspects of Phonological Theory.* Harper and Row, New York.

Pott, A.F. 1833. *Etymologische Forschungen auf dem Gebiete der indo-germanischen Sprachen, mit besonderem Bezug auf die Lautwandlung im Sanskrit, Lateinischen, Littauischen und Gotischen.* Meyerische Hofbuchhandlung, Lemgo.

Pott, A.F. 1870. Die Umstellung des Hauches. *Kuhns Zeitschrift für vergleichende Sprachforschung auf dem Gebiete der indogermanischen Sprache* 19: 16–41.

Rabeler, Th.H.F. 1911. Niederdeutscher Lautstand im Kreise Bleckede. *Zeitschrift für deutsche Philologie* 43: 141–202, 320–77.

Ralph, B. 1975. *Phonological Differentiation: Studies in Nordic Language History.* Acta Universitas Gothoburgensis, Göteborg.

Rapola, M. 1933. *Suomen kirjakielen historia I.* Suomalaisen Kirjallisuuden Seura,

Redenbarger, W.J. 1976. Vowel lowering and *i*-epenthesis in Classical Latin. In Luján and Hensey (eds.), 1–13.

Reibel, D.A., and S.A. Schane (eds.) 1969. *Modern Studies in English.* Prentice-Hall, Englewood Cliffs, N.J.

Rice, L. 1967. *Hungarian Morphological Irregularities with Contributions to Feature Theory.* Unpubl. Ph.D.diss., Indiana University.

Rigsby, B. 1965. Continuity and change in Sahaptian vowel systems. *IJAL* 31: 306–11.

Rigsby, B., and M. Silverstein. 1969. Nez Perce vowels and Proto-Sahaptian vowel harmony. *Language* 45: 45–59.

Robinson, O.W. 1972. *Synchronic Reflexes of Diachronic Phonological Rules.* Unpubl. Ph.D. diss., Cornell University.

Robinson, O.W. 1976. A 'scattered' rule in Swiss German. *Language* 52: 148–62.

246

Ross, J.R. 1973. Leftward, Ho! In Anderson and Kiparsky (eds.), 166–73.

Sadock, J.M. 1973. Word-final devoicing in the development of Yiddish. In Kachru et al. (eds.), 790–7.

Sadock, J.M., and A.L. Vanek (eds.) 1970. *Studies presented to Robert B. Lees by his Students*. Linguistic Research, Edmonton.

Samuels, M.L. 1972. *Linguistic Evolution with Special Reference to English*. Cambridge University Press.

Sanžeev, G.D. 1959. *Sovremennyj mongol,skij jazyk*. Izdatel,stvo vostočnoj literatury, Moskva.

Sapir, D. 1965. *A Grammar of Diola-Fogny*, Cambridge University Press.

Sapir, E. 1915. Notes on Judeo-German phonology. *The Jewish Quarterly Review*, n.s. 6: 231–66. Reprinted in Mandelbaum (ed.), 252–72.

Sapir, E. 1922. The Takelma language of Southwestern Oregon. In Boas (ed.), 1–296.

Sapir, E. 1930. Southern Paiute, a Shoshonean language. *Proceedings of the American Academy of Arts and Sciences* 65, nos. 1–3.

Saussure, F. de 1916. *Cours de linguistique générale*. Bayot, Paris. English translation as Saussure (1959).

Saussure, F. de, 1959. *Course in General Linguistics*. Ed. by C. Bally and A. Sechehaye, transl. by W. Baskin. Philosophical Library, New York.

Schane, S.A. 1968. *French Phonology and Morphology*. MIT Press, Cambridge, Mass.

Scherer, W. 1868. *Zur Geschichte der deutschen Sprache*, Weidmann, Berlin.

Schindler, J. 1974. Fragen zum paradigmatischen Ausgleich. *Die Sprache* 20: 1–9.

Schirmunski, V. 1962. *Deutsche Mundartkunde. Vergleichende Laut- und Formenlehre der deutsche Mundarten*. Deutsche Akademie der Wissenschaften zu Berlin, Veröffentlichungen des Instituts für deutsche Sprache und Literatur 25, Akademie-Verlag, Berlin.

Sebeok, T. (ed.) 1973. *Current Trends in Linguistics*, Vol. II: *Diachronic, Areal, and Typological Linguistics*. Mouton, The Hague.

Shuy, R.W. and Ch.-J.N. Bailey (eds.) 1974. *Towards Tomorrow's Linguistics*. Georgetown University Press, Washington, D.C.

Skorik, P.Ja. 1961. *Grammatika čukotskogo jazyka*, vol. 1. Jzdatelgstvo Akademii Nauk, Moscow/Leningrad.

Skorik, P.Ja. 1968a. Čukotsko-Kamčatskie jazyki (vvedenie). *Jazyki narodov SSSR* 5: 235–47.

Skorik, P.Ja. 1968b. Čukotskij jazyk. *Jazyki narodov SSSR* 5: 248–70.

Skousen, R. 1972. On capturing regularities. In Peranteau et al. (eds.), 567–78.

Skousen, R. 1975. *Substantive Evidence in Phonology: the Evidence from Finnish and French*. Mouton, The Hague.

Smith, F., and G.A. Miller (eds.) 1966. *The Genesis of Language*. MIT Press, Cambridge, Mass.

Smith, N.V. 1967. The phonology of Nupe. *Journal of African Languages* 6: 153–69.

Smith, N.V. 1969. Review of Schane (1968). *Language* 45: 398–407.

Stampe, D. 1967. Lecture presented at the Texas Conference on Universals in Linguistic Theory, Austin.

Stampe, D. 1969. The acquisition of phonetic representation. In Binnick et al. (eds.), 443–54.

Stampe, D. 1972. On the natural history of diphthongs. In Peranteau et al. (eds.), 578–90.

Stanley, R. 1967. Redundancy rules in phonology. *Language* 43: 393–437.

Stechow, A. von. (ed.) 1971. *Beiträge zur Generativen Grammatik: Referate des 5. Linguistischen Kolloquiums*, Regensburg, 1970. Vieweg, Braunschweig.

Stockwell, R.P., and R.K.S. Macaulay (eds.) 1972. *Linguistic Change and Generative Theory*, Indiana University Press, Bloomington, Ind.

Streitberg, W. 1963. *Urgermanische Grammatik. Einführung in das vergleichende Studium der altgermanischen Dialekte*. Winter, Heidelberg, third ed.

Thomason, S. 1973. Paper presented at the 1973 Summer Meeting of the Linguistic

Society of America. Revised version published as 'On the Analysis of Inflectional Change', *Papers in Linguistics* 7: 351–79, 1974.

Thomason, S. 1976. Analogical change as grammar complication. In Christie (ed.), 401–9.

Trubetzkoy, N.S. 1962. *Grundzüge der Phonologie*. Vandenhoeck und Ruprecht, Göttingen, third ed. English transl. by C.A.M. Baltaxe as *Principles of Phonology*, University of California Press, Berkeley, Cal.

Tucker, A.N., and J. Tompo Ole Mpaayei. 1955. *A Maasai Grammar*. Longmans, London.

Twaddell, W.F. 1935. *On defining the phoneme*. Language Monograph 16. Page references to the reprint in Joos (ed.), 55–80.

Twaddell, W.F. 1938. A note on Old High German Umlaut. *Monatshefte für deutschen Unterricht* 30: 177–81. Page references to the reprint in Joos (ed.), 85–7.

Vennemann, T. 1968. On the use of paradigmatic information in a competence rule of Modern German phonology. Paper read at the Summer Meeting of the Linguistic Society of America, Urbana, Ill.

Vennemann, T. 1970. The German velar nasal: a case for abstract phonology. *Phonetica* 22:65–81.

Vennemann, T. 1972. Phonetic analogy and conceptual analogy. In Vennemann and Wilbur (eds.), 181–204. Reprinted in Baldi and Werth (eds.), 258–74.

Vennemann, T. 1974a. Phonological concreteness in Natural Generative Grammar. In Shuy and Bailey (eds.), 202–19.

Vennemann, T. 1974b. Words and syllables in natural generative grammar. In Bruck et al. (eds.), 346–74.

Vennemann, T., and T. Wilbur (eds.) 1972. *Schuchardt, the Neogrammarians, and the Transformational Theory of Phonological Change*. Athenäum, Frankfurt.

Verburg, P.A. 1950. The background of the linguistic conceptions of Franz Bopp. *Lingua* 2: 438–68.

Vetter, D. 1968. *Abstractness in Phonological Representations*. Unpubl. Ph.D. diss., MIT, Cambridge, Mass.

Vincent, N. 1974. Analogy reconsidered. In Anderson and Jones (eds.), 427–45.

Wackernagel, J. 1896. *Altindische Grammatik I*. Vandenhoeck and Ruprecht, Göttingen.

Wackernagel, J., and A. Debrunner. 1954. *Altindische Grammatik II:2*. Vandenhoeck und Ruprecht, Göttingen.

Wang, W.S.-Y. 1969. Competing changes as a cause of residue. *Language* 45: 9–25. Reprinted in Baldi and Werth (eds.), 236–57.

Wanner, G. 1941. *Die Mundart des Kantons Schaffhausen*. Beiträge zur schweizerdeutschen Grammatik 20. A. Bachmann, ed., Frauenfeld.

Wartburg, W. von, 1969. *Problems and Methods in Linguistics*. Barnes and Noble, New York. Translated by J.M.H. Reid. (Originally publ. in German in 1943).

Watkins, C. 1969. *Indogermanische Grammatik III:1, Formenlehre*. Ed. by J. Kuryłowicz. Winter, Heidelberg.

Watkins, C. 1972. *Indo-European Origins of the Celtic Verb*. Institute of Advanced Studies, Dublin.

Weinreich, U. 1963. Four riddles in bilingual dialectology. *American Contributions to the Fifth International Congress of Slavists*, 335–58. Mouton, The Hague.

Westphal, R. 1869. *Philosophisch-historische Grammatik der deutschen Sprache*. Jena.

Whitney, W.D. 1889. *Sanskrit Grammar*. Harvard University Press, Cambridge, Mass. 2nd ed., reprinted 1961.

Wiik, K. 1969. *Suomen kielen morfofonemiikkaa* (Turun yliopiston fonetiikan laitoksen julkais ja 3).

Williamson, K. 1965. *A Grammar of the Kokoluma Dialect of Ijo*. West African Language Monographs 2, Cambridge.

248

Wurm, S.A., and D.C. Laycock (eds.) 1970. *Pacific Linguistic Studies in Honor of Arthur Capell.* Australian National University, Canberra.

Zhukova, A.N. 1968a. Alyutorskij jazyk. *Jazyk narodov SSSR* 5: 271–293.

Zhukova, A.N. 1968b. Kerekskij jazyk. *Jazyk narodov SSSR 5:* 310–333.

Zimmer, K.E. 1967. A note on vowel harmony. *IJAL* 33: 166–71.

Zwicky, A.M. 1967. Umlaut and noun plurals in German. *Studia Grammatica* 6: 35–45. Akademie Verlag, Berlin.

Zwicky, A.M. 1970a. More on Nez Perce: on alternative analyses. *Ohio State University Working Papers in Linguistics* 4: 115–26.

Zwicky, A.M. 1970b. A double regularity in the acquisition of English verb morphology. *Ohio State University Working Papers in Linguistics* 4: 142–8.

# Index